The Soap Opera Evolution

To Carol and Harry,
who have always provided me
with a "guiding light."

The Soap Opera Evolution

*America's Enduring Romance
with Daytime Drama*

by
Marilyn J. Matelski

McFarland & Company, Inc., Publishers
Jefferson, North Carolina, and London

Library of Congress Cataloguing-in-Publication Data

Matelski, Marilyn J., 1950–
  The soap opera evolution.

  Bibliography: p. 207.
  Includes index.
  1. Soap operas—United States. I. Title.
  PN1992.8.S4M27 1988   791.45′75′0973   87-43168

ISBN 0-89950-324-1 (acid-free natural paper) ∞

Manufactured in the United States of America.

McFarland & Company, Inc., Publishers
  Box 611, Jefferson, North Carolina 28640

Acknowledgments

Writing a book is seldom an exclusively individual experience. Accordingly, this book would have never been completed without some assistance from several of my dedicated friends, colleagues and students. I would like to express my deepest gratitude to the following people: to my parents, Carolyn and Harry Matelski, who helped collect my research data, assisted in proofreading, and provided useful suggestions and support throughout my endeavor; to the students in my Fall 1985 Broadcast Programming class at Boston College, who interviewed over 600 persons for audience analysis; to Teri and Matt Haymer and Nancy Street, whose editing contributions and continuing moral support were invaluable; to Dale Herbeck, whose computer knowledge and daily banter were most welcome; and to the many well-wishers (both friends and "mice"), who made my life as unlike a soap opera as possible during this time. Thank you all.

Table of Contents

Introduction

"Like sands through the hourglass, so are the *Days of Our Lives*."

Each weekday afternoon, most Americans are able to supplement the days of their lives with endless vicarious experiences of love, loss and libido, courtesy of network daytime dramas . . . or, as we commonly refer to them, "the soaps." Soap operas have been a staple in American broadcasting since the early thirties, and are likely to continue as such for a very long time to come. Today, an estimated fifty million people are considered to be regular soap opera viewers, including two-thirds of all American women in households with television. This dramatic figure translates into more than $900 million in total network revenues each year—one-sixth of all annual network profits.[1]

However, despite the popularity and profitability of daytime dramas (or "washboard weepers," as they were once described in *Variety*), soap operas were never considered an important vehicle for prolific academic research until quite recently in broadcast history. Initial studies in the late thirties were conducted by network research departments as small portions of larger, more general radio listener analyses.[2] And in the early forties, most independent research on soaps was solicited by broadcasters in retaliation to charges from a highly publicized New York psychiatrist named Louis Berg.

Berg assumed a "hypodermic theory" of mass media effects for his analysis of soap operas. This "hypodermic theory" postulated that information from mass media channels, when "injected" into American listeners, directly precipitated certain types of reactions which were impossible to overcome. Thus, according to Berg, soap operas were directly responsible for severe psychosomatic maladies, including "acute anxiety state[s], tachycardia, arrythmias, increase[s] in blood pressure, profuse perspirations, tremors, vasomotor instability, nocturnal frights, vertigo and gastrointestinal disturbances."[3] Broadcasters were concerned that these charges might persuade the Roosevelt administration to impose wartime programming controls. Consequently, they acted to weaken Berg's accusations by critiquing his research methodology. They also decided to generate new studies by independent firms. When his methodology was analyzed, Berg's data was found to be dubious at best, Berg having conducted his "research" by recording only his *own* blood pressure and pulse. As for gathering new research, the networks commissioned several respected social scientists to respond to Berg's accusations.

Among these scholars was a man named Paul F. Lazarsfeld, whose Bureau of Applied Social Research replaced Berg's hypodermic theory of mass communication with a more moderate, diffusive perspective of media. Lazarsfeld saw the soap opera as an *indirect* source of influence, which, in turn, was influenced by outside factors such as audience, social climate, economic factors and politics. Together with Frank N. Stanton, Lazarsfeld compiled a collection of articles in a book, *Radio Research: 1942-1943,*[4] which adapted his perspective to specific studies in daytime drama.[5] It quickly became a standard text of research and remained relatively unchallenged until the early seventies, when soap operas entered the world of academia as a topic of serious scholarly inquiry.

Since 1972, researchers such as Cantor,[6] Katzman,[7] Goldsen,[8] Greenberg,[9] and Cassata[10] have updated Lazarsfeld's research to include television. In addition, they have asked different questions and used other means of inquiry such as content analysis to understand better the popularity and significance of soap operas in today's society. Among the new directions of inquiry have been the growth of a more diverse audience of soap opera devotees and the change of character profiles in dramatic plotlines as well as the potential positive effects of daytime drama in educating the public about important social issues in a dramatic setting.

The purpose of this book is to combine previous research with new content analyses as well as quantitative methodology to trace the evolution of soap operas over the past several decades. It is important to note that while much of the research for this text is new (see Appendices A and B), it has been essential to include past significant studies by others to better understand the total picture of daytime drama in America today.

Chapter 1 focuses on plotlines: a comparison of familiar themes in the forties to present-day storylines; an assessment of how much reality is reflected in today's plots; a correlation between themes and ratings sweep periods; and similarities and differences among individual daytime dramas.[11] Chapter 2 addresses the subject of soap opera characterizations and their evolution in psychological make-up, occupational opportunities, age and sociological status. Chapter 3 deals with viewer demographics: the gradual shift from housewives to multi-dimensional groups over the past forty years; specific demographics which are associated with specific programs; and the reasons most people watch today's soap operas. Common themes in daytime drama as well as individual programming characteristics emerge for each soap in the eighties. Chapter 4 summarizes the specific plotlines for each of the thirteen soap operas on television today. Chapter 5 gives a summary and some final conclusions about soap opera trends over the last forty years as well as some predictions for the future. Finally, Appendices A and B and an annotated bibliography should provide readers with useful sources for further information.

Chapter 1

The Plots

While this book does not begin its comparative study until the early forties (since most serious research was not conducted until then), it is important to note that the first daytime dramas began as early as 1930, with the introduction of Irna Phillips' *Painted Dreams*. Their subsequent success was due to several factors at that time: creative programming; advertiser support; and a post–Depression environment.

Initially, the notion of serial drama was considered risky and programmatically unwise. Most network executives felt that the listening audience would accept only those storylines that were resolved within a series episode. However, in the early thirties, programmers experimented with an open-ended evening comedy called *Amos 'n' Andy*. This program, along with other serial comedies like *The Goldbergs* and *Myrt and Marge*, became popular immediately, proving that the serial could be a successful form of radio entertainment.[1] However, despite the demonstrated popularity of open-ended storylines, network programmers were still hesitant to move prime-time serial form to daytime audiences. Their concerns centered around the seemingly unattractive listening population (housewives) during this time block and the questionable cost efficiency of providing serious drama in continuous segments. Despite these reservations, however, the networks decided to experiment with several fifteen-minute "episodes," provided at discounted prices to interested sponsors in the early thirties. Most advertising support for these daytime dramas came from corporations like Colgate Palmolive–Peet and Procter and Gamble, who sold household products to interested female listeners. Thus, the term "soap opera" was developed, to describe the melodramatic plotlines sold by detergent companies.[2]

The introduction of daytime drama met with as immediate a success as had its evening serial counterpart. Devoted listeners faithfully followed the lives and loves of their favorite soap opera characters. And, much to the networks' surprise, housewives were not an unattractive listening demographic to possess. In fact, programmers soon discovered that house-

1

wives, while not directly in the labor force, often controlled the purse strings of the household economy. Accordingly, by 1939, advertising revenue for the popular serials had exceeded $26 million.[3] Housewives had indeed found an alluring substitute for previous programming fare (such as hygienic information, recipe readings and household tips), and were demonstrating their consumer power as well. Network programmers and advertisers had inadvertently stumbled onto an undiscovered gold mine. However, creative programming was not the only reason for the immediate popularity of radio soap operas. To better understand the success of daytime drama in the thirties, it is important to look at two additional factors: the story formula and its relationship to post–Depression America.

The "assembly-line" approach towards developing the soap opera genre we know today began in the early thirties, when many of the first serials were created by two advertising executives, Frank and Anne Hummert. They originated many of the popular early daytime dramas like *Just Plain Bill, The Romance of Helen Trent* and *Ma Perkins*.[4] The Hummerts based most of their stories in the Midwest — an ideal setting for several reasons. First of all, the Hummerts' ad agency was located in Chicago. They felt their soap operas should be produced there because as the creators, they would be conveniently located and could produce programs less expensively than in New York.[5] After making this decision, it followed that the Hummerts would choose much of their talent from the immediate area, thus creating more authentic drama from the Midwest than from other areas of the country. Finally, the Hummerts felt that the Midwest carried with it an accurate reflection of American values, attitudes and lifestyles. It seemed to be an ideal part of the country for audiences to associate with the familiar themes of daytime drama, known as the "Hummert formula."

The Hummerts' story formula was really quite simple: They combined fantasies of exotic romance, pathos and suspense with a familiar environment of everyday life in a small-town or rural setting. Combined with an identifiable hero or heroine, this formula produced an overwhelming audience response. For example, each episode of *Our Gal Sunday* began with the following:

> (Voiced over the song, "Red River Valley"):
> *Our Gal Sunday* — the story of an orphan girl named Sunday from the little mining town of Silver Creek, Colorado, who in young womanhood married England's richest, most handsome lord, Lord Henry Brinthrope. The story asks the question: Can this girl from a mining town in the west find happiness as the wife of a wealthy and titled Englishman?[6]

Listeners flocked to hear the adventures of the small-town girl they "knew" and "loved" in predicaments they might only experience vicariously. And, while the settings and characters varied from soap to soap, the underlying premise in Hummert daytime drama was always the same: that people everywhere shared common needs, common values and common problems.

This broadcast unity of beliefs and attitudes was especially important during the post–Depression era, when poverty, unemployment and general political pessimism threatened the very fiber of American family life. Listeners found courage through soap opera characters such as Ma Perkins and "Just Plain Bill" Davidson—common folks who could survive despite overwhelming odds. Their victories over the trials and tribulations of daily living gave many Americans the feeling that they, too, could and would survive.

Another formidable contributor to early soap opera formula and content was Irna Phillips, whose style differed from the Hummerts' somewhat, but was equally successful nonetheless. Phillips rose to fame as the creator of radio's first serial, *Painted Dreams,* and was an equally powerful force in the development of many serials thereafter. She concentrated on characterization more than plotline fantasy (as in the Hummert dramas), and later became noted for introducing "working professionals," i.e., doctors and lawyers, to daytime serials. Phillips' approach to characterization was not always as popular as the Hummert storyline fantasies in the thirties. However, in the early forties, when post–Depression escapism was not so necessary in America, her "more realistic" approach to daytime drama caught on quickly. In addition to *Painted Dreams* (1930), Phillips' credits during the early days of soap opera history included *The Guiding Light* and *The Road of Life* (1937), *Woman of White* (1938), and *The Right to Happiness* (1939).

It can be said that daytime drama entered the decade of the forties with several firmly established tenets of serial writing. First, characterization was simple, straightforward and easily recognizable[7] A good example of a character description in the forties was Ma Perkins, who was portrayed as:

> a woman whose life is the same, whose surroundings are the same, whose problems are the same as those of thousands of other women in the world today. A woman who spent all her life taking care of her home, washing and cooking and cleaning and raising her family. And now, her husband's death pitched her head foremost into being the head of the family as well as the mother.[8]

Since most daytime radio listeners were women, they could identify with a woman who led a simple life, yet was also a solid citizen and model for others in her mythical community.

Second, characters found themselves in predicaments that were easily identifiable by their listeners, with settings easily imaginable to those who had never travelled far beyond their home environment. As Rudolf

Arnheim discovered in his study "The World of the Daytime Serial,"[9] soap opera characters seemingly preferred common-day occurrences in their own home town, as opposed to problems in an unknown environment. And, when circumstances necessitated travel, the new setting invariably took place in the United States. Arnheim surmised that soap opera producers refrained from international travel because they felt that listeners would not enjoy a foreign setting which would demand that they imagine a place outside their own realm of experience.[10]

Third, most of the action centered around strong, stable female characters, who were not necessarily professionals, but community cornerstones, nonetheless. Men were very definitely the weaker sex in soap opera life—a direct reflection on the primary listening audience during the daytime hours.

Finally, daytime drama was often used as a vehicle for moral discussions or a rededication to American beliefs and values. Soap opera heroines often voiced the platitudes of the Golden Rule as well as the rewards that would come to those who could endure the trials and tribulations of living in a troubled society. Take, for example, Ma Perkins' philosophy in 1938:

> Anyone of this earth who's done wrong, and then goes so far as to right that wrong, I can tell you that they're well on their way to erasing the harm they did in the eyes of anyone decent.[11]

While it is true that the basic soap opera formula was established during the thirties, other important characteristics which are present in today's soaps evolved during the forties, fifties, sixties and seventies. For example, as mentioned earlier, career women became more numerous in the forties because of writers like Irna Phillips. Phillips also introduced mental problems and amnesia to daytime drama, to reflect America's post-war interest in psychology. Usually a central character suffered some type of emotional malady such as memory loss, a nervous breakdown, alcoholism or shellshock as a result of wartime stress. Also, psychosomatic paralysis was a common affliction to the long-suffering soap opera heroes and heroines.

Toward the end of the forties, crime emerged as an important plotline theme, especially in the area of juvenile delinquency. This direction was also reflective of the times, for Americans were becoming increasingly concerned about youth crime in their country. Criminal storylines continued throughout the early fifties and are still an important theme in today's daytime drama (although the situations have been updated considerably).

In 1956, another significant change was made, as television soap operas developed a half-hour format (as compared to the fifteen-minute capsules of early radio days). At first, networks winced at the notion that soap plots could sustain themselves for such a long period of time each day; but, once again, Irna Phillips erased their doubts by creating the very successful, innovative drama *As the World Turns.* Almost immediately, advertisers saw the popularity of this new innovation, and soon, half-hour soap operas became standard fare. This phenomenon repeated itself a little over a decade later, when several daytime serials moved from a half-hour to an hour-long format.

The late sixties was referred to as the "era of relevance," when soap opera giant Agnes Nixon created a new trend in daytime drama at ABC. Nixon's characters on *All My Children* and *One Life to Live* explored such topics as drug abuse, ethnic and cultural minorities and sexual promiscuity. Not so surprisingly, these plotlines also met with immediate success, and were responsible for ABC dominating the daytime ratings for most of the seventies. Also, Nixon's "soap opera facelift" caused some of the older, more traditional soaps to include similar storylines to maintain audience popularity.

Thus, soap operas have been said to mirror societal changes, while still keeping the early formulas set by the Hummerts and Irna Phillips. But how much have soaps *really* changed? To judge the evolution of plotlines in daytime drama from forty years ago to the present, it is important to look at the types of themes used in today's stories versus those used in the past.

A Comparison Between Radio Soap Operas in the Forties and Television Soap Operas in the Eighties

In Rudolf Arnheim's analysis of daytime serials in 1941, he isolated the following recurring themes:
1) family
2) courtship
3) marriage
4) crime
5) economic/professional/public affairs
6) illness/accidents.[12]

In general, Arnheim felt that soap opera plotlines covered a vast array of social problems. However, he was concerned that daytime drama displayed a tendency to weaken problems by giving them atypical causes. Business and professional problems were used in his study as a glaring example of misrepresentation:

> Much more often than by economic conditions, business or professional troubles are caused by other people who want to damage the "sufferer" for personal reasons which have nothing to do with the business situa-

tion. Arline asks her father, a banker, to dismiss his female lawyer, Portia Blake, because her husband fell in love with the lawyer. A girl wants to prevent Bess Johnson from becoming Dean of a school, because the woman thwarted the girl's attempt to marry against her father's wishes. In both cases the connection between the business situation and the private situation is purely accidental. Gordon is unemployed — why? Are jobs scarce in his field? No, he is an artist who became blind and therefore had to give up his job. An individual case is chosen in which illness instead of the economic situation causes the trouble.[13]

Arnheim concluded that societal problems were actually portrayed as individual crises, and hence were not addressed as effectively as possible. Instead, he suggested that more emphasis should be placed on the individual as a member of a community and that outside influences should be showcased instead of ignored. In this way, Arnheim felt that daytime drama could become more valuable in other areas besides entertainment.[14]

To compare Arnheim's research with plotlines in the eighties, a content analysis was conducted from 1983–1985.[15] Specific data from this study can be found in Appendix A. However, a brief summary of the results illustrates several differences between popular themes in the forties and those used today.

First of all, Arnheim's six categories of plotlines — family, courtship, marriage, crime, economic and illness/injury — correspond favorably to those used today. However, additional themes of travel and mystery/intrigue figure prominently in today's soap operas also. No longer are daytime audiences as content to "stay at home" with stories of love and romance as they were forty years ago. Investigations, especially those involving some form of international travel, seem to be standard fare on today's soaps. In addition, other differences should be noted:

1. More soap operas are set in real-world, non–Midwestern locales today than forty years ago. *Ryan's Hope* (New York City), *Santa Barbara* (Santa Barbara, California) and *Capitol* (Washington, D.C.) all represent a movement away from fictional rural areas in the nation's breadbasket.

2. As for parenthood themes, major plotlines are no longer concerned with tiny babies, for the most part. Instead, the story usually revolves around a teenager or young adult recently "discovering" his/her true parentage.

3. Romance is still a very popular theme in today's soap operas. However, marriage is not the ultimate goal of the romance, as in the past. Perhaps this is due to society's permissiveness in issues of living together.

4. Alcoholism is not as common a theme as it was in the forties. Today, most instances of drinking occur as one-night binges in desperation or combined with drugs to become "substance abuse," as compared with the

post-war fixation with chronic mental problems. More detail about drinking in the eighties' daytime dramas will be discussed in the next section of this chapter.

5. Jobs are still a very popular part of soap operas. Getting jobs, keeping jobs and reconciling professional responsibilities with personal lives seem to occupy today's daytime serials even more than those in the forties. Probably the major difference between eras is the types of desirable, available jobs in today's soap world. In addition to doctors, lawyers and politicians, there are many more journalists, detectives, police officers, show business performers and bartenders than before. Also, women occupy the work force at all levels in a much more significant way than before. They are evident in all professions, and at all economic levels.

6. Some illnesses in today's soap operas, such as temporary blindness and psychosomatic paralysis, are similar to those forty years ago. However, others, such as amnesia and nonspecific "terminal illnesses," are not as popular as they have been in the past.

It is clear that certain themes and storylines have been added, deleted, or modified in the basic soap opera formula over the past forty years. But are Arnheim's criticisms about serial plot crises having "atypical" causes still valid? To answer this question, one must address a more basic issue: How well do soap operas mirror reality in today's world?

The Reflection of Reality in Today's Soaps

As indicated earlier in this chapter, most critics would agree that daytime drama, like other broadcast programming, changed drastically during the fifties and sixties. These changes were due in part to advancing technology as well as the prevailing political climate of the time.

In the early fifties, most soap operas moved from radio to television, and the resulting change in technology was felt at all levels, including scriptwriting. First of all, daily serials soon became thirty minutes in length as compared to the fifteen-minute capsules of the thirties and forties. Because viewers could now see their characters, plotlines became more slowly paced to capitalize on all the advantages of the visual medium, such as character reactions and new locales. In fact, a common plotline, such as a marriage proposal, could last for weeks in a fifties' television soap. After the male character "popped the question" in *Secret Storm,* for example, several days of programming would be spent learning the reactions of both principal and supporting characters to this event: the bride-to-be, her mother, her old boyfriend, his old girlfriend or ex-wife, his secret admirer, her secret admirer, etc., etc. The possibilities were endless. Thus, one major plotline could sustain itself for weeks longer on television than would be possible on radio despite the added fifteen minutes of programming each day.

Relatedly, the visual medium of television allowed for a wider choice in soap opera settings, because writers were not forced to limit themselves to the experiential world of radio listeners. Instead, they could take their characters anywhere, as long as they visually established the appropriate setting. However, the visual element in television also had distinct limits, for soap writers could no longer rely on "imagination" to set a scene. Instead, they would have to create the mood visually, which was a time-consuming and potentially expensive venture. As a result, stories with more true-to-life settings, such as *The Guiding Light* (created by Irna Phillips) and *Search for Tomorrow* (written by Roy Winsor) became more popular to both networks and viewers.

The late sixties has been previously described as the "era of relevance," due mainly to Agnes Nixon's contributions to soap opera drama on the ABC network.[16] Nixon, among other things, included different racial and ethnic groups (Jews, Blacks, Irish and Polish) in her soaps, and these characters were often confronted with societal problems of drug addiction, child abuse and venereal disease as well as the more traditional fare of love, marriage and children. Sex was freer, women were more independent, and community problems were addressed more directly than in the past. This new programming trend was lauded by both viewers and critics: ratings skyrocketed and scholars now asserted that daytime drama was both entertaining and informative. In fact, much of the research in the early seventies centered on the positive educational effects viewers had from watching soap operas.

When reviewing these trends, it is easy to see that daytime drama has reflected more reality in recent decades than during the time of Arnheim's 1941 analysis. And, in some cases, it can even be said that daytime drama has played a direct role in changing certain social behaviors. For example, in the late seventies, when South American coffee prices skyrocketed, most soap opera characters diverted from their usual practice of offering coffee and served tea or another beverage instead. The apparent correlation between the use of a non-coffee beverage on soaps and the decline in American coffee consumption was astonishing. While no one would argue that soap operas were solely responsible for the American coffee cutback, the "non-coffee" behavior on daytime drama was nevertheless acknowledged as having a distinct influence on resulting social attitudes and behavior in this area.

Despite certain instances of social action in soap operas, however, research indicates that daytime dramas generally do not address serious societal issues in a continuing, in-depth manner. Instead, controversial plotlines are introduced sporadically, and kept only as long as they receive positive viewer response.[17] If topics are unpopular, such as the 1983 lesbian storyline in *All My Children,* they are usually dropped within a few weeks and never reintroduced.[18]

There are certain social problems which do occur regularly in daytime drama. However, all too often, they are portrayed less realistically than most social activists would prefer. Consider the following:

1. In the past several years, alcoholism has been combined with drug use many times to create a new problem of "substance abuse." However, most of these instances occur in one of several ways: a) one-night drinking binges which ultimately lead to other problems; b) overuse of prescription drugs, but on a short-term basis; c) an unwitting involvement with an illicit drug ring; or d) an innocent character being deceptively fed drugs. It is important to emphasize that in most cases, fictional alcohol/drug abuse does not occur over a long period of time ... as generally happens in real life.

2. Psychological problems have always been common in soap operas, but today's trends diverge from traditional mental health maladies. Most often, emotional problems in eighties' daytime drama are linked to hypnotic suggestion (after the character has been kidnapped), mysticism or extrasensory perception. Usually, characters who have been seen as having psychological problems are later diagnosed as having been victimized by sinister outside sources. For example, a 1985 storyline in *The Guiding Light* involved a character named Billy Lewis, who was programmed to kill his half-brother, Kyle Samson, by an evil secret organization known as "Infinity." For months, Billy's friends and relatives noticed his odd behavior, but assumed a mental problem rather than a wicked plot. Only through a dramatic courtroom scene was Billy Lewis revealed as a crime victim instead of an emotionally troubled man.

3. As noted previously, jobs are a distinctly important storyline in soap operas, but rarely are people fired or laid off due to economic conditions as in the real world. More often, soap opera characters quit and form their own businesses (usually a nightclub or bar); or they are suspended for several weeks, later to be rehired and lauded for their courage despite the suspension.

In summary, then, it can be said that today's daytime serials reflect social reality more accurately than during the time of Arnheim's 1941 study. However, the depth and risk of issue-taking are directly related to viewer response and storyline popularity. And, given the economic foundations of television, this trend is likely to continue.

Soap Opera Plots and Ratings

As discussed previously, societal concerns, political issues and economic climate have some influence on soap opera stories. However, other factors, such as prime-time television, the film industry, and television rating structures, seem even more powerful in dictating the way daytime serial plotlines are written. Over the last several years, for example, storyline segments in most daytime serials have imitated scenes from such prime-time television fare as *Dynasty* and *Knots Landing,* and movies such as *Flashdance, Raiders of the Lost Ark,* and *Witness.* Since prime-time series and movies are much more expensive to produce than soap operas, it's obvious that there have been limitations to daytime serial imitation. However, soap opera producers seem to feel that success in any context is worthy of replication; and this feeling has been most directly conveyed in daytime drama through longer program segments (changing from half-hour to hour-long shows) and larger budgets over the last several years.

Daytime drama has also adopted a "prime-time" attitude toward ratings and their importance to program survival. Thus, it is not very surprising to learn that soap operas save most of their key dramatic action for ratings sweep periods, much like their counterparts in prime-time drama. In fact, the intelligent viewer's key to watching soap operas over the past several years has been to concentrate on programs during the months of February, May, July and November—the sweep periods—because, as in prime-time shows, more action, adventure, passion and problem resolution are likely to occur during these times.

In reviewing the occurrences of plotline themes between 1983–1985, it is important to note several observations as they relate to television ratings and the sweep periods. First of all, the storylines most likely to be aired during a ratings sweep period include:

1) marriage
2) investigations (usually involving international travel)
3) the discovery of key clues in some type of crime or secret
4) court cases
5) criminal arrests
6) dramatic accidents such as fires, explosions, airplane trouble or car crashes
7) the discovery of a character with a false identity
8) life-saving surgery
9) death

Also, it is not unusual for a person suffering from a traumatic injury or psychosomatic illness to recover dramatically in February, May, July or November.

In contrast to "sweep period" storylines, certain themes occur consistently throughout the year, thus classifying them as part of the general soap opera formula. Not surprisingly, these themes have been characteristic of daytime drama since its inception in the early thirties. They are the following:

1) parenthood
2) romance
3) love

4) jealous lovers
5) romantic stumbling blocks
6) romance break-ups
7) making love
8) passion
9) rebounding
10) psychological problems
11) crime
12) deception
13) secrets
14) jobs
15) money
16) illness/injury

Clearly, it can be said that soap opera plots in the eighties still revolve around issues of love, family, health and security — much like the storylines in early radio daytime drama. And even today, soap opera characters respond to these issues with the same philosophy as their predecessors, which was best expressed by Kay Fairchild, a central character in a forties' radio serial called *Stepmother:*

> All we can be sure of is that nothing is sure. And that tomorrow won't be like today. Our lives move in cycles — sometimes that's a good thing to remember, sometimes bad. We're in a dark valley that allows us to hope, and to be almost sure that we'll come out after awhile on top of a hill. But, we have to remember, too, that beyond every hill, there's another valley.[19]

The essence of soap opera plots is that they are ever-changing. As it can be said that no character can be content for very long, so it also can be said that misery and despair are temporary states in a character's soap opera life. Most significantly, in the eighties, it can be said that a character can project his/her situation to last no longer than the next ratings sweep; for these periods represent a time of conclusion as well as a time for renewal.

Individuality in Daytime Drama

It was established earlier in this chapter that all soap operas have similar thematic styles and a specific formula. However, today's programs also have special identities of their own, including different program lengths, storyline pace, numbers of plots and thematic emphasis (see Table 1.1). These individual differences are useful in finding correlations between specific shows and their appeal to specific target audiences. However, soap opera audiences will not be addressed until a later chapter. For the

TABLE 1.1

SOAP OPERA STORYLINES, JULY 1983–1985*

Soap Opera	Program Length	Avg. # of Themes/Day	Initial Year of Broadcast	Most Popular Themes**
ALL MY CHILDREN (ABC)	60 min.	3.1	1970	1. Mystery/Intrigue Crime/Punishment (tie) 2. Romance/Love/Sex
ANOTHER WORLD (NBC)	60 min.	2.3	1964	1. Mystery/Intrigue Crime/Punishment (tie) 2. Finance/Professional
AS THE WORLD TURNS (CBS)	60 min.	3.0	1956	1. Mystery/Intrigue 2. Crime/Punishment
CAPITOL (CBS)	30 min.	2.6	1981	1. Romance/Love/Sex 2. Mystery/Intrigue
DAYS OF OUR LIVES (NBC)	60 min.	2.8	1965	1. Crime/Punishment 2. Romance/Love/Sex Mystery/Intrigue (tie)
GENERAL HOSPITAL (ABC)	60 min.	2.8	1963	1. Crime/Punishment 2. Finance/Professional Mystery/Intrigue (tie)
GUIDING LIGHT (CBS)	60 min.	3.1	1937	1. Crime/Punishment 2. Mystery/Intrigue Romance/Love/Sex (tie)
LOVING (ABC)	30 min.	2.4	1983	1. Mystery/Intrigue Romance/Love/Sex (tie) 2. Finance/Professional
ONE LIFE TO LIVE (ABC)	60 min.	2.9	1968	1. Crime/Punishment Finance/Professional (tie) 2. Mystery/Intrigue
RYAN'S HOPE (ABC)	30 min.	2.3	1975	1. Mystery/Intrigue 2. Romance/Love/Sex
YOUNG AND RESTLESS (CBS)	60 min.	2.5	1973	1. Mystery/Intrigue 2. Romance/Love/Sex

*See n.11, Introduction
**in order of most coverage

moment, it is more useful simply to compare today's soap operas in plotline structure, pace and presentation.

Table 1.1 reveals that plot pacing was quite different among several of the soap operas surveyed from 1983–1985. Within the hour-long soaps, *Another World* seemed to move its stories most slowly (by averaging 2.3 themes per day). On the other hand, *All My Children* and *The Guiding Light* seemed to present the most plot action (with an average of 3.1 themes per day). The median pace for sixty-minute soap operas was 2.81 themes per day, making *Another World* and *The Young and the Restless* slower-paced than average; and *All My Children, As the World Turns* and *The Guiding Light* faster than average.

There were only three half-hour soap operas surveyed in 1983–1985, and the plot pacing of each was relatively similar. The median number of themes presented in a thirty-minute soap was about 2.43 per day. Most noteworthy about this statistic is the fact that even the slowest-paced half-hour soap opera used the same number of themes in half as much time as the hour-long *Another World*. Also, it is important to observe that doubling the time slot from thirty to sixty minutes did not greatly change the average number of themes plotted in each soap opera each day.

As for thematic popularity, it is clear that storylines involving mystery/intrigue and crime/punishment seemed to dominate soap operas from 1983–1985. However, the way in which each drama combined these themes with others as well as the number of times each was actually used (see Appendix A, Table 2) provides evidence that within the general formula labeled "soap opera form" lie creative latitudes.

One final note should be added to the 1983–1985 findings on page 12. They represent only a small portion of time in the forty-year evolution of soap operas. As the reader will discover in Chapter 4, each of these eleven daytime dramas has undergone both large and small changes since its inception. And each change has been reflective of the socioeconomic and political climates as well as other media influences and listener/viewer response.

Chapter Two

The Characters

Soap opera characters—and the actors who portray them—have undergone enormous changes since the inception of radio daytime drama in the early thirties. The relationship between actors and their roles has become more complex and intertwined since the beginning of serial drama, and the resulting configuration has meant that actors can earn more money and fame than in years past. However, most contemporary soap stars would agree that many of today's rewards are counterbalanced by obligations that go far beyond the daily TV studio tapings.

During the Depression, actors were paid as little as $10 per fifteen-minute episode if they were paid at all; sometimes they worked simply for the broadcasting credit on their resume.[1] Despite the low (or no) pay, however, most cast members in daytime drama were not disenchanted, for radio serials were not terribly demanding. They required no make-up, script memorization or specific physical characteristics. In fact, in the thirties and forties, one actor might be able to portray two or three people in several soaps because the radio audience could not "see" the characters. They could only discern vocal differences—not dual roles or physical incongruities between the actors and their characters.[2] As Robert Landry noted in *Variety:*

> ...memory acclaims radio actors as remarkably versatile and amazingly busy. They rushed from studio to studio, show to show, role to role. It never mattered if they were too young or too old, too fat or too scrawny, so long as they could maintain the illusion vocally.[3]

Today's soap opera actors average an annual salary of over $35,000 (although many of the more established and highly popular actors can earn at least three times that amount).[4] The salary allows them to subsist in New York or Los Angeles while also working (or waiting for work) in theatre, films, prime-time television and/or commercials. Thus, soaps have come to be known as a popular stepping stone or rite of passage to bigger and better things. Among the hundreds of well-known actors who list soap operas in their early credentials are Lee Grant, Donna Mills, Jill Clayburgh, JoBeth Williams, Alan Alda, Robby Benson, Don Knotts, Daniel J. Travanti . . . the list goes on and on.[5]

Production time for today's televised soap operas is much longer, more tedious and expensive than in early radio drama. For one thing, each daytime TV soap program lasts thirty to sixty minutes – at least twice as long as radio serials in the thirties and forties. In addition, pre-production and taping time are much more intense. In fact, soap opera actors usually begin their workday by 8:00 a.m., and work until 6:00 p.m. or later. Between these hours, they go through the following steps:

1) "line rehearsal" – the actors read through their scripts for pacing and interpretation;

2) "blocking rehearsal" – the actors run through the movements they'll have to make and where they must stand for a certain line or camera angle with the show's director;

3) "technical run-through" – the actors rehearse their lines with sets and props so that the production crew can experiment with lighting, camera shots, etc.;

4) "dress rehearsal" – the actors rehearse in costume and make-up;

5) the taping; and

6) re-taping (if there are any mistakes).

In some cases (especially in New York), the show must be finished by 4:30 p.m. so that different producers can prepare for another program, like the network news. In other situations, actors may not complete taping until 6:00 p.m. or later. And when the actors have finally finished their work at the studio, they usually go home and memorize the script for the next day's taping.[6] The process repeats itself day after day.

To the media critic, the cast members' studio schedules seem extremely rigorous in themselves. However, the actors' responsibilities to their respective shows do not end after the programs have been taped. Outside the studio, soap stars must deal with a huge amount of visibility and character identity. They must have publicity shots taken for over a dozen soap opera fan magazines, and they often travel on extended promotional tours. The schedule can be quite overwhelming; but the most difficult part for the actors is that often their fans cannot separate the stars from their characterizations. Consider the following:

> Peter Reckell is one of the hottest actors on daytime television. His stardom has brought many things: a six-figure salary and a $1 million home in Hollywood, 4,000 loyal members of his fan club, letters from women who want him to father their children, and an identity crisis.
>
> Reckell . . . is better known as Bo Brady, the sexy anti-hero on NBC's *Days of Our Lives,* and that's his problem. Fans call him Bo. They write to him as Bo. Some apparently believe he really *is* Bo. Call it a tribute

to his acting talent, but it's also the reason why success on daytime television, for all its rewards, can easily become a trap. Reckell would like to leave daytime, but to do so, he's going to have to shed the character of Bo Brady.[7]

The characters—and the actors who portray them—are often intrinsically interwoven and seen as one and the same. Consequently, separating the soap character from the actor's image is often a difficult, if not impossible, task to undertake. The reason is that characterization is the main component of audience interest in soaps (see Chapter 3). As established earlier in this book, many similar plotlines occur in soap operas. And since most devoted viewers have come to recognize the stories associated with the genre of daytime drama, they are usually not challenged by the serial themes. Rather, the audience intrigue lies in *how* their favorite characters respond within the familiar plots, and not in the plotlines themselves.

Because of the overwhelming popularity of soap opera stars, Chapter 2 is devoted to the characters and the actors who portray them. It will also address the evolution of daytime dramatic characterization over the last several decades—psychologically, occupationally and socioeconomically.

Psychological Profiles: Then and Now

In the early years of serial drama, the audience often used the radio announcer as well as actors' voices to help them determine whether their story characters were basically good or bad. An authoritative voiceover describing each actor's entrance or exit might use phrases like, "the kindly man walking down the stairs," or "that half-gangster" to slant feelings about the goodness or badness of specific characters.[8] Also, the characters themselves, through dialogue or mere tone of voice, could contribute to the listeners' perceptions of their moral fiber.

When soap operas began in the early thirties, most characters in the storylines were either "good" or "bad." However, scriptwriters soon realized that serial drama could not last long without using characters who possessed less distinguishable moral qualities. By the early forties, researcher Rudolf Arnheim noted that there were three basic psychological profiles of soap opera characters: the "good," the "bad," and the "weak."

"Good" people were not without fault; they often did bad things. But the main difference between "good" characters and the other two types was that the problems they caused were to themselves or their immediate families—not to innocent victims. According to Arnheim:

Good people create trouble, e.g., by deceiving others for their own good: a wife "gives hope" to a blind husband by making him believe she is expecting a child; an actor plays the role of a blind girl's brother to save her from knowing that the brother is in prison under a murder charge; another actor offers his services to make a neglecting husband jealous. A "good" man may fall in love with somebody else's wife, or being married himself, to another woman, but such a love relation is never "consummated," and generally the person's faultiness tends to justify the slip. Good people also accuse themselves of crimes in order to shield others. An exemplary woman was allowed to try keeping an adopted child from the real mother by dubious tricks, these being apparently excused by virtue of motherly affection.[9]

"Good" troublemakers in the forties were rarely punished; scriptwriters felt that their motives, while somewhat imperfect, were directed toward ultimate justice. In a sense, "good" characters were acceptable Machiavellians — their ends justified their means.

Because of the demographic composition of daytime drama's listening audience, it is not surprising to note that there were many more "good" women than "good" men as primary characters. Also, "good" troublemakers succeeded in their goals much more often than "bad" or "weak" troublemakers. Arnheim surmised that these phenomena were presented to reassure the listening housewife that her life's work was invaluable, even though it may not be lauded by certain other sectors of society.

"Bad" characters, on the other hand, were devious, reprehensible and beyond redemption. They clearly set out to cause trouble for others — most often to innocent bystanders. "Bad" people were hardly ever victimized; any trouble caused to their families or themselves was clearly accidental. And, not so surprisingly, "bad" characters were more often men than women, especially in public affairs crime and economic problems.[10] "Bad" people were to blame for many of the "good" people's problems. Their indiscretions ranged from neglect to maniacal revenge. In short, "bad" characters, rather than external conditions, were responsible for most of the unhappiness.

"Bad" people in serial drama rarely showed any inner conflict. They never worried about their lack of goodness; instead, they made others worry about them. Fortunately, however, "bad" characters were rarely able to see their devious plans executed to completion. Audiences were often in suspense until the last, but ultimately, the "good" was victorious. Thus, the moral guidelines of the soap opera genre were once again intact.

"Weak" characters were not as clear-cut to the audience as "good" or "bad" because their behaviors were often the same as in the other groups. The real difference was not in their actions, but in their lack of conviction within those actions. Arnheim described "weak" characters as follows:

They excel in unpleasant qualities such as jealousy, vindictiveness, lack of balance, deceitfulness, selfishness, but it is clearly stated that these defects do not spring from an evil nature, but are weaknesses resulting

from bad experiences or lack of control. It is suggested that they may
eventually be brought back to their better selves.[11]

Most often, "weak" characters were devious troublemakers. However, the
damage they inflicted was usually on themselves or their families (like the
"good" characters). Unlike the "good," however, "weak" characters were
found largely in both genders—they occurred as often as "bad" males, and
almost twice as frequently as "good" or "bad" females.

After the "weak" characters were established in radio serials, writers
found that they were the most intriguing to their listeners. This was because
the "weak" individuals provided a more multi-dimensional presence than
"good" or "bad" people, making their actions much more difficult to
predict. As such, they quickly became an integral part of the triadic
characterization formula found in daytime drama.

These three established psychological profiles—the "good," the "bad,"
and the "weak"—continued their established formulaic roles throughout
the fifties and sixties. However, during the early seventies, daytime television changed a bit, becoming more sexually explicit. "Good," "bad," and
"weak" characters didn't change their profiles much during this time either;
but their focus became much more clearly pointed toward sexual relationships rather than friendships, jobs and economic conditions. Edith Efron,
in "The Soaps—Anything but 99-44/100 Percent Pure,"[12] described soap
opera characters of this era as falling into a mating/marriage/baby cycle
(although not necessarily in that order). Most "good," "bad," and "weak"
characters' actions during this period reflected some attitude toward sex
and its effect on marriage and reproduction.

"Good" people's sex, for example, was often passive and apologetic.
Efron identified this characteristic when describing a scene from a (then)
popular soap:

> In *The Doctors,* Sam, after an unendurably long buildup, finally takes
> Dr. Althea, a troubled divorcee, in his arms, and kisses her once, gently
> on the lips. He then looks ruefully, says, "I'm sorry," and moves to look
> mournfully out the window. "I'm not," murmurs Althea softly, and
> floats out of the room.[13]

"Good" people's sex most often led to love, marriage and a baby, for babies
were a necessary focal point in daytime drama of the fifties, sixties and early
seventies. "Good" people were obsessed with pregnancy, and most female
soap characters during this era were constantly thinking about having
children—when, where and with whom. Many of the storyline themes also
addressed the psychological aspects of childbearing, including the frustra-
tions of not being pregnant, carrying the unborn child through medical
difficulties, and the heroic fight for survival of both mother and baby during the actual childbirth. Each dramatic aspect—from conception to

delivery—filled daytime storyline capsules for months, much to the audience's delight. And the emotional strain of pre-natal and post-natal traumas also justified certain irascible and irrational behaviors of "good" female characters. Audiences empathized with the "good" people and found that some of their actions, while seemingly bad, were simply reflective of the enormous strain of raising a family.[14]

Conversely, "bad" characters were much more interested in sex than in love, and were definitely anti-baby. "Bad" or "weak" women were often portrayed as career-oriented people, who, out of spite or ignorance, did not center their lives around (what should be) the most important value—the home. Obviously, these characterizations reflected the writers' desire to appeal to their largest audience segment, housewives. However, as the early seventies developed into the mid- and late-seventies, more families became two-income households. The number of daytime audience housewives began to diminish, and soap opera writers found themselves appealing to a new set of demographics.

As a result, daytime drama entered into the mid-seventies with changes in the "black-white" moral fiber of soap characters as well as a shift away from the homemaker emphasis. Characters began to be seen as "primarily good," "primarily bad," or "primarily weak," as compared to the harsher previous categories. In fact, researchers like Cassata and Skill found that their viewer subjects seemed much less judgmental when describing often-watched characters. Take Karen Wolek, from *One Life to Live,* for example. Cassata and Skill described her character in the following way:

> Karen is seen as a "mostly good" person whose portrayal of women falls in the gray area of being a combination of "realistic" and "unrealistic." For the most part, Karen's emotional view of the world seems to cloud good judgment and even common sense. She seems to lack a strong focus as to where her life is headed, which in a goal-oriented society makes her a poor role model for women. Beyond these weaknesses, Karen is seen as a warm, caring human being whose vulnerability seems to attract a loyal and sympathetic following.[15]

This change in characters' moral evaluations was due to several factors: viewer power; writer realism; and actor power.

1. *Viewer Power.* The rising audience demographics for daytime television gave soap opera fans a stronger voice in character development. If they were unhappy with the turn of events on a particular soap, they often wrote to the producers and spearheaded a change in plot or character direction. Also, the shift toward male soap viewers was directly responsible for modifying certain percentages of "good," "bad" and "weak" male characters in daytime drama.

2. *Writer Realism.* Many new and innovative writers were added to soap opera staffs during the mid-seventies. This change was due in part to the expansion of many daytime programs to an hour-long format. The result of this expansion was two-fold: more writers contributed more ideas for characterization; and the newer writers seemed to inject a greater realism when composing character profiles. As Jeff Ryder, one of the head writers on *The Guiding Light,* commented:

> I like them (the characters) all, which is why it is difficult to create a character who is one-hundred percent mean. I understand their motivations, the ups and downs of these friends of ours that we created. Indeed, they're based on composites of people we know. We've nourished them; we watch them grow.[16]

3. Actor Power. Actors themselves began to grow in power and status. Consequently, their demands to have a voice in developing their character were often heeded through plotline changes or interpretation. A good example of an actor influencing storyline development occurred over ten years ago with actress Francesca James, who played Kitty Shea on *All My Children* from 1972–1977. It seems that the character Kitty began a downward spiral of fatigue, depression and loneliness. The character's mental state began to affect Francesca's own personality, since she was involved with the character daily. As a result, she asked creator Agnes Nixon to change Kitty's fate a bit. Nixon then decided to have Kitty see a therapist. Her life improved drastically—and so did that of Francesca James.[17]

As for changes in interpretation, Larry Keith, who played Nick Davis on *All My Children,* recalled his character changes, even when the scriptwriters changed nothing:

> This guy I play[ed] was supposed to be (an out-and-out villain), but I didn't want to make him that black-and-white. Actors, you see, can help shape the role—they can play *against* the material, the way they move, the way they speak, their expressions—that can change the feeling of a character. That's what I did with "Nick Davis."[18]

In summary, it can be said that the moral composition of most soap opera characters today is drastically different from that in radio daytime drama. Viewers rarely see a totally "good" or "bad" character in eighties' soap operas. Instead, characters are described as "primarily" good or bad. Finally, the numbers of "primarily" good male characters have grown substantially due to changing audience demographics, writing strategies and acting freedom.

Occupations: Then and Now

Like the evolution of "good," "bad" and "weak" characters, the occupational levels among fictional residents in soap opera towns have changed substantially over the last several decades. Housewives and professionals have been around since the early Hummert serials; however, their numbers and prominence in daytime drama have fluctuated in accordance with the changing work force in America.

In early radio, most of the main soap opera characters were considered economically middle-class. Their homes, their dress and the towns in which they lived were usually described by radio announcers as plain, simple and not overly impressive. Rudolf Arnheim noted that homemaking and professional occupations continued to be most prevalent in soap operas during the early forties. The large numbers of housewives in serial drama were easy to explain: They were easily identifiable to most of the listening audience. However, the presence of characters with professional careers was more difficult to understand; while most of the professional characters featured (such as physicians, attorneys and artists) were probably better off economically than most listeners, they were usually not rich enough to be considered fantasy objects. On the other hand, society people, high political officials and big businessmen — characters who inspired fantasy and wish fulfillment — usually gave way to independent but small shopkeepers.

Arnheim suggested three reasons for this phenomenon. First of all, serial drama required much conflict and trouble to keep the stories moving from month to month and year to year. Doctors and lawyers were thus essential to have around for unknown illnesses, life-saving surgery, mental problems, felonious crimes and courtroom cases — the storylines for which a dramatic climax was necessary.

Secondly, Arnheim noted that most of the professionals in daytime drama were men. And, while they might have an occasional heroic role in an isolated crisis, their main function was to be friends or husbands to the central female characters. As Chapter 1 established, most storylines were very personal and inner-directed. The listening audience rarely experienced professional people *actually working* (except during a dramatic climax); it was their *personal* life that was most interesting.

Finally, since leadership and success were based on personal qualities much more often than on professional credentials,[19] professional characters often served as foils for the "common folk" to show their knowledge and expertise. Thus, housewives and small shopkeepers often succeeded in their endeavors when those most qualified were unable.[20] Arnheim described the following characters from popular forties' serials, who saw simple truth in areas where other, more professional people had failed:

> The "leave-it-to-me" man, storekeeper Scattergood Baines, convicts the respected president of the local school of a grave professional error. Ma Perkins, the country woman, provides a senatorial committee with the

decisive clues for the disclosure of a large scandal, and the owner of a small second-hand book store at the lower East Side of New York, an old Jew, gives philosophical advice to a famous physician, to his son, and to last year's number 1 debutante, who, excited by their troubles, rather foolishly buzz among the bookshelves.[21]

Like the moral evaluation of characters, storylines dealing with professional status versus personal worth persisted for at least two decades, including the soap opera transition from radio to TV. However, in the late sixties and early seventies, new daytime serial programs entered the network competition. These new shows began to focus more on professional careers as well as representation from other areas of the workplace. This movement was initiated by story creator Agnes Nixon and executive producer Gloria Monty at ABC; and as other network competitors saw ABC's success with their character innovations, most followed suit. CBS and NBC began to revamp their older, more traditional shows, reflecting the new demographics of their changing American audience. In the late sixties, networks realized that daytime audiences had become younger, more male, more educated, more career-oriented, and more ethnically diverse than in the past. But they probably would not have signalled any changes had they not seen the results of Agnes Nixon's creation and Gloria Monty's execution.

When introducing *One Life to Live* and *All My Children* in the late sixties and early seventies, Nixon tried several ideas that were considered quite unique for their time. For one thing, black doctors and lawyers became central characters, providing substance for added professional storylines as well as a more varied ethnic representation in daytime drama. Also, certain female characters became more career-oriented; and now these professional women could also be "good." They were no longer seen as villainesses for wanting to share their home life with a career.[22]

In short, the late sixties and early seventies brought more minorities to the soap opera workplace. Additionally, new soap operas created during this period were situated in larger towns and cities, thus giving a more cosmopolitan look to their new fictional demographics. More blue-collar workers, skilled as well as unskilled laborers, were featured in storylines. However, as critic Marya Mannes observed:

...(the) soap opera still concern(ed) itself basically with one kind of America: the comfortable suburban life of white, middle-class Protestants, the homes always impeccably neat and ultra-conservative, the men either lawyers, doctors, small-businessmen or newspaper types, the women always perfectly coiffed and smartly attired, the forces of good and the forces of evil neatly opposed, love finally triumphant over obstacles that would have mired Eros himself.[23]

Thus, despite some of the innovations begun in the late sixties and early seventies, the basic premise behind most soap operas was still primarily white, middle-class, and oriented toward hearth and home.

The mid-seventies brought with them more drastic changes than those prompted by social activists in the late sixties. These changes were due primarily to the introduction and immediate popularity of prime-time soap operas. The meteoric ratings success of shows like *Dallas* and *Dynasty* led daytime serial producers to expand their budgets, shoot more scenes on location, and develop more action/adventure plotlines. In addition, new character types, such as the millionaire entrepreneur, emerged in daytime drama. Usually, this nouveau-riche big businessman was a strong male character who had made a fortune through wildcat oil wells, diamond mines, marketing and/or investments.[24] And, unlike rich, strong males in past soaps, these men were not necessarily evil (although they might be ruthless at times). Media critic Terry Ann Knopf described five different types of "midday millionaires" who dominated the soap opera screen in the late seventies and early eighties. They were typed as follows:

1. *Romantic.* This type was most aptly portrayed by the character James Stenbeck in *As the World Turns.* James was rich, cultured and elite. He cared only for those people and things that were in good taste. Stenbeck was tall, dark and exotically good-looking; his major passions were beautiful women and racehorses. James Stenbeck could be despicable to his enemies, but his genuine charm and good manners were irresistible to most women.

2. *Sexy.* The character of Travis Sentell on *Search for Tomorrow* was a "sexy" millionaire with a macho, beefcake physique. Sentell was highly educated—he spoke three languages fluently—and could feel comfortable at any high society affair. However, his experiences in Vietnam brought him closer to people less wealthy than himself. In short, Travis Sentell was daytime television's answer to *Dallas'* Bobby Ewing ... a rich, handsome hero who was a common man at heart.

3. *Saintly.* This rich character type was "primarily good." As portrayed through Mac Cory of *Another World,* the saintly millionaire continued to be patient, kind and forgiving, even though he was constantly victimized by conniving wives, children and friends.

4. *Aristocratic.* A good example of the aristocratic millionaire was Alan Spaulding in *The Guiding Light.* He wore wealth and good breeding like a finely cut suit. He came from the finest, most exclusive private schools and his family was one of the established rich in Springfield. Spaulding was a ruthless businessman, but an equally passionate lover—a desirable fantasy partner in many ways.

5. *Big Daddyish.* Asa Buchanan from *One Life to Life* best personified this type. He was an older version of *Dallas'* J.R. Ewing, with Texas wealth and an insatiable hunger for power. Buchanan owned oil wells, cattle, horses, a football team and a record company called Lone Star Productions. This "big daddy" type of millionaire was the most "bad" of all big businessmen, and, like J.R. Ewing, viewers loved to hate him.

In addition to the influence of prime-time television, soap opera writers felt the impact of other, larger societal conditions. For example, beginning with the 1974 Watergate scandal and continuing through Wilbur Mills' escapades with Fanne Foxe in Washington, D.C.'s Tidal Basin and Wayne Hays' admission to placing his mistress, Elizabeth Ray, on Congressional payroll, public opinion of governmental officials was extremely low. As a result, political characters became more numerous and villainous than ever before in daytime drama. Politicians like Mitch Williams *(General Hospital),* Ted Adamson *(Search for Tomorrow),* Kellam Chandler *(Days of Our Lives)* and Zachary Colton *(Another World)* entered the world of soaps as "overly ambitious, weak, inept, ruthless and corrupt scoundrels."[25] Knopf noted that these characterizations reflected, not only daytime television's reaction to the demographic success of prime-time soaps, but also the public feeling that America was out of control economically, socially and politically. Audiences seemed to want more "take charge" figures in their television lives.

Thus, occupationally speaking, soap opera characters have changed enormously since their early radio days. While there are still high percentages of middle-class "common folk" who dispense simple wisdom, there is also a large contingent of materialistic fantasy figures in the eighties. And the trend seems likely to continue over the next few years.

Economic and Social Status: Then and Now

In 1941, Rudolf Arnheim surveyed the existing radio serials and found the following socioeconomic groups:

1) society people (sons of millionaires, families with big money, etc.) — 19 percent
2) high officials — 21 percent
3) big business — 33 percent
4) professionals — 73 percent
5) housewives — 65 percent
6) small business — 31 percent
7) wage earners — 19 percent
8) destitute people — 6 percent[26]

Arnheim saw in this breakdown a peculiarly American twist to the European tradition of writing about rich, high-society people. Like much European literature, soap opera writers included certain "upper crust" characters in their storylines. However, unlike European fiction, the role of these characters was usually to honor the down-to-earth qualities of the middle class. As Arnheim observed:

> The fiction of mutual intercourse on an equal level is stressed, e.g., in the case of a famous Broadway actor who consumes his time and nervous energy in helping the humbler middle-class family next door. Marriage with a member of the upper-class conveys honor on the just plain people. There is the spectacular career of the "orphan girl who was reared by two miners and who in young womanhood married England's wealthiest, most handsome lord." Ma Perkins, an elderly housewife and lumberyard owner in the country, has her daughter married to a brillant young congressman in Washington. Mrs. Stella Dallas, who is a lower, middle-class woman and wants to remain one, was married to a diplomatic attache in the Capitol, and her daughter "went out of her mother's life" by marrying a man who is prominent in Washington society. At the same time, proud self-assertion and a certain resentment against people who draw high prestige from wealth or a professional position is often clearly expressed. A rich businessman's marriage proposal is rejected. A bankrupt real estate agent protests against his daughter's desire to marry an attractive young millionaire. The elegant and rich physician courting a simple "government girl" is a "heel" who well deserves to be murdered by an equally rich "glamour girl." A taxicab driver wrote a symphony worth $25,000 and receives but scarcely appreciates the attentions of an unscrupulously wealthy wangler and his elegant wife.[27]

As discussed earlier in this chapter, many soap opera characters reflected a middle-class bias because of the networks' desire to mirror the beliefs, attitudes and values of their listening audience. And, as noted in Arnheim's research, the audience responded most favorably to the notion of middle-class characters having more inner strength and power than those who might be better off educationally, financially and occupationally.

In the eighties, this same type of theme is still very desirable, as can be seen in some of the most popular storylines of the 1984–1985 and 1985–1986 seasons:

• The son of a prominent senator, who himself seeks political office, falls in love with a hooker. Unknown to him, she bears his child, and tries to live in the shadows of Washington, D.C. He finds her, however, along with his young son, and they plan to marry—alienating him from his wealthy, prominent family.

• A ruthless attorney—the son of a rich, ruthless businessman—finds happiness with a poor but proud nurse, who has recently left the convent. He may still be a villain-like character to many; but to his "innocent" woman friend, he repeatedly acts like a knight in shining armor.

• A beautiful young woman from "the other side of the tracks" finds herself the object of competition between men from two opposing wealthy families. While she ultimately chooses one, the other is perpetually seeking weaknesses in the links that bond her marriage.

- A suave, charming, rich young man moves into town to invest in several businesses. Despite his financial successes, however, he feels lonely and unloved, since his wife has died recently and he has no one with whom to share his wealth and happiness. While supervising one of his restaurants, he encounters a pretty college student—the daughter of a successful physician—and she changes his life overnight.
- The former merchant-marine son of an Irish immigrant overcomes his checkered past to marry the stunning daughter of a nightclub entrepreneur. While their class differences plague their marriage from time to time, they always reconcile after discussing their problems with the husband's blue-collar family.

As anyone can see, the storyline of the "rich serving the poor" has survived for over fifty years as a soap opera staple. Perhaps this is due to the fact that the primary audience of middle-class women has not changed drastically since Arnheim's study; and that a popular fantasy among this group of viewers focuses on the rich, who need "more ordinary" people to help them achieve ultimate happiness.

Despite the prominence of plotlines based on conflicting social status, however, there have been several efforts over the years towards better representation of each economic class. The success in this area has come mainly from introducing more realistic representatives of different ethnic groups and, accordingly, presenting a more "human" assessment of each social group. No longer is there a "good-bad" value judgment implicit within a character's social standing; all types of morality are present in all economic classes.

The "humanization" of socioeconomic classes began with Agnes Nixon's creation of *One Life to Live* in 1968. To develop her characters, Nixon used the "triple threat"—ethnic, economic and social diversity. Consequently, her very first storyline was vastly different from other soap opera fare. It involved a poor Polish-American who fell in love with the daughter of a wealthy Protestant publisher in the community. This daughter was a bit unstable—a result of pressures from her father—so she, unaware of the Pole's love for her, promptly fell for an Irish-American. However, the ethnically mired plot did not end there. The publisher's other daughter had an affair with the Polish-American's doctor brother; the Irish-American's sister married a Jew; and the Polish-American's sister romanced a doctor who had once been involved with a black woman.[28]

The ratings soared on *One Life to Live,* and predictably, new soaps as well as the more established daytime serials followed ethnic suit with characters like the Leshinsky family *(Search for Tomorrow),* the Ryans *(Ryan's Hope)* and the Grants (a black family in *Days of Our Lives).* ABC became the undisputed leader in this area; CBS was the most conservative network in changing its WASP orientation. In fact, in one of CBS's new seventies' soaps, *The Young and the Restless,* most of the characters were not only white, Anglo-Saxon and rich, they also were glamorous types who rarely associated with the blue-collar workers, much less different ethnic groups. *The Young and the Restless* was the exception to the ethnic diversification rule of the late sixties and early seventies. Most writers of daytime drama followed the popular trend of introducing ethnically different characters to "socially relevant" storylines.

As certain ethnic groups grew in popularity, the corresponding soap characters became more central to the plotline. And, although most critics would agree that blacks and other minorities have never been adequately represented, several ethnic and racial groups have come a long way from portraying visiting out-of-town consultants, foreign psychoanalysts or occasional police officers. Some minority characters have actually become significant enough to the soap storylines to rate moral evaluations. Examples of such characters include Abe Carver, a black police detective on *Days of Our Lives* (primarily good); Heather Dalton, a black singer and law student on *As the World Turns* (primarily good); and Stefano DiMera, a wealthy Greek magnate on *Days of Our Lives* (bad).

Like the evolution of racial and ethnic representation in daytime drama, the introduction of a more balanced economic and social class distribution started in the late sixties. More blue-collar and lower income families entered the world of soaps, and, as Schemering noted in *The Soap Opera Encyclopedia,* "every adult female on *Ryan's Hope,* set in New York City, held down a job — from barmaid to doctor — to support herself or her family."[29]

By the late seventies, the upper end of the social strata also began to expand so that scholars began to identify several types of serial personalities that were different and more complex than the more traditional middle-class common folk. Rondina, Cassata and Skill developed twelve such categories: five primary personalities and seven secondary types.[30] These character types are still present in today's daytime dramas.

Primary Types

1. *The Chic Suburbanite.* This category is comprised of well-educated, achievement-oriented, upper-middle-class men and women. They are usually single or divorced, range in age from 20 to 34, work a professional job, and are primarily concerned with their overall image and social status. The "chic suburbanites" are rarely interested in happy relationships with family or friends; they usually interact with others for the sheer need to impress them or for the ultimate enhancement of their social standing. Viewers see this character type as flashy because of his/her attention to fashion and the latest "in" trends. As exemplified by Erica Kane *(All My Children)* and Mason Capwell *(Santa Barbara),* this type is seen as carefree and frivolous, and extremely selfish towards others.

2. *The Subtle Single.* Like the "chic suburbanites," these characters are young, upper-middle-class and well-educated. Women are much more numerous than men in this category, but both genders are professional and career-oriented. The major difference between "subtle singles" and their "chic" counterparts lies in their basic system of values. While characters like Erica Kane and Mason Capwell are power-hungry and selfish, characters of this type (as personified by Ross Marler in *The Guiding Light* and Marlena Brady in *Days of Our Lives*) are most interested in their bonds with family and friends. Though they are heavily committed to their careers, their professional activities are considered secondary to maintaining a strong sense of love and acceptance at home. "Subtle singles" dress much less flamboyantly than "chic suburbanites" and are "modest and dependable extroverts, who nevertheless enjoy a serene existence in today's fast-paced world."[31]

3. *The Traditional Family Person.* This category has been an integral part of the soap opera genre since 1930 and is still the backbone for most of today's daytime drama. Typically, characters who are "traditional family" people are married; however, they are not limited to one specific type of occupation. They can be professionals, blue-collar workers or homemakers. Likewise, their age range varies significantly between 20 and 64. Their common bond lies in their major concern that the family unit function smoothly. Members of the Horton family (in *Days of Our Lives*), the McCandlesses *(Capitol)* and the Webbers *(General Hospital)*, for example, are often preoccupied with pregnancy, childbirth, and their children's growth into adulthood. For women like Alice Horton *(Days of Our Lives)*, "family" is the cornerstone from which all other things are built; they believe in their husbands and children and often seek guidance from God to make their lives better. "Traditional families" are usually quite conservative in fashion, profession and philosophy of life.

4. *The Successful Professional.* Characters in this group are usually middle-aged upper- or middle-class professionals, like Clint Buchanan *(One Life to Live),* Fletcher Reed *(The Guiding Light),* and Jack Fenelli *(Ryan's Hope).* Usually, these people are single or divorced because of their single-minded devotion to their career. Work is their life, such that most of their leisure-time activities are also related in some way to their career. "Successful professionals" are "primarily good," but are often portrayed as incomplete, for their work has become far too important in their lives.

5. *The Elegant Socialite.* Characters of this type are usually middle-aged, married, widowed, or divorced, upper-class women like Myrna Clegg *(Capitol)* and Alexandra Spaulding *(The Guiding Light).* They often flaunt their wealthy, "upper crust" origins, and are constantly using their money to impress upon others that they are tasteful, civic-minded, and extremely cultural. These people are politically conservative and can be quite eccentric in dress and behavior. Often, they are not as much concerned with their own inner values as they are with their outward appearance to "the masses."

Secondary Types

1. **Self-Made Businesspersons.** As exemplified by C.C. Capwell *(Santa Barbara)* and Asa Buchanan *(One Life to Live)*, these characters are wealthy, ruthless and autocratic. Their lives and loves are run like an accountant's ledger; they perceive other characters as "friends" or "foes," depending on their needs at the time.

2. **Contented Youths.** Characters like Andy Dixon, Dusty Donovan (on *As the World Turns*) and T.R. Kendall *(Search for Tomorrow)*, represent this popular category — middle-class, high-school teenagers or college students who are members of traditional family units. They have strong ties to friends and family, and often suffer from the typical pains of growing up. Many of these youths have been featured since their birth, leading viewers to identify with them personally.

3. **Troubled Teens.** This group bears a demographic similarity to the "contented youths"; however, they suffer from the inability to cope with their transition from childhood to adulthood. As a result, they frequently fall prey to drinking, drugs, sex, and ill-suited friends. They are often classified as the "rebels" of the traditional families, and soap opera viewers often experience a love-hate relationship with them. Characters in this group include Brenda Clegg *(Capitol)*, Frannie Hughes *(As the World Turns)*, and Jennifer Rose Horton *(Days of Our Lives)*.

4. **Happy Homemakers.** These women, like Maeve Ryan *(Ryan's Hope)*, are seen as the true "pillars of love, strength and virtue" in the family unit.[32]

5. **Dissatisfied Homemakers.** Characters in this group, such as Vanessa Chamberlain Lewis (in *The Guiding Light*) and Liz Chandler Curtis (in *Days of Our Lives*), are often frustrated with their assigned roles as wives, mothers and homemakers. They yearn for more self-fulfillment — usually in the form of a professional career rather than charity work or civic duties. And, because they feel no one truly understands them, they cause strain in their relationships with family and friends.

6. **Retired Homebodies.** These people, like Nancy and Chris Hughes (in *As the World Turns*), have often been members of their soap opera family since its first program; as such, they carry with them a wisdom and strength to reconcile even the most discordant members of the family. They are known for their stability in a crisis and are considered to be very pleasant, congenial people who help without meddling, give advice without seeming dictatorial, and provide overwhelming and unselfish love for each and every member of their families.

7. **Frustrated Laborers.** Mostly comprised of males, this general type falls into two subcategories: the young (19–34), unsettled blue-collar workers who have no clear-cut direction to their lives; and the middle-aged (50–64) lower-middle- or middle-class laborers who have become bored and dissatisfied with their work and lives and are contemplating ways to change

their fates. Examples of the former subgroup include Wally McCandless *(Capitol)* and Holden Snyder *(As the World Turns)*. The character Stu Bergman *(Search for Tomorrow)* provides a good representation of the latter subgroup.

When reviewing today's "primary" and "secondary" typology, it is clear that economic and social roles have expanded in each category since Arnheim's study in the forties. Also, it is important to note that the upper classes are no longer filled with villains; in fact, many wealthy soap opera characters are attractive, heroic types.[33] Conversely, the lower classes are not completely made up of "good," long-suffering victims. An example of a despicable character who happens to be poor is the scheming, manipulative Ava Rescott Forbes in *Loving*. She was born "on the wrong side of the tracks" in the fictional town of Corinth, and has been making people's lives miserable ever since. Just a brief part of her soap opera life involved trapping the wealthy Jack Forbes into marrying her by becoming pregnant, losing the baby, and then secretly adopting her sister's baby so that she could deceive Jack into thinking it was theirs.[34]

In summary, soap opera characters are no longer as easily definable as in years past. And their complexities cross over moral, social and psychological boundaries. To be sure, this trend is likely to continue, due to the obvious viewer pleasure with the multi-dimensional natures of today's character types.

Chapter Three

The Audience

Probably the largest amount of research found in broadcasting is in the area of audience studies, and daytime drama is no exception. Audiences are a very powerful force in broadcasting. Programs often succeed or fail based on audience popularity; networks formulate their reputations — and their balance sheets — on whether or not audiences find their programs attractive; advertisers spend millions of dollars annually on commercial announcements within these popular programs; and social scientists constantly marvel at the reflective effects of commercially successful programming on audiences, and vice versa. In short, audiences are a key element in television and radio, and, as such, have been studied from various perspectives. To better understand the broadcast audience as it relates to daytime drama, it is necessary to explore the existing research from three major areas: ratings, network audience studies, and scholarly investigations.

Ratings

Ratings (or some type of ratings system) have existed almost since the rise of commercial sponsorship in radio. In the mid-twenties, several independent researchers set up agencies to study the audience popularity of radio programming, thereby showing advertisers how much their commercial dollars were worth in total listeners. Their efforts were met with great enthusiasm by those sponsors.

One of these early entrepreneurs, a man named Claude Hooper, emerged during this time as the proprietor of one of the most popular audience ratings systems in the business.[1] Hooper used "checkers" to telephone people and conduct interviews while listeners were tuned in to a specific show. Arguably, his results were not very scientific, for these "checkers" had no clear figures as to who listened to particular programs and who did not. Still, the Hooper ratings system was highly regarded by sponsors as the primary source of knowledge about their audiences.[2]

Hooper continued his ratings service supremacy until the mid-forties, when a newer, more advanced system took hold. This was the A.C. Nielsen Company, whose introduction of the "audimeter" (an automatic metering device which recorded the times the radio was turned on and to which programs it was tuned) revolutionized scientific methodology in broadcast ratings. Soon, Nielsen became the most sought-after ratings service in radio, and it has continued its strong reputation today as one of the two largest TV ratings services in the country.[3] The other giant is Arbitron, an offshoot of Control Data Corporation, which began measuring television audiences in 1949.[4]

For several years now, the two major services, A.C. Nielsen and Arbitron Company (ARB), have dominated the ratings market in television. They provide the necessary demographic information (audience age, gender, etc.) for networks as well as for individual stations in all of the larger broadcast areas. From these two sources, programmers, producers, writers and actors can discover their "ratings" and "share" popularity for specific programs.[5]

Methodologically speaking, Nielsen and Arbitron differ somewhat. A.C. Nielsen Company is made up of two divisions: the Nielsen Television Index (NTI) and the Nielsen Station Index (NSI). The NTI is the national division, providing information for network programmers; the NSI is the resource center for local television. Both divisions use a sample selection (e.g., the NTI measures 1260 households)[6] which is chosen randomly from telephone directories. Willing subjects agree to have an audimeter installed on their television sets, and they promise to fill out diaries to provide more detailed information for the company.

From the audimeters and diaries, Nielsen is able to provide the following information:[7]

1) the ratings and shares of audience for each televised program;

2) the program's ranking as compared with other shows during the same time block;

3) audience demographics, including age, gender, educational level, income, marital status, etc.;

4) "season-to-date" averages of program audiences;

5) estimates of average audiences for certain program types (like miniseries, soap operas, game shows, etc.);

6) a comparison of total TV use to years past; and

7) TV set use by time slots.[8]

Arbitron entered the broadcast market a few years later than A.C. Nielsen, but rapidly built its reputation by instituting such innovations as "ratings sweep" periods and "overnights." "Ratings sweeps" use the months of February, May, July and November to measure the audience popularity of specific shows as well as the relative ranking of competing stations or networks. It is for this reason, by the way, that most blockbuster prime-time television programming and soap opera cliff-hangers are presented at these times (see Chapter 1). The higher the rating, the more power networks have at the advertising bargaining table. "Overnights" provide networks and large TV stations with information about their shows within twelve hours of their airing. This information enables programmers to make decisions about retaining or cancelling certain shows within a relatively short period of time.

Arbitron Company answers the same types of programming questions as Nielsen, but performs this service for both local and network radio *and* television. They also use diaries for their local market research as well as a monitoring device similar to the audimeter for their network research. Sometimes, they add another element to their data-gathering—the "telephone incidental." This technique involves phoning subjects during a particular program or shortly thereafter to determine their reactions to the show.

Arbitron Company selects its sample by dividing the country up geographically. A computer selects certain households within each sample unit from master tapes distributed by a direct mail advertising company.[9] Because of its attention to such sophisticated statistical detail in its data gathering, Arbitron (like A.C. Nielsen) claims a very high degree of accuracy in its survey results.

When reviewing these brief summaries of the research techniques used by Nielsen and Arbitron, it is easy to see that they compare very favorably to each other in the ways they acquire data for their demographic analyses. There is no question that they are extremely credible research vehicles for networks, advertisers and producers.

Ratings are very important to commercial broadcasters. They determine who the audience is for specific programs; from that analysis, advertisers and networks (or stations) can negotiate for the price of commercial time. Then, the agreed-upon advertising prices feed back into the production system, so that audiences may receive better quality programs in the future. The process continues, as the ratings-commercial price-production budget cycle repeats itself over and over again.

Muriel Cantor noted that a network's daytime ratings are usually lower than its prime-time ratings because more television sets are turned on in the evening. Still, the budgets of daytime dramas are often determined on the basis of their demographic popularity. For example, the ABC soaps have been more heavily funded because of their overall ratings popularity since 1977.[10] And NBC usually provides larger budgets for its most successful soap opera to date, *Days of Our Lives.*

Despite their popularity among networks and sponsors, however, the Nielsen and Arbitron companies have not been without their critics. Todd Gitlin, in *Inside Prime Time,* described several of the systems' major weaknesses.[11] According to Gitlin, one of the major flaws in the Nielsen ratings set-up is its lack of true representativeness. Contrary to the usual criticisms of the survey's initial sample size of 1260, Gitlin found little fault in representative *size;* he felt that the number was statistically well-founded. However, the true problem lay in the fact that not everyone in the initial sample agrees to install an audimeter; in fact, in 1963, less than 50 percent of the people cooperated with the service. Since then, the figure has fluctuated dramatically, rising to 75 percent in 1966, dropping to 70 percent in 1979, and finally dipping to 67 percent in 1980. Based on this data, critics have asked whether the final sample is vastly different from the initial one. In other words, are people who refuse the survey different from those who agree to it?[12]

Subsequent research has answered that question, and indeed, those who cooperate are very different from those who don't. For one thing, cooperators tend to watch more television. They are also younger, more educated and come from larger families than non-cooperators. Finally, cooperators are generally more active television viewers; they choose specific programs because they truly want to watch them, not because they don't have anything else to do.

Other criticisms by Gitlin included the following:

1. Neither Nielsen and Arbitron can guarantee the accuracy of their diaries. Sometimes they are not written well; sometimes they are mere facsimiles of the *TV Guide* program descriptions. In either case, it is difficult to decipher the subject's true reaction to the show.

2. It is still not possible to ascertain whether viewers *actually* watch the show. There have been known cases where households, whether out of sympathy to a third-place network or to impress the researchers with the shows they watch, have turned the TV set on to a specific channel and not watched the show.

3. Nielsen keeps some of its sample households for several years (sometimes as many as twelve). There's no question that in that period of time, the distinct possibility of changing demographics exists in such households.

4. Nielsen counts only viewers in houses or apartments with listed phone numbers. This does not take into account persons living in military barracks, boarding houses, dormitories, multi-family units, hotels or motels. It also does not recognize many poor, older or minority people who may not own telephones.

Despite all the criticism, though, networks and advertisers seem quite pleased with the overall performances of Nielsen and Arbitron. As Gitlin noted:

> The limits of numbers are clear: They always have to be interpreted, and, of course they measure only the past, not the future. But absent a clear standard of taste or a strong sense of traditional form, absent any clear aesthetic or moral values in the mass market or in the executive suites,

the numbers have the great virtue of being there, looking radiantly exact.[13]

Together with statistics from the networks' own in-house audience research, firms like Nielsen and Arbitron help network executives feel confident that their programs reflect current audience taste.

Network Audience Research

Like Nielsen and Arbitron, the networks vary in their specific approaches to audience research. However, their goals are similar: Each network wants as many testing strategies as possible to help it determine its programming for the season.

CBS is the pioneer of audience testing. In fact, its first equipment to measure audience reactions was designed in the forties by Frank Stanton and Paul Lazarsfeld (editors of *Radio Research: 1942-1943*). At CBS, there are two basic screening facilities—one in New York and one in Los Angeles.[14] At each spot, staff assistants give away free tickets to tourists so that they may evaluate possible pilots for the following year. The tourists are said to be a more representative sample than Californians or New Yorkers. These volunteers are ushered into a screening room, where they find their seats equipped with two buttons—a red one and a green one. After the screening, they are given questionnaires to be completed.[15]

Usually, CBS audience researchers collect surveys of this type until they have reached their demographic requirements; then they throw out the extras.[16] After the significant data have been collected, they rate the pilots as Below Average, Average and Above Average, rank them accordingly, and later choose as many as they need for the next broadcast season.

ABC, on the other hand, contracts most of its testing to Audience Studies Incorporated (ASI) and uses Preview House in Los Angeles for its screening procedures. Volunteers are obtained in two different ways: the tourists, whom they gather in much the same way as CBS; and phone invitations. Instead of a series of small screening rooms (like CBS), Preview House uses a 400-seat auditorium, where chairs with five-position switches allow viewers to rate the shows they see as Very Dull, Dull, Fair, Good and Very Good.[17] Preview House gathers the electronic data as well as some post-show questionnaires, and fits the information into appropriate demographic categories; afterwards, like CBS, it disposes of the extras.

NBC uses cable subscribers for its research, and, like ABC, hires Audience Studies Incorporated to conduct the study. ASI rents unused cable channels in large market areas that are representative of many groups and classes of viewers. Twenty-four hours before the broadcast, staff members call about 125 subscribers in four areas of the country and ask them to watch a new show at a specific time the next evening. After the "pilot" has been shown, ASI follows up with phone interviews and records the answers according to their demographic breakdown.[18]

The above summaries illustrate that the three commercial networks share very similar audience testing procedures. It's also evident that some of the research gathering is not necessarily error-free. But because networks are not in the sole business of doing research, they are usually not very concerned about sloppy methodology. Their business is programming.

Scholarly researchers, on the other hand, pay a great amount of attention to theory formulation, methodology and data-gathering. They are usually more sensitive to these issues because of their background as well as their non-affiliation with specific networks or businesses. This non-affiliation is both an advantage and a handicap, for another important difference between academic research and audience testing is that it is more commonly read by academic colleagues rather than by programmers and advertisers. In other words, academic research is not likely to be accepted as quickly nor acted upon as dramatically as audience testing or ratings. It can, however, provide very insightful views of broadcasting and its effect on audiences.

Scholarly Studies

As established earlier, much of the existing scholarly research has dealt with the audience and its relationship to the mass media. Soap opera studies are no exception. As with the other evolutionary aspects of soap operas, audience research in daytime drama began in the forties, dropped off for several years, and resumed in the late sixties and early seventies.

In the early forties, Herta Herzog and Helen Kaufman studied daytime radio listeners and their habits for Lazarsfeld's Bureau of Applied Research. More of their research will be cited later in this chapter. However, it is important to note that Herzog and Kaufman, along with Summers, Roper and others, found that the "average serial listener" at that time was young (18–35), female and middle-class, with a high school education.[19] This portrait of the "typical" soap opera fan continued for two decades until researchers like Rose Goldsen, Bradley Greenberg, Natan Katzman and Ronald Compesi studied viewers of daytime drama and their gratifications in the early seventies. The popularity of these studies encouraged more academic research, as soap operas were finally acknowledged as legitimate vehicles for analysis. Today, a large percentage of daytime audience research is often dispatched through convention papers, dissertations, scholarly journals and textbooks. The following sections of this chapter utilize this very valuable previous research as well as a new study conducted in 1985[20] to better understand the evolution of soap opera audiences over the last fifty years.

Comparison Between Radio Soap Opera Audiences in the Forties and Television Soap Opera Audiences in the Eighties

There is no question that the common thread linking most soap opera listeners in the early forties was their gender. While differing in age, economic class, lifestyle and geographic location, the fact remained that women were the greatest fans of radio serial drama. However, as researchers investigated the audience demographics more carefully, they found that a more describable soap opera follower *did* exist — one definable in terms more specific than "female."[21]

One clearly notable observation about most daytime listeners in the early forties was that they had been measurably affected by the Depression in the late twenties and early thirties. The effect was usually indirect, however, since women of that time were not a large factor in the workplace. Instead, their husbands, fathers, sons or brothers were often unemployed, and the women were left to compensate for their income loss at home. The few women who found work outside the home were usually single, and not career-oriented. Their primary goal was to get married; they generally worked at their jobs until they found husbands and had children. Thus, it is safe to say that the typical soap opera listener was married and part of a single-income household. As Robert Allen noted:

> The job of the typical woman in the 1930s was enormous but clearly defined: it was her task to "keep things going," to hold family and home together against the economic ravages of the Depression, to minimize the deterioration in living standards most families suffered. For all the talk of flappers and changing roles for women during the 1920s, what carried over into the 1930s was the division of family, social, and economic roles according to sex.[22]

Further, according to Herta Herzog,[23] the typical forties' serial listener did not have a formal education beyond high school; in fact, many of the listeners surveyed had not gone past elementary school. Non-listeners, on the other hand, seemed to graduate from high school and beyond more often. Despite the comparative gap in education between soap listeners and non-listeners, incomes between the two groups were not radically different. Both seemed to be affected by the post–Depression environment and were members of single-income households.

Herzog also found that most listeners lived in rural settings rather than in large metropolitan areas or small cities. She reasoned that one possible explanation for this phenomenon was that more citified environments provided more activity choices for people. Thus, they were able to choose other things over listening to the radio.

Finally, Herzog developed a "sophistication index" to compare serial listeners with non-listeners. This "sophistication index" was made up of

TABLE 3.1

AGE AND ECONOMIC CLASS BREAKDOWNS FOR THE 1985 STUDY*

GENDER/AGE	LOWER	LOWER-MIDDLE	MIDDLE	UPPER-MIDDLE	UPPER
Males 1-10 (12)	8.3%	8.3%	50%	25%	8.3%
Females 1-10 (12)	8.3%	8.3%	66.7%	8.3%	8.3%
Males 11-20 (59)	5.1%	3.4%	47.5%	39%	5.1%
Females 11-20 (128)	1.3%	10.9%	46.2%	40.3%	1.3%
Males 21-40 (93)	5.4%	8.6%	44.1%	38.7%	3.2%
Females 21-40 (156)	1.3%	10.9%	46.2%	40.3%	1.3%
Males 41-60 (36)	-	11.1%	41.7%	41.7%	5.5%
Females 41-60 (63)	1.5%	4.8%	50.8%	33.3%	9.6%
Males 61+ (16)	6.3%	12.5%	50%	3.2%	-
Females 61+ (25)	3.8%	11.5%	46.2%	38.5%	-

*NOTE: The numbers in parentheses indicate the actual numbers of people surveyed in each group.

various components, such as an interest in reading, owning a telephone,[24] and participation in outside activities and hobbies. After tabulating the results, Herzog found that reading amounts between the two groups did not vary greatly. However, the types of preferred books and magazines differed between listeners and non-listeners. Listeners read more mystery novels,

TABLE 3.2

AGE AND EDUCATIONAL BREAKDOWNS FOR THE 1985 STUDY*

GENDER/AGE	ELEMENTARY SCHOOL	HIGH SCHOOL	COMMUNITY COLLEGE	COLLEGE	M.A.	PH.D
Males 1-10 (12)	100%	-	-	-	-	-
Females 1-10 (12)	100%	-	-	-	-	-
Males 11-20 (59)	3.4%	33.9%	3.5%	59.3%	-	-
Females 11-20 (128)	9.4%	18%	4.7%	67.9%	-	-
Males 21-40 (93)	-	4.3%	6.5%	75.3%	11.8%	2.1%
Females 21-40 (156)	-	10.3%	2.6%	73.1%	12.8%	1.2%
Males 41-60 (36)	5.6%	33.3%	-	38.9%	13.9%	8.3%
Females 41-60 (63)	-	28.6%	12.6%	49.2%	4.8%	4.8%
Males 61+ (16)	12.5%	62.5%	12.5%	12.5%	-	-
Females 61+	11.5%	42.4%	19.2%	19.2%	7.7%	-

*NOTE: The numbers in parentheses indicate the actual numbers of people surveyed in each group.

while non-listeners enjoyed historical novels. Also, Herzog observed that serial listeners tended to spend more time at home, preferring vicarious experiences to those that were first-hand.[25]

Thus, in summary, the "typical" radio soap opera listener of the early forties was a married female, between the ages of 18 and 35, living in a rural area, with a high school education or less. She also enjoyed activities at home more than outside entertainment or other hobbies.

In contrast, the 1985 survey reflects a much more varied audience composition. While it is still true that most soap opera fans are female, further descriptions of economic class, education and sophistication are more difficult to make than in years past. For example, Tables 3.1 and 3.2 illustrate the demographic breakdowns of the 600 people surveyed. When looking at the figures in 3.1 and 3.2, it's very clear that educational levels and economic situations have changed greatly since the early forties. However, neither component seems to be related to soap opera viewing.

In 1985, the main factors that determined soap opera viewing were age and gender; not marital status, income, education or career orientation. In general most subjects who had a "free afternoon" often listed watching TV as one of their primary choices (see Appendix B, Table B.1). However, different age groups voiced different priorities for their various viewing habits. For example, children between the ages of 1 and 10 often substituted daytime television for some outside activity or getting their homework finished (so they could watch TV later). An overwhelming number of 11- to 20-year-old females chose television as their primary recreation; and many of the male college-aged students were also heavy viewers.

However, as the 11- to 20-year-olds moved into the 21–40 age category (and left school), an interesting change occurred. Men continued to watch the same amounts of daytime television, but women declined in their viewing amounts. When interviewed, these females commented that a change in marital status, a professional commitment, having children, and/or maintaining a household accounted for their changes in habit. However, an impressive number of females from age 21 to age 40 said they still watched soap operas occasionally, and many times videotaped them during the day so they could view them at their convenience.

From age 41 to age 60, total viewing was less than in the previous two age groups. Both men and women preferred to use their free time for shopping, errands, lunch with friends, etc. And, not surprisingly, TV viewing dramatically increased for persons 61 and over.[26]

Of the people who chose television viewing as their primary activity, Table 3.3 illustrates their general programming choices. For specific groups, the results can be found in Appendix B, Table B.2. However, the following generalizations can be made:

1. *Ages 1-10.* Not surprisingly, both girls and boys chose cartoons as their favorite type of daytime programming. However, girls were evenly split in making their second choice: they found soap operas and game shows to be equally enticing. Boys, on the other hand, showed no strong preference for anything outside of cartoons.

2. *Ages 11-20.* Males and females in this age group watched all categories of programming (soap operas, game shows, movies, talk shows,

TABLE 3.3

PROGRAM PREFERENCES OF DAYTIME TELEVISION AUDIENCES

Soap Operas	77.7%
Game Shows	16.8%
Movies	11.9%
Cartoons	11.7%
Other (News, PBS, Sports, Reruns, Talk Shows, First-Run Syndication)	11.4%

---

sports, cartoons and old reruns), but soap operas were by far the most watched. The most popular second choice for males seemed to be cartoons; women were almost totally devoted to soaps, but if forced to make another selection, chose game shows. It is important to note that many people in this age category were college students; this evidence serves to support other research claiming that college students are the second largest soap opera audience in television.

3. *Ages 21–40.* Members of both sexes in this category also overwhelmingly chose serial drama as their favorite form of daytime TV programming. However, men in this age group were more open to second- and third-choice categories (cartoons, old reruns) than their female counterparts. Women were almost totally committed to soap operas (91.4 percent). Their next preference, game shows, drew only 14.4 percent of the interviewees.

4. *Ages 41–60.* Again, soap operas were extremely popular with this group (74.5 percent); movies were chosen as a distant second (21.3 percent). However, males in this age range were the first adult group not to select soap operas as their first choice. Instead, most preferred movies as a 2:1 favorite over soaps and game shows. Two surprising observations should be noted. First, it seemed amazing that a fairly large percentage of men in this age range watched soap operas at all—they were not identified initially as a soap-oriented group. Second, a fairly large percentage of men seemed to enjoy cartoons. Apparently, we never outgrow our affection for cartoons.

5. *Ages 61 and over.* Slightly over half of this age group selected soap operas as their first choice. Game shows were chosen next most often. An

interesting characteristic of people in this age group was that the viewers were most adamant about their program choices. For example, those who watched soaps usually watched many; those who disliked them were extremely vocal and watched *only* game shows, movies, news or PBS.

Despite some possible weaknesses in this 1985 study,[27] its audience analysis seems quite clear. Today's "typical" soap fan is female and usually between 18 and 35, like soap opera fans in the early forties. However, beyond this simple classification, it is difficult, if not impossible, to define a "typical" daytime audience more specifically. Soap opera viewers have evolved to be younger, more male, more career-oriented, more educated and in general, more diverse than their earlier counterparts. However, as will be established in the next section, specific soap operas tend to attract a more specific set of viewers.

Which People Watch Which Soap Operas

Soon after the ratings systems began, social scientists realized that the notion of one general description for daytime listeners was hardly enough to gain an understanding of the total radio serial audience. Thus, in the early forties, Helen Kaufman, a researcher at Lazarsfeld's Bureau of Audience Research, studied the appeals of specific radio serials to certain sectors of the listening public.[28] Through her efforts, networks, advertisers and scholars learned of the diversity needed to attract varied audiences to radio serial programming.

In her study, Kaufman focused on four popular radio serials: *Life Can Be Beautiful, The Romance of Helen Trent, Stella Dallas* and *Against the Storm.*

Life Can Be Beautiful

According to Kaufman, *Life Can Be Beautiful* appealed to the younger segment of the total number of radio listeners.[29] Taking place in a small bookshop in Manhattan, *Life Can Be Beautiful* was a story about the owner of the store — a wise, gentle, elderly Jewish man, his foster child and her crippled fiance — and how they dealt with the famous, wealthy and important people who visited them at the bookstore. The basic lesson in this soap was that good people would ultimately be happy, and the storylines dealt with many of the problems all people face — romance, love, parenthood, economic survival, etc. But the major emphasis in this show (as compared to some others) was the youthful view that the future was full of change, progress and hope. Characters were not limited to mere survival; they would actually succeed. And they had their entire lives ahead of them to do exactly that.

The Romance of Helen Trent

Conversely, *The Romance of Helen Trent* was more likely to appeal to older radio listeners. Trent was a Hollywood fashion designer who was in her mid- to late thirties.[30] She "proved" that life and love could exist beyond 35. Helen had many romances (despite the title) throughout her serial life, but they never seemed to culminate into marriage; and, as Kaufman suggested, this was an appealing trait of the serial. Audiences waited and wondered whether Helen's newest romance would be the "right" one.

Stella Dallas

Stella Dallas was a lower-middle-class, middle-aged divorced woman who was constantly helping those she cared about. Audiences listened as Stella languished through her daughter's ill-fated marriage to a prominent Washington man; and they loved the way she protected poor, unsuspecting victims from richer, more powerful, but cruel individuals. Stella Dallas was not highly educated, but she possessed a great amount of credibility with those in very high social or political positions. For these reasons, Kaufman surmised that *Stella Dallas* was most appealing to rural, lower or lower-middle-class listeners. As they "lived through" Stella's adventures, it was impressed upon them that money and social position often compromised integrity and ethics. She truly demonstrated time after time that wealth and power were secondary to strong personal qualities (which she found more readily among the "common" people).

Against the Storm

Kaufman felt that *Against the Storm* most directly appealed to younger, more highly educated, upper-middle-class women. It involved upwardly mobile, professional people who were politically active and traveled around the world. One of the messages in *Against the Storm* was that people had responsibilities to society as well as to themselves. This focus was radically different from most other storylines (see Chapter 1), and was considered more attractive to highly sophisticated, metropolitan listeners.

After completing her analysis, Kaufman warned that it was dangerous to overgeneralize about audiences of specific programs. Many listeners had very personal reactions to radio serials, and they were not easy to classify socially, economically, educationally or geographically. In her study, Kaufman discovered that different people saw different things within the same storyline. As evidence, she cited the following four reactions to the radio soap, *Road to Life:*

> It is concerning a doctor, his life, and how he always tries to do the right thing. Sometimes he gets left out in the cold, too.

Dr. Brent is a wonderful man, taking such good care of a poor little orphan boy. He is doing God's work.

It is a drama, Jim Brent and Dr. Parsons — jealousy, you know. There are several characters, but Jim Brent is the important one. He will win out in the end.

It is about a young doctor in Chicago. I like to hear how he cures sick people. It makes me wonder whether he could cure me too.[31]

Keeping this tendency to differentiate in mind, the 1985 study carefully defined specific audiences for most of today's soap operas.[32] It is important to note that the following comments serve only as partial audience descriptions; as Kaufman observed, many people have very personal reasons for identifying with certain soap operas. They are not necessarily limited to demographic statistics.

All My Children

This soap opera was extremely popular with both men and women in the college-aged and 21–40 age groups. Females aged 41–60 showed some interest in it, but the overwhelming majority were men and women aged 18–35. When asked why they enjoyed it, common responses included the fact that *All My Children* combines serious themes with a sense of humor. Viewers also liked the various ethnic and economic groups as well as the mix between traditional and contemporary issues. Some of the most popular plotlines in *All My Children* between 1983 and 1985 included themes of parenthood, romantic jealousy, crime, deception, secrets and career choices.

Another World

Statistically, *Another World* seemed most popular with males and females in the older demographic groups (50 and over). However, due to the fact that only a small number of people surveyed claimed to watch this soap opera, this analysis may be misleading. In any case, *Another World* was characterized as very traditional in nature. Popular themes from 1983 to 1985 were romance, drugs, criminal investigations, job-related problems and illness/injury.

As the World Turns

Not many of the viewers surveyed listed this soap as one of their favorites, but of those who did, the "over 50" age group was by far the leading viewership. Of those interviewed, many people had been fans of *As the World Turns* since its first year, and felt it was a very strong daytime drama. The most popular themes between 1983 and 1985 — parenthood, romance and romantic problems, criminal investigation, deception and illness/injury — seemed very traditional in nature.

Capitol

As with *As the World Turns,* the 1985 survey did not talk to large numbers who watched this program. However, of those who did, the "over 50" group was again prominent. Many of the people interviewed said that they started watching *Capitol* because it fell between two of their favorites, *As the World Turns* and *The Guiding Light.* From 1983 to 1985, the most popular themes in this soap were parenthood, romantic problems, criminal investigations and illness/injury.

Days of Our Lives

The two age groups most devoted to this soap were male college students and females aged 41–60. It seemed that *Days of Our Lives* appealed to two different audiences: one that was made up of young males, interested in themes such as investigations of exotic crimes and action/adventure; and another audience of older women who enjoyed romance, love and marriage. Also, it was interesting to note that many of the younger viewers watched *Days of Our Lives* and *General Hospital* each day because of similar storylines.

General Hospital

After 22 years, *General Hospital* was still a very popular soap opera in 1985. High percentages in all age groups from 11 to 60 listed this drama as one of their favorites; in fact, female college students and males from ages 21 to 40 listed it most often as their top choice. However, some of the people interviewed at this time indicated that they were becoming disenchanted with *General Hospital* because of increasingly unbelievable storylines and slow plotline development. Themes they preferred were along the lines of those found in the 1983/1984 season — international travel, criminal investigations and job concerns.

The Guiding Light

The Guiding Light seemed to collect audience support from all age groups, with females over 50 registering as the most numerous viewership group. The latter figure may have been due to the fact that this is the longest survivor in daytime drama. Having started in radio in 1937, and moving to television in 1952, *The Guiding Light* is still going strong today. Some of the younger persons interviewed indicated that they had recently switched from *General Hospital,* preferring *The Guiding Light*'s pace and storylines. Other, more mature people said that they had "grown up" with the Bauer family and had never left "home." Popular plotlines for *The Guiding Light* from 1983 to 1985 included pregnancy and parenthood issues, marriage proposals and marriages, secrets, career decisions, divorce and illness/injury.

One Life to Live

While the percentages are somewhat lower than in *All My Children* and *General Hospital, One Life to Live* has considerable popularity with men from ages 18 to 35. Several persons indicated that they had really started watching this soap opera because it aired between *All My Children* and *General Hospital.* However, they now listed it as their favorite daytime drama. Popular themes in the 1983–1985 seasons were romance (with jealous lovers lurking in the background), crime investigations involving action/adventure, and money and career concerns.

The Young and the Restless

The Young and the Restless seemed strongest in viewer appeal for women in the 21–45 age group. When asked about this soap, most said they like the wealth, glamour and fantasy-like lives of the characters. (This, by the way, was in direct opposition to those who liked *All My Children*). Popular plotlines between 1983 and 1985 included pregnancy/parenthood issues, romantic rebounding, heroes versus villains, and high-powered careers and finance.

After analyzing some of the current audience trends in soap operas, it is important to make a few additional programming comments. First of all, the data presented for consideration were gathered during the 1983–1985 seasons; since then, network programmers have made major and minor changes in soap opera storylines and characterizations. Changes are made because network executives constantly seek to maintain a certain set of audience demographics or try to shift from one age/gender group to another. As indicated earlier in this chapter, the ratings are the name of the network-advertiser game; so the quest for preferable demographics is ever-present. Relatedly, "preferable" demographics are no longer defined only as the female age group between 18 and 35; for example, advertisers have noted recently that men and women over 50 usually have a relatively large disposable income, and more leisure time in which to spend it. As such, this age group has become a very attractive demographic to hold. Thus, the strategy of appealing to two totally different age/gender groups (as in *Days of Our Lives*) may become a more popular trend in the future.

Finally, it is important to note that the desired audience demographics for any soap opera can usually be determined by looking at the characters' demographics as well as the storyline themes. They will reveal the programmer's desires.

Why People Watch Soap Operas

As established earlier in this chapter, soap opera fans often watch specific shows because the storylines mirror their own living situations.

However, sometimes viewers prefer dramas that take place in very different environments from the ones they are used to; in these cases, viewers seem to make program choices that reflect different motivations altogether. This "dual-purpose" phenomenon has been a basis for study since the early years of radio serials.

Among those who first explored the reasons behind soap opera popularity — both demographic and psychodynamic — was researcher Herta Herzog. She created her classic study of daytime listener habits in 1942, and it is still used as a strong foundation for much of today's soap opera research.[33]

Herzog cited three primary reasons why daytime listeners enjoyed radio serials. First of all, many seemed to look forward to the "emotional release" they received through the storylines and characters presented. They could laugh, cry or be surprised with each dramatic turn of events. Also, listeners said that it "made them feel better to know that other people [had] troubles too."[34]

Secondly, the fantasy dimension of daytime drama provided opportunities for wishful thinking. In fact, many listeners readily admitted that while their own lives might be sad or tedious, they could always abandon them for a short while to live the lives of their fictional friends.

Finally, and most surprisingly, radio listeners often sought information and advice from their favorite serial characters. Herzog suggested two reasons for this behavior. First, women without much formal education did not appear to have many other sanctuaries for simple information; and second, women seemed to worry more than men — soap operas were seen as one of several knowledgeable sources that could relieve their anxieties. To further explain this feeling, listeners cited several examples of situations where they felt they were aided by listening to radio soaps. Included among them were marital difficulties, problems with children, and being able to accept growing old gracefully. Herzog cautioned, however, that these comments were very subjective in nature. Like Kaufman, Herzog observed that certain things seen as positive by one fan might often be construed as negative by another.

In the mid-eighties, these three factors — emotional release, fantasy fulfillment and information — still seem to play an important role in America's enduring love affair with daytime drama. By sheer time commitment alone, viewers seem to be quite devoted to their soaps. In fact, the 1985 survey revealed that male and female daytime viewers in each age group averaged seeing between 2 and 3.81 soap operas on a regular basis (see Table 3.4). It was not unusual in this survey to find that some women between the ages of 21 and 55 watched six or seven soaps habitually — they simply used a multi-programmable VCR and viewed the taped stories later in the day.

TABLE 3.4
AVERAGE NUMBER OF SOAP OPERAS WATCHED BY VIEWERS

AGE GROUP	NUMBER OF SOAP OPERAS
1-10	2
11-20	3.81
21-40	2.32
41-60	2.34
61+	2.17

The overwhelming popularity of today's soap operas suggests that they still fulfill certain needs for the viewing public. According to the 1985 audience survey, these needs include emotional release, fantasy, advice and certain types of information. The following points serve to detail today's viewers' comments:[35]

1. Overall, viewers claimed that they chose specific soap operas because they enjoyed seeing certain characters' reactions to the situations in which they found themselves. Plotlines were the second most important reason for watching daytime drama. From this information, it was clear that viewers actively *chose* their programs. They did not watch them because they simply fit into their schedules or because other friends watched them. In fact, a considerable number of those interviewed arranged their work schedules *around* their favorite soap operas (if they couldn't videotape them).

2. Heavy soap opera viewers (those who regularly watched three or more programs) seemed to be loyal to specific networks; i.e., they tended to watch *all* ABC, *all* CBS or *all* NBC dramas. However, many of those who watched two soaps chose them because of specific storyline content, pacing or characters, despite differences in networks. One of the best examples of this phenomenon was the popular dual combination of *Days of Our Lives* (NBC) and *General Hospital* (ABC). Another popular mix was *All My Children* (ABC) and *The Guiding Light* (CBS).

3. Time slots for competing soap operas were no longer considered to be as important an issue as in the past, largely because of the increasing amount of VCR use. Many of those interviewed said that they regularly viewed two soaps broadcast at the same time, either by watching one while

taping the other or by having friends tape them. Also, as indicated earlier, the ability to tape programs for later viewing allows more people from different demographic groups to become fans; no longer are soap operas available only to those who are home during the day.

4. Viewers were very loyal to their specific soap operas, many having watched the same ones for years and years. However, loyalty to past habits was not their main reason for continued watching. As a matter of fact, some persons stated that while they "grew up" with one soap, they switched to another because they preferred the latter drama's characters and plots. In the last analysis, audiences were most dedicated to programs that provided good storylines and characters; they did not remain loyal for long if they were continually disappointed.

5. While the 1985 survey showed that ABC led in overall numbers, the other two networks claimed equally devoted fans. And soap operas were very definitely an intended choice for viewing (whether on ABC, CBS or NBC). With so many programming alternatives available through cable, satellite and home video, audiences were not forced to select daytime drama because it was the least objectionable choice. They were happy to be active, dedicated fans of this genre.

In summary, soap opera fans have grown more sophisticated, in keeping with the nation's economy, educational system and technology. They can no longer be quantified as a homogeneous group of married, middle-class housewives, with little or no formal education. However, despite their new sophistication, fans are still extremely zealous when discussing their favorite stories and the characters within them. For most viewers of daytime drama, fictional families like the Tylers, Quartermaines, Buchanans and Bauers contain very real friends . . . and foes.

Chapter Four

A Synopsis of Trends
in Today's Soap Operas

As discussed in Chapter 1, many storyline trends in daytime drama have adapted to societal changes as well as to those within the broadcast industry. In fact, during the past several decades of soap opera development, serial characters have faced a series of "timely" traumas, including alcoholism, loss of mental health, juvenile delinquency, terminal illness, divorce and impotence. They've also had to address issues of women's lib, minority representation, birth control, drug abuse, sexual freedom and venereal disease—combined within the context of more traditional fare, such as romance, courtship and marriage.

The purpose of this chapter is to look more specifically at serial trends, i.e., to see how each of today's soap operas has reacted to the outside influences mentioned earlier. In the following pages, condensed histories of major plotlines in thirteen contemporary daytime dramas will be presented, complete with their dates of first broadcast, family trees and "predictable" programming trends for the immediate future.[1] In terms of plotline prediction, however, the reader should exercise some caution; for it is important to remember that these same plotlines might change drastically, depending on unforeseeable otuside influences in the future. Still, it's always fun to imagine the possible conflicts that lie ahead for our favorite fictional friends. The following sections accomplish just that.

All My Children
First Broadcast: January 5, 1970 (ABC)

When the now-famous photo album first turned its pages in 1970, *All My Children* introduced three families who were major forces behind the daily happenings in Pine Valley (see Figure 1). The first was the Tylers— Phoebe and her husband, Charles, as well as their children, Ann and

FIGURE 1

Prominent Families on ALL MY CHILDREN (1970)

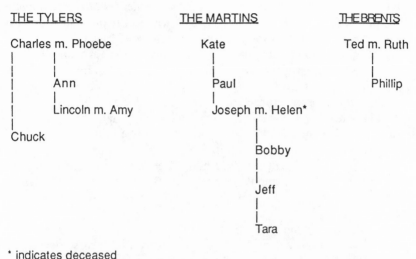

THE TYLERS

Charles m. Phoebe
| |
| |
| Ann
| |
| Lincoln m. Amy
|
Chuck

THE MARTINS

Kate
|
|
Paul
|
Joseph m. Helen*
|
Bobby
|
|
Jeff
|
|
Tara

THE BRENTS

Ted m. Ruth
|
|
Phillip

* indicates deceased

Lincoln, and Charles' grandson, Chuck (whose parents had died while he was still a small infant). The Tylers were very wealthy and considered to be one of the most influential names in Pine Valley. Phoebe, the strong matriarch of the group, was portrayed as an elegant socialite, forever concerned with her family's reputation within the community. As a result, she meddled in everyone's affairs ... although she nearly always meant well while she was meddling.

One of Phoebe's greatest concerns in the first years of *All My Children* was her son Lincoln's marriage to his love, Amy. Amy and her sister, Ruth, were considered middle-class and socially beneath the Tylers. To further complicate matters, Amy was usually in trouble with the municipal authorities because her liberal political views often led her to participate in peace marches and environmental demonstrations. Needless to say, Phoebe was not pleased at all with Amy's economic class nor her activist leanings, and she totally disapproved of her as a daughter-in-law.

Amy Tyler had other problems besides Phoebe, however. Her sister Ruth, and Ruth's husband, Ted Brent, had been known as the proud parents of Phillip. Phillip, though, was not truly their son — he was Amy's illegitimate son, who had been adopted by Ruth and Ted at birth. This deep, dark secret had apparently been kept for years until Nick Davis, Phillip's natural father, came to Pine Valley. Nick had no ill will toward the Brent family and agreed to keep Phil's parentage a secret; however, unbeknownst to him, Erica Kane, a town troublemaker, told everyone about it. Feeling betrayed by what he felt was Nick's deception, Ted Brent decided to confront Nick Davis about revealing his secret. He never got there, though. Unfortunately, on the way to Nick's house, Ted was involved in a fatal car accident. Ruth was left a widow, with a small "son" to care for.

The third family of note in Pine Valley was the Martin brood. Dr. Joe Martin, a widower, was the father of three children, Tara, Bobby and Jeff. (According to one report, though, Bobby went upstairs to polish his skis one day and has never returned to the storyline.) Joe Martin was a strong, upstanding member of the community, and, along with Grandma Kate, he tried to raise his children with ethics and moral fiber.

This moral fiber provided a source of strength and attraction to many, but especially to the Brent family. Phillip Brent and Tara Martin became high school sweethearts, and Ruth Brent, after being widowed by Ted (with whom she was never very happy, anyway), romanced and married Dr. Joe.

Needless to say, however, these relationships did not remain the same for very long in Pine Valley. For one thing, Amy Tyler was so devastated by Erica Kane's gossip about Phil's true parentage that she left Linc and drifted away from Pine Valley altogether. Linc subsequently fell in love with a friend and business partner of Ann's, Sydney Scott, and followed her to New York. Erica Kane, on the other hand, stayed in Pine Valley and seduced Dr. Jeff Martin, Joe's son. Later, they eloped, and Erica became pregnant. She then had a secret abortion. Erica ultimately asked Jeff for a divorce, having met a new man named Jason Maxwell. Unfortunately, Jason was murdered in his hotel room and Jeff was arrested as a prime suspect in the case. Jeff was defended by his brilliant attorney-uncle, Paul Martin; but without Erica's help, Jeff's case was bleak. Finally, Erica's mother, Mona Kane, came forward and admitted that she had accidentally killed Jason when a struggle ensued after she'd asked him to stop seeing Erica. Jeff was soon freed, and he later married a wonderful nurse named Mary Kennicott. Mary and Jeff enjoyed a happy marriage, although it was only for a short time; the Jeff Martin home was broken into by a band of convicts, and Mary was fatally shot. Jeff, overcome with grief, decided to leave Pine Valley (but he returned months later).

In addition to these interwoven relationships, two long-lasting romantic triangles emerged early in *All My Children*:

1. ***Phil Brent–Tara Martin–Chuck Tyler.*** Phillip Brent, emotionally overwhelmed by the discovery that Ruth and Ted were not his "real" parents, suffered a psychosomatic loss of memory, left Tara Martin and Pine Valley, and wandered the streets of New York. When he finally recovered, he returned to discover that Tara had found a new love, Chuck Tyler, and she rejected Phil's attempts to reconcile. On the day of Chuck and Tara's wedding, Nick Davis tried to prevent the ceremony from taking place, claiming that his son, Phillip, still loved Tara. His announcement did little to postpone the ceremony. However, Chuck's sudden kidney infection, which caused him to be rushed to the hospital, did preempt the marriage vows. Tara and Phillip were once again reunited, although they vowed to maintain a platonic relationship while Chuck was recovering from his illness.

Phil and Tara's "good" intentions were short-lived, however. Phil was soon drafted and ordered to Vietnam. Before he left, they tried to elope; but hindered by a blinding snowstorm, they "said their vows" informally and later consummated their "marriage." Shortly thereafter, Chuck recovered, Tara found herself pregnant with Phillip's child, and Phil was reported missing in action. Despite Tara's pregnancy, Chuck wanted to marry her; after their marriage, Tara bore a son, whom she named Phillip.

2. *Nick Davis–Ann Tyler–Paul Martin.* Nick Davis, in spite of his low social status as a dance instructor, was very attracted to Ann Tyler. Despite Phoebe's objections, Ann eloped with Nick, and they lived happily for a short time after. However, Nick, upset by the (false) notion that he might no longer be able to produce children, gradually became distant from Ann. He ultimately asked for a divorce, which she agreed to, because she didn't think he loved her anymore. Shortly after the divorce, and her quick marriage to Paul Martin, Ann discovered she was pregnant by Nick. And, of course, by the time Nick found out, it was no longer possible to tell Ann he'd loved her all along.

Thus, after a few short years, the Martins, Brents and Tylers brought several changes into their family lives. (See Figure 2.) Later in the seventies, though, new characters and previously minor characters became more important to the daily drama in Pine Valley.

One such character was Kitty Shea, a dance instructor who had an affair with Nick Davis. Nick, depressed over losing Ann and the child that he had unknowingly fathered, had a brief fling with Kitty. The result was another pregnancy; and Nick, not wanting another illegitimate child, asked Kitty to marry him. Kitty accepted Nick's proposal; but after she discovered that he still had feelings for Ann, she tried to commit suicide, lost the baby and eventually had to be placed under psychiatric care. Nick still yearned for Ann, and planned to reconcile with her after Kitty was well.

Other popular characters during this time were the Cortlandt family and Dr. Cliff Warner. Palmer Cortlandt was a wealthy widower who was suspiciously overprotective of his ailing daughter, Nina. When Nina became infatuated with Cliff Warner, Palmer was jealous (since he seemed to want Nina all to himself), and did whatever possible to separate them.

FIGURE 2

Prominent Families on ALL MY CHILDREN (mid 1970's)

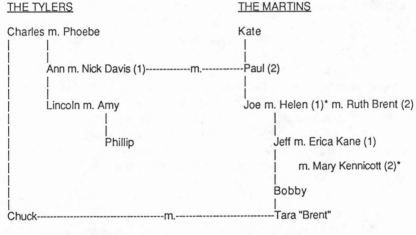

THE TYLERS

Charles m. Phoebe

Ann m. Nick Davis (1)------------m.------------Paul (2)

Lincoln m. Amy

Phillip

Chuck------------------------------------m.------------------------Tara "Brent"

THE MARTINS

Kate

Joe m. Helen (1)* m. Ruth Brent (2)

Jeff m. Erica Kane (1)

m. Mary Kennicott (2)*

Bobby

* indicates deceased

One such ploy was to convince Nina that she was going blind (because of her diabetes) and that her "deteriorating" condition made it unwise to marry Dr. Cliff. Despite Palmer's interference, however, Cliff persuaded Nina to marry him.

Meanwhile, at the Tyler and Martin households, the older, more established characters were changing partners once again.

Tara Martin "Brent" Tyler discovered that Phil Brent had not died in Vietnam, although he had been missing for some time. When Phillip eventually returned to Pine Valley, he discovered that his "wife" had married Chuck Tyler, and he mistakenly surmised that little Phillip was Chuck's son. Despite his love for Tara, Phil Brent left the Chuck Tylers alone, and instead, turned to Erica Kane Martin for solace. Erica, having lost Jeff Martin to Mary Kennicott, was on the rebound from her broken marriage. She welcomed Phil with open arms. Erica soon became pregnant in the affair, and Phil married her (while still in love with Tara). When Erica found out that Phillip was not totally involved with her, she developed psychological problems, suffered a miscarriage, and was committed to a sanitarium for awhile. Soon after, Phil discovered (because of a needed blood transfusion) that little Phil was his. As a result, Phillip and Tara wanted to be married; but Erica was unwilling to grant a divorce. And, since Tara felt that little Phil would suffer emotionally with the discovery that Chuck was not his father, Phil did not pressure Erica into action.

Consequently, Phil and Tara continued their troubled love affair until they were finally wed in the late seventies.

After Phillip and Tara were married, Erica turned to Nick Davis for comfort, and their "romance" almost ended in marriage. Nick, however, decided against it before the ceremony took place. He later left Pine Valley and left Erica along with it. Not remaining depressed for long, Erica began seeing an ex–football player, Tom Cudahy. They soon married; but before too much time had elapsed, the honeymoon was over. Erica had met a man named Brandon Kingsley, who promised her a successful modeling career. She subsequently became disenchanted with Tom's down-to-earth approach to life, divorced him, and went after Brandon. Brandon, however, neglected to tell her that he was already married and had a small child. When she discovered his deception, she simply moved on to a richer, more prominent prospect, Kent Bogard. Kent's father, Lars, owned a large cosmetics company, and Erica immediately set about to further her career.

At another home in Pine Valley, Ann Tyler Martin finally understood that Nick had divorced her because he had thought he was sterile; not because he'd stopped loving her. They met briefly, and tried to reconcile. However, Ann soon discovered that her true love was Paul, and she told Nick of her feelings when he pursued her in New York. Unfortunately, on their return to Pine Valley, Nick and Ann were involved in an auto accident, and both were left unconscious. Nick recovered first, though, and lied about Ann's love for Paul. Paul, believing Ann wanted to divorce him, began a romance with Margo Flax, a friend of Erica's. Ann recovered later, and found out about Paul's affair. She left the hospital and Pine Valley as well, moving to Seattle with her brother, Linc.

Linc and Ann ultimately returned to their home, Ann having realized she had misunderstood Paul's relationship with Margo. But Paul divorced her and married Margo. Margo went to great lengths to try to keep Paul — her deception abounded everywhere. After tremendous setbacks, including Margo's attempted murder of Ann, Paul and Ann were finally remarried. Margo later died, without giving them further trouble.

Upon Linc's return, he fell in love with Kitty Shea. Kitty was unquestionably below the Tylers in social status, so matriarch Phoebe set about to break up their relationship. Among her conniving attempts, she bribed a street woman, Myrtle Lum, to pose as Kitty's long-lost mother. Unfortunately for Phoebe, Myrtle liked Kitty, and actually began thinking of her as a real daughter. Phoebe was foiled in her attempts to separate Linc and Kitty. However, Kitty soon discovered that she had a terminal neurological disease — nature had intervened where Phoebe had failed.

Despite her hollow victory, Phoebe was not beyond reproach for her actions. She lost much of her power as matriarch, and her own marriage was suffering for her misdeeds. Charles Tyler had tolerated Phoebe's

FIGURE 3

Prominent Families on ALL MY CHILDREN (1980)

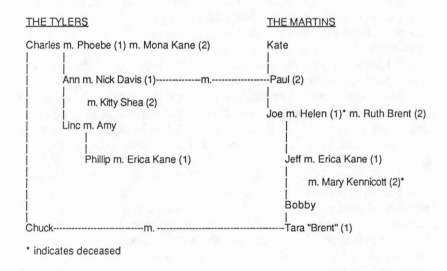

THE TYLERS   THE MARTINS

Charles m. Phoebe (1) m. Mona Kane (2)   Kate
| | |
| | |
| Ann m. Nick Davis (1)--------------m.--------------------Paul (2)
| | |
| | m. Kitty Shea (2) |
| | Joe m. Helen (1)* m. Ruth Brent (2)
| Linc m. Amy |
| | |
| | |
| Phillip m. Erica Kane (1)   Jeff m. Erica Kane (1)
| |
| | m. Mary Kennicott (2)*
| |
| Bobby
| |
Chuck--------------------------m. -------------------------------------Tara "Brent" (1)

* indicates deceased

meddling for a long time; however, her interference in Linc and Kitty's life as well as her insistence that he fire his longtime secretary and friend, Mona Kane, were all he could tolerate. Charles finally demanded a divorce, and later married Mona. Phoebe, in turn, became an alcoholic.

Thus, by 1980, Pine Valley was once again restructured (see Figure 3). And the action continued from there.

Chuck Tyler, bereft by his divorce from Tara, found a fragile happiness with a young woman named Donna Beck. Their initial friendship turned into a romance, and the couple was soon married. However, Chuck and Donna's marriage was not secure for long; Palmer Cortlandt was attracted to Donna's youthful vulnerability (much like his daughter, Nina's), and was determined to have her for himself. Palmer bedazzled Donna with his charm, money and good manners. And because of her past as a teen prostitute, Palmer's attention gave Donna a sense of self-worth she had not felt previously. Eventually, Chuck and Donna's marriage ended in divorce; Donna then married Palmer, and Chuck married a woman named Carrie Sanders.

However, Chuck and Donna, despite their marriages to other people, continued to be brought together by fate. On one occasion, they came across each other on a skiing trip and made love in the heat of passion.

While they agreed to keep their momentary indiscretion a secret, this soon became impossible: Donna was pregnant, but Palmer was sterile. However, despite Palmer's anger at Donna's betrayal, he had his own deceptions to address. For one thing, his former wife, Daisy, whom he had banished from town (telling everyone she was dead), returned to Pine Valley. But unbeknownst to Nina, Daisy was not actually her mother; for Palmer had fathered Nina with a housekeeper named Myra Murdoch. Palmer ultimately became obsessed with his ex-wife, Daisy; Carrie became tired of dealing with Chuck's love for Donna and left town; and Donna and Chuck renewed their romance. Donna's baby, however, carried the Cortlandt name. Palmer refused to give up his custody of the little boy—he wanted an heir to carry on his name.

The problems with Chuck and Donna's and Tara and Phillip's romances had yet another repercussion—they began to place a strain on Ruth and Joe Martin's marriage. After a brief affair with a man named David Thorton, however, Ruth returned to Joe, and they adopted Tad Gardner soon after.

In another incident, Ann Tyler Martin was killed when a bomb exploded in her car. The bomb was intended for her husband, Paul, because of his investigation of mob connections in Pine Valley. Paul, bereft by his loss, later left his home for a job in Washington, D.C.

Ann Tyler Martin's was not the only death in Pine Valley, however. Phillip Brent, Tara's new husband, was killed in a helicopter crash over the Caribbean. Tara, overcome by grief, sought comfort from Dr. Jim Jefferson, a child psychologist who was treating little Phillip. They ultimately married and left Pine Valley.

Elsewhere, Nina Cortlandt Warner continued to be happy in her marriage to Cliff, although Palmer, determined to keep troubling the couple, encouraged a handsome new character, Steve Jacobi, to complicate their marital bliss. Steve continued to plague Nina and Cliff's marriage.

As for other new characters in the early 1980s, the Gardner family emerged as the most popular. The Gardners had been in Pine Valley before: Ray Gardner, Tad's natural father, had been extorting money from Ruth and Joe Martin for quite awhile. He had even raped Ruth out of anger that they had reported the extortion to the police. He vowed to come back one day for revenge. Indeed, he did return after his prison stay ... and after his ex-wife, Opal, and their daughter, Jenny, moved to Pine Valley. Soon after their move, Jenny became involved with a handsome young man named Greg Nelson. Their love was true, but Jenny and Greg had their ups and downs due to Jenny's father's reputation. They ultimately became happy, although Jenny died shortly thereafter.

Meanwhile, Phoebe Tyler continued to have her own problems. Her niece, Brooke English, was constantly finding the wrong people with whom to associate. Phoebe's drinking problems also continued; and romantically,

FIGURE 4

Prominent Families on ALL MY CHILDREN (mid 1980's)

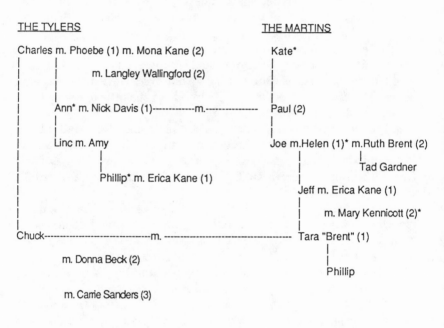

THE TYLERS   THE MARTINS

Charles m. Phoebe (1) m. Mona Kane (2)   Kate*

              m. Langley Wallingford (2)

      Ann* m. Nick Davis (1)------------m.---------------- Paul (2)

      Linc m. Amy   Joe m.Helen (1)* m.Ruth Brent (2)

              Phillip* m. Erica Kane (1)   Tad Gardner

                                                Jeff m. Erica Kane (1)

                                                        m. Mary Kennicott (2)*

Chuck------------------------------m. ----------------------------------- Tara "Brent" (1)

      m. Donna Beck (2)   Phillip

      m. Carrie Sanders (3)

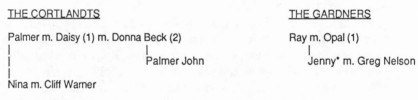

THE CORTLANDTS   THE GARDNERS

Palmer m. Daisy (1) m. Donna Beck (2)   Ray m. Opal (1)

                    Palmer John   Jenny* m. Greg Nelson

Nina m. Cliff Warner

* indicates deceased

she entered into a rocky marriage with Langley Wallingford—a money-hungry charmer, who later left her for Opal Gardner and others. Their marriage improved a bit a few years later, but seemed to be destined for more ups and downs.

And Erica Kane continued her marital and career escapades. She married Adam Chandler, a wealthy businessman, in 1984. This marriage was really no different from the other three, although the stakes were higher. To Erica Kane, husbands would always be in constant competition with her love of money, power and recognition. She ended up divorcing Adam and looking for other loves.

Such was life in Pine Valley in the mid-1980s (see Figure 4).

After reviewing the patterns established since 1970, it is safe to make several predictions for future storylines in *All My Children:*

1. Phoebe Tyler Wallingford and Erica Kane are the two mainstays of Pine Valley. While other friends and family members have come and gone, these two have remained strong, popular and interesting. *All My Children* is likely to continue with these characters as a major part of their future stories, while at the same time introducing newer, but equally formidable, foils for them. Count on new loves and power connections for Erica; and Phoebe is bound to have heretofore unknown relatives and past relationships return to her.

2. Some of the most popular storylines in Pine Valley's history have included romantic triangles and young love. These themes have come to be an integral part of *All My Children,* and will go on as such. However, they probably will involve new characters, not those from the traditional families with whom fans have associated for many years.

3. Another popular theme in this soap has been money and its relationship to power. This trend is likely to continue because of its fantasy-like possibilities as well as its adaptability to current issues like drugs, political elections, etc. Palmer Cortlandt is also likely to be involved in these storylines — his penchant for money and power is legendary.

Another World
First Broadcast: May 4, 1964 (NBC)

Another World began its first broadcast by introducing one of Bay City's most respected families — the Matthews (see Figure 5). As the story opened, the Matthews family was mourning the loss of brother William, who had died leaving his widow, Liz, and their two children, Bill and Susan. William was one of the wealthier brothers in the family, and Liz took great pride in emphasizing this fact to his more middle-class brother, Jim, and Jim's wife, Mary.

Liz was little more than a small annoyance to Jim and Mary at this time, however, for they had bigger problems to deal with. For one thing, their daughter, Pat, was accused in the murder of Tom Baxter. It seemed that several months earlier, she had had an affair with Tom, became pregnant, and was then pressured by him to have an abortion. Pat believed that the abortion had caused her to become infertile, and, in a moment of despair, had confronted Tom with disastrous results.

Jim and Mary worried about their daughter's fate; they also worried about being able to afford good legal counsel for her case. Fortunately, a talented attorney, John Randolph, was able to reduce Pat's plea to temporary insanity, and she was freed. The Matthews family was delighted

FIGURE 5

Prominent Families on ANOTHER WORLD (1964)

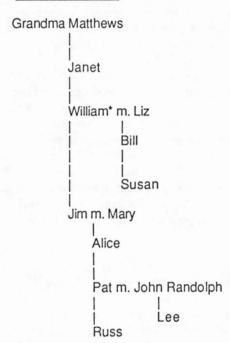

THE MATTHEWS

Grandma Matthews

Janet

William* m. Liz
        Bill
        Susan

Jim m. Mary
    Alice
    Pat m. John Randolph
              Lee
    Russ

* indicates deceased

with the outcome, as was John Randolph — for he had fallen in love with Pat while working on her case. They were soon married.

Pat and John Randolph were not completely happy in their marriage, however. Shortly after their wedding, Lee Randolph, John's daughter from a previous marriage, came to Bay City to wreak havoc in her stepmother's home. The daily upheavals brought undue pressure to the Randolph household, and relationships among everyone were strained at best. In fact, the only relief in Lee's antagonism towards Pat came when John was paralyzed in an unfortunate auto accident. However, the "armed truce" soon ended when lawyer Mike Bauer and his daughter, Hope, moved into town.

Mike's wife had just committed suicide, and to better handle his despair, he plunged into his work, helping the paralyzed John Randolph with some of his caseload. In the process of assisting John, Pat and Mike fell in love. Lee was devastated by their love because she, too, had fallen deeply in love with Mike and could not tolerate his rejection. Lee reacted to her distress by running away from home and taking up with a drug pusher, becoming addicted to LSD, and finally perishing in a car crash. Mike, realizing the stress he had brought to the Randolph home, decided to leave Bay City. He and Hope were not heard from again. As for the Randolphs, Pat and John were reconciled eventually; John fully recovered from his accident; and the couple later became the parents of twins, Michael and Marianne.

Meanwhile, at the William Matthews home, trouble was brewing as well. Bill had fallen in love with a sweet young woman named Missy Palmer, who decided she could not return his love because she was illegitimate. She ran away from Bay City, met some sleazy people in Chicago, married a crook named Danny Fargo, and ultimately was arrested for the murder of her criminal husband. Bill tracked her down, successfully defended her in court, and (despite the protestations of his mother, Liz) married Missy. They moved to California, along with Missy's baby, Ricky. Shortly thereafter, however, Bill drowned accidentally, and Missy was left a widow.

Susan Matthews, Bill's sister, was also upset with their mother, Liz. Susan's maternal problems were quite different from her brother's, though; she and her mother were competing for the affections of the same man, attorney Fred Douglas. Susan ultimately won out by marrying Fred; she then divorced him and found true happiness by marrying Dr. Dan Shearer. Liz, in turn, responded to Susan's romance by rebounding to a devious gigolo, Wayne Addison, who was responsible for much of the corruption in Bay City. Addison spent much of his time paying off government officials and leading heretofore respected citizens into criminal dealings. One such citizen was Walter Curtin, who wanted more money to provide a better life for his new wife, Lenore.

Liz Matthews became insanely jealous of Lenore because she mistakenly thought Lenore was having an affair with Wayne Addison. Liz subsequently told Walter, who in turn murdered Wayne. Unfortunately for Lenore, however, she had been seen earlier at Wayne's apartment, and she was eventually accused of his murder. Liz Matthews continued to make Lenore's life miserable with her spitefulness during the trial; but Walter, Lenore's attorney, got her acquitted anyway. Walter finally admitted to Lenore that he had murdered Wayne; but Lenore kept his admission a secret, since he was killed shortly thereafter.

Finally, Bill and Susan's cousin, Russ Matthews, had equally severe romantic problems during this time; but unlike his rich cousins, Russ' problems were rooted in money. A struggling intern, Russ met and fell in love with a young patient named Rachel Davis. Rachel and her mother, Ada, had always been very poor; when Rachel learned of Russ' love as well as his family name, she jumped at the chance to marry him. Unfortunately for Rachel (and Russ), Russ was a member of the *Jim* Matthews family—his economic status was neither high nor enviable. Rachel soon grew bored with the life of a budget-conscious intern's wife, and turned her attention to a handsome, rich, self-made businessman, Steven Frame. Steven, however, was in love with Alice Matthews, Russ' sister; he refused Rachel's flirtations ... for awhile, at least. One night, Steven succumbed to Rachel's seductive efforts, and she became pregnant. Steven realized that Alice's middle-class morality would not allow her to accept his momentary transgression, so he begged Rachel to keep their secret. Of course, she refused—in fact, she told Alice that he was the father of her baby at Steven and Alice's engagement party. Predictably, Alice, mindful of the fact that her sister-in-law was carrying her fiance's child, left Bay City to save her brother and the rest of her family from hurt and embarrassment. But Steven's love for her was true; when she returned, she forgave him, and they married anyway. Rachel had her baby and named him Jamie. This event added to the changing family structure in 1970 (see Figure 6).

In the early seventies, the drama of *Another World* continued with the troubled marriage of Russ and Rachel Matthews. After several months, Russ finally discovered that Jamie was Steven Frame's son. He divorced Rachel immediately and became interested in a young nurse named Cindy Clark. As it happened, Cindy's brother, Ted, began to fall in love with Rachel at the same time. Rachel did not feel the same way; however, her lack of feeling did not stop her from marrying him for convenience while keeping her sights on Steven Frame.

Meanwhile, Steven, torn between his concern for his son, Jamie, and his troubled marriage to Alice, unwittingly became a victim for Rachel. One day, Alice, who had recently miscarried, heard Rachel talk about being with Steven on the day Alice lost her baby. Without asking him, Alice ran away to New York and sued for divorce. Since Steven was confused and hurt by Alice's actions, he decided to marry Rachel and give his son his proper birthright. Needless to say, however, when Alice finally returned to Bay City, both she and Steven reconciled their differences, and after some painful times (including Alice's psychiatric problems), Steven divorced Rachel and remarried Alice.

Rachel, utterly rejected and alone, was at the lowest point in her life after losing Steven. However, much to her surprise, a new romance was soon introduced in the form of MacKenzie Cory. Mac was the father of another Bay City villainess, Iris Cory Carrington, who jealousy tried to ruin Mac's affair in every way. Despite Iris' attempts, though, Mac and Rachel were married; and, much to everyone's amazement, Rachel was

FIGURE 6

Prominent Families on ANOTHER WORLD (1970)

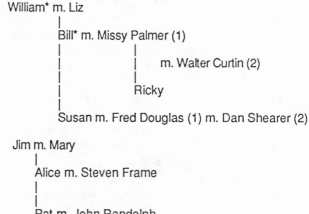

THE MATTHEWS

William* m. Liz
|
Bill* m. Missy Palmer (1)
| |
| | m. Walter Curtin (2)
| |
| Ricky
|
Susan m. Fred Douglas (1) m. Dan Shearer (2)

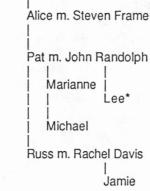

Jim m. Mary
|
Alice m. Steven Frame
|
|
Pat m. John Randolph
| | |
| Marianne |
| | Lee*
| |
| Michael
|
Russ m. Rachel Davis
|
Jamie

* indicates deceased

---

actually happy . . . and nice! Mac had an unbelievable effect on Rachel — he seemed to see good in her when no one else could. Rachel soon began to live up to his expectations by reconciling with many of her old enemies.

Iris never gave up hating Rachel, however. She continued to spread rumors about her, and even paid a gigolo, Phillip Wainwright, to seduce her. For a time, Mac believed Iris, but ultimately found out that she was lying. Mac and Rachel then patched up their marriage.

In other households, times were changing also. Pat Randolph began drinking after seeing her husband, John, with Wayne Addison's ex-wife, Bernice (who was later killed). Pat separated herself from everyone for awhile until she was struck by two tragic events: Russ' love, Cindy, had become terminally ill — he married her just before she died; and John Randolph, too, began drinking, losing much of his legal business. After seeing the grief of others, Pat decided to reconcile with John.

Russ' problems continued after Cindy's death. He became engaged to the scheming Iris Carrington, but later broke up with her after discovering her vindictive plot against Rachel and Mac. Iris then rebounded to Robert Delaney (who had been previously married to and lost Lenore Curtin). Because of their mutual loneliness, they decided to get married. Robert, though, was unaware that he had fathered a child by a woman named Clarice Hobson. After discovering his child (and finding out that Iris had known all along), Robert started drinking and left Iris and Bay City. Iris did not stop with Robert's departure, however — she continued to harass Clarice for custody of the baby.

Finally, toward the mid-seventies, Bay City was drastically altered by two deaths — Mary Matthews (who had a heart attack during her "second honeymoon" with Jim) and Steven Frame (who presumably died in a helicopter crash). The Matthews family was once again changed (see Figure 7), and new characters began to filter into town.

One such notable character was Willis Frame (Steven's brother), who came to Bay City to gain control of his dead brother's business. Together with his lover, Carol Lamonte, Willis preyed upon the devastated Alice Frame. For a while, it seemed that Willis would claim everything; but Alice, after getting over some of her grief, soon discovered his motives and sent him packing.

Meanwhile, at the Cory household, Mac and Iris had reconciled their differences, but Rachel and Mac's marriage was on shaky ground. Rachel, after losing a baby, had turned to a new hobby, sculpture. Mac felt she was entirely too devoted to it — as well as to her instructor, Ken Palmer. On the other hand, Rachel was jealous of Mac's attentions to Pat Randolph (who was divorcing John). Rachel was mistaken, however. Mac's interest in Pat was purely work-related. And Pat was truly interested in a doctor named Dave Gilchrist — although this interest was only temporary. Pat had other problems to address.

For one thing, Pat and John's daughter, Marianne, was nagging Pat continually about reconciling. She never really let up, even after the divorce was final and John remarried. Why was she so insistent, even then? Probably because John had entered into a marriage with the unsavory, money-hungry Olive Gordon. Marianne, after investigating the situation, discovered that Olive didn't really love John; in fact, Olive was having an affair with an architect named Evan Webster. After telling her twin brother, Michael, they confronted John, who then confronted Evan, and accidentally killed him. John didn't go through a murder trial, however. He soon had a nervous breakdown and was committed to an institution. He later divorced Olive and was rehabilitated.

FIGURE 7

Prominent Families on ANOTHER WORLD (mid 1970's)

THE MATTHEWS

William* m. Liz
|
   Bill* m. Missy Palmer (1)
   | |
   | | m. Walter Curtin (2)
   | |
   | Ricky
   |
   Susan m. Fred Douglas (1) m. Dan Shearer (2)

Jim m. Mary*
|
   Alice m. Steven Frame*
   |
   |
   Pat m. John Randolph
   | | |
   | | Lee*
   | |
   | Marianne
   | |
   | Michael
   |
   Russ m. Rachel Davis (1) m. Cindy Clark (2)*
          |
          | m. Ted Clark (2)
          |
          |__m. Steven Frame (3)*
             |
             Jamie

          m. MacKenzie Cory (4)
             |
* indicates deceased   Iris m. Eliot Carrington

Pat could truly sympathize with John's problems; she had to contend with a murder of her own. It seemed that Marianne had become engaged to Greg Barnard, a new member of John's law firm and, in Pat's estimation, a snake. He had first tried to seduce Pat (after his engagement to Marianne), then accused Pat of seducing him. Finally, when she confronted him about his lies, he tried to rape her. She killed him, trying to ward off his advances. Pat was eventually acquitted for her actions, but she suffered enormous emotional stress in the meantime.

Back at the Corys, life continued to be rocky, at best. After reconciling their differences over Ken Palmer and Pat Randolph, Rachel and Mac set about to have a child. After several attempts, Rachel was convinced she'd never carry Mac's child full-term. Mac, on the other hand, mistakenly thought he'd become sterile, and he tried to hide this fact from her. Iris, seeing the vulnerability of Mac and Rachel's marriage, started making trouble almost immediately. She hired a man named Sven Petersen to pose as a butler, while wreaking havoc. Indeed, he did. By the time he was (justifiably) driven out of town, Sven had drugged Mac and put him into bed with Sven's pregnant illegitimate daughter, then claimed Mac was the father of the girl's baby; and he had murdered the chauffeur, Rocky, for discovering his deception.

After the Sven Petersen affair, Rachel and Mac once again reconciled. However, their relationship continued to sail through troubled waters, encompassing Rachel's interference with Jamie's marriage to Blaine Ewing; Rachel's jealousy over the flirtations of Steven Frame's sister, Janice, with Mac, which led to Rachel and Mac's divorce; Janice's subsequent attempted murder of Mac; and Iris' discovery that Mac was not her real father. Luckily, by the early 1980s, Mac and Rachel had survived everything, remarried, and were now living together with their little girl, Amanda.

Elsewhere, the Matthews household was changing also. Russ, ever unlucky in love, married a past prostitute, Sharlene Watts. The marriage soon failed, and Russ subsequently engaged in several other affairs before he moved to Texas (and, at least temporarily, out of *Another World*). His cousin, Susan Matthews Shearer, on the other hand, returned to Bay City, with her mother (Liz) determined that she would reconcile with her estranged husband, Dan Shearer. Susan refused, and Dan became engaged to Alice Frame instead. Shortly after their engagement, disaster occurred. Olive Gordon, in love with Dan, tried to kill Alice by setting fire to her house. Alice was saved by John Randolph (who, unfortunately, died in the fire); but Alice and Dan later broke their engagement. (This, by the way, was not new for Alice—she had been engaged several times before and broken each one.) Susan and Dan were then reunited and moved to Boston.

Finally toward the end of the seventies, a new family—the Perrinis—came to *Another World*. They included Angie, Rose and Joey. Angie came to Bay City and fell in love with the dastardly Willis Frame. Her mother, Rose, cautioned her about him, so Angie married Willis' brother Vince instead. But Angie soon discovered that she really loved Willis, and she later divorced Vince—only to find out that Willis was involved with someone else. She left Bay City.

FIGURE 8

Prominent Families on ANOTHER WORLD (1980)

THE MATTHEWS

```
William* m. Liz
    |
    Bill* m. Missy Palmer (1)
    |        |
    |        |    m. Walter Curtin (2)
    |        |
    |       Ricky
    |
    Susan m. Fred Douglas (1) m. Dan Shearer (2)

Jim m. Mary*
|
Alice m. Steven Frame (1)*
|        |
|       Sally
|
Pat m. John Randolph (1)*
|   |    |
|   |    |    m. Olive Gordon (2)
|  Marianne |
|   |    |
|   |   Lee*
|   |
|  Michael
|
Russ m. Rachel Davis (1) m. Cindy Clark (2)* m. Sharlene Watts (3)
              |
              |   m. Ted Clark (2)
              |
              |_m. Steven Frame (3)*
              |        |
              |       Jamie m. Blaine Ewing
              |
              |_m. MacKenzie Cory (4) (5)
                  |         |
                Amanda    Iris m. Eliot Carrington (1) m. Brian Bancroft (2)
```

* indicates deceased

Joey, Angie's brother, stayed on and became infatuated with a pretty girl named Eileen Simpson. She returned his love. However, Joey had another admirer — Sally Frame (Alice's adopted daughter). Sally was determined to have Joey, and even went so far as to have Eileen kidnapped and sold into white slavery. Joey saved Eileen, though, and they planned to be married. Unfortunately, they soon found out that Eileen had a terminal blood disorder. Joey married her anyway, and she died the next day.

A diagram of the characters and stories in 1980 (see Figure 8) makes it obvious that Bay City was drastically different from years before. Some characters had died off; others had moved on to spinoffs, like *Texas*. In any case, *Another World* began to reflect a new look, along with some older favorites.

Russ Matthews, still looking for the "right" woman, returned to his home and found Iris Carrington Bancroft's old friend, Tracy Dewitt. Russ romanced her, they fell in love, and were married. However, Jason Dunlap, Tracy's personal manager, was terribly jealous of Russ, and paid a mob member to blow him up. Unfortunately, Tracy, not Russ, was in the car at the time the bomb exploded. Russ had lost yet another wife.

Rachel and Mac Cory continued their roller coaster marriage. For a short time, however, things seemed to be quite calm. Jamie finally divorced Blaine Ewing (much to Rachel's relief) and Mac and Rachel continued to try for another baby. Rachel ultimately did become pregnant; unfortunately, though, it was not with Mac's child. Instead, she fell in love with a man named Mitch Blake and they had an affair which had drastic consequences: Mitch was thought dead and Rachel was convicted as his murderess. Of course, she later was freed when Mitch returned, and she ran away with him and their little boy, Matthew. Mac was devastated and fought back the only way he could: He gained custody of little Amanda.

Amanda was not Mac's only child, as he later discovered. He befriended a young man, Sandy Alexander, and gave him a job at Cory Publishing Company. Several months later, Sandy told him that he was his illegitimate son. The news delighted Mac, but it only infuriated Jamie, who began "proving" himself a better "son" to Mac. He overworked himself, and then started taking amphetamines to keep up his pace. Jamie lost his second wife, Cecile, in the process, and was on a downward spin ... that is, until he discovered that his real father, Steven Frame, had never died.

Steve Frame returned to Bay City with his wife, Alice, apparently having suffered a severe case of amnesia. He immediately set about to right the wrongs done to his family, and to become acquainted with son Jamie and adopted daughter Sally. Jamie continued being troublesome for awhile, writing a sordid novel about Pat Randolph, and coming between Susan Matthews Shearer and her daughter, Julia. However, he soon began to straighten himself out, when he fell in love with attorney Stacey Winthrop.

Steven Frame's life, on the other hand, had begun to get very complicated. He still planned to remarry Alice; but on the eve of his wedding date, due to some tragic events, he realized that he still really loved Rachel. He immediately broke off his engagement to Alice. Alice was broken-hearted, and her despair only increased when she heard the news that her dad, Jim, had died. Alice, without many friends and most of her family, decided to leave Bay City permanently. With her exit, the Matthews family became a mere memory on *Another World.*

Meanwhile, Steven moved in with Rachel, and they were actually married just before Steven died in a car accident. Rachel, overwhelmed by her grief, turned once again to Mac, and they were again remarried.

As for the new faces in Bay City, several prominent ones emerged at this time. There was Cass Winthrop, attorney Stacey Winthrop's brother. He was having simultaneous affairs with Cecile de Poulignac (who had previously been married to Jamie Frame) and Felicia Grant, a romance novelist. As if this weren't enough activity to keep a man busy, Cass was involved in the murder of a nasty woman named Alma Rudder. Cecile, however, was the prime suspect, and tried to run away. She was ultimately cleared of the charges, but vowed revenge on all those who accused her. She blackmailed, threatened and corrupted most of Bay City on her bloodlet-ting spree, but she still couldn't deny her feelings for Cass. Cass, on the other hand, used Cecile for all she was worth; he got information from her about Mac Cory's business deals, and seduced her while he was doing it (even though she was seeing wealthy Peter Love—one of the very elite new families in Bay City). Cass eventually mellowed, though, when he fell in love with Kathleen McKinnon. He tried to mend his evil ways, and even proposed to Kathleen. However, Cecile wanted revenge—and she got it when she kidnapped Cass on the day of his wedding.

Other new characters at this time included Catlin Ewing (Blaine's half-brother), who met, romanced, married and remarried Sally Frame (Alice and Steve's adopted daughter), despite his constant trouble with the law; and Carl Hutchins, who along with Cecile, provided treachery and crime to Bay City (see Figure 9).

Probably more than most other soaps, *Another World* has changed its writing direction many times since its first broadcast in 1964. These changes are due to two main factors: unstable ratings, and writer migration to other, more popular serials. With such a history, it is particularly difficult to predict future trends for *Another World.* However, some patterns seem evident:

1. Rachel and Mac Cory will still be prominent members of Bay City society, but their personal woes will be secondary to more outside concerns such as their grown (or growing) children, friends and community prob-lems. Rachel and Mac provide a history for *Another World;* however, their personal traumas have been played out so fully that there seems little else to cover.

2. While romance, marriage and illegitimate pregnancy still play a key

FIGURE 9

Prominent Families on ANOTHER WORLD (mid 1980's)

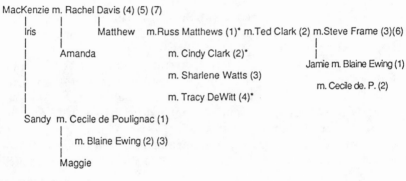

THE CORYS

MacKenzie m. Rachel Davis (4) (5) (7)

Iris | Matthew   m.Russ Matthews (1)* m.Ted Clark (2) m.Steve Frame (3)(6)

Amanda   m. Cindy Clark (2)*   Jamie m. Blaine Ewing (1)

m. Sharlene Watts (3)   m. Cecile de. P. (2)

m. Tracy DeWitt (4)*

Sandy m. Cecile de Poulignac (1)

m. Blaine Ewing (2) (3)

Maggie

* indicates deceased

role in some characters' stories, the main emphases have been on crime and financial investment in recent years. This trend is likely to continue, at least for as long as it seems popular on prime-time television.

3. Families will not be so prominent as the Matthews were in the sixties. The emphasis will be on action/adventure plots (see point 2), and professional "families," e.g., doctors and nurses, instead of biological families.

4. Look for more extravagant settings, celebrity guest cameos and exotic storylines, especially during ratings sweep months. It seems that the producers of this show are taking an even more aggressive stance towards ratings than ever before.

As the World Turns
First Broadcast: April 2, 1956 (CBS)

When the world began turning at CBS in 1956, little did Procter and Gamble know that Irna Phillips' serial would continue to be extremely popular thirty years later. Set in the fictitious town of Oakdale, *As the World Turns* focused on two families—the Hugheses and the Lowells. The Hughes family was composed of Grandpa Will, his daughter Edith and son Chris, as well as Chris's wife Nancy, and their children, Donald, Penny, Bob and Susan. The Lowell family was a little smaller, but no less important in the first serial plotlines. They included Judge Lowell; his son, Jim; Jim's wife, Claire; and Jim and Claire's daughter, Ellen (see Figure 10).

FIGURE 10

Prominent Families on AS THE WORLD TURNS (1956)

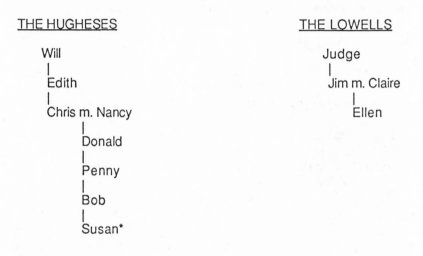

THE HUGHESES   THE LOWELLS

Will   Judge
| |
Edith   Jim m. Claire
| |
Chris m. Nancy   Ellen
    |
    Donald
    |
    Penny
    |
    Bob
    |
    Susan*

* indicates deceased

Jim Lowell and Chris Hughes were partners in a very successful law firm, and both of their families enjoyed a certain prominence in Oakdale. Despite their compatibility in economic and social status, however, the Hughes family was quite different from the Lowells — they believed much more strongly in the basic family values which had been passed on to them from previous generations. From time to time, this value difference created only minor social strains on the Hughes-Lowell friendship; but one day, a major upheaval occurred in both households. Edith Hughes was found having an affair with the married Jim Lowell (who died a short time later). The ramifications of this shocking discovery were many and long-lasting.

One of the more revealing immediate reactions came from Chris Hughes, who felt very guilty about Edith's indiscretions. This was because he had never lived up to his promise of giving her money for college after he had started his first law job. Chris had married Nancy while he was in law school, instead. To him, Edith had lost her direction from that point on; her affair with Jim was one of many misguided mistakes.

Far more devastating, however, were the reactions of the younger members of both the Hughes and Lowell families. Penny Hughes (Nancy and Chris' daughter) and Ellen Lowell were terribly shaken by this embarrassing situation. Combined with their insecurities that their parents didn't really love them, Penny and Ellen went on to somewhat reckless paths of their own. They each sought love and security from any source they could find. In Ellen's case, this meant falling in love with a married doctor, Tim Cole. She became pregnant shortly thereafter, and had the baby; she then gave it up for adoption to a young physician named David Stewart and his wife, Betty.

Penny, on the other hand, became infatuated with the young and careless Jeff Baker. Her parents disapproved totally of Jeff, so after a few family battles, Penny and Jeff decided to run off and elope. Chris and Nancy were too late to stop them from running away, but they did succeed in forcing an annulment when Penny and Jeff returned. Later, however, when Jeff straightened himself out and became a more suitable choice for their daughter, the Hugheses heartily endorsed their marriage plans. Penny and Jeff were happy at last.

By January of 1960, the Hughes and Lowell families had already started changing (see Figure 11); but this was just a small beginning of much, much more on *As the World Turns*. In addition to the already established characters, Oakdale was about to be introduced to newer, even more controversial people in its serene setting. Probably the most notorious of these was Lisa Miller, who set her marital sights on young Bob Hughes shortly after she arrived in 1960.

Lisa met Bob in college, and when she heard that he had come from a wealthy, upstanding family (unlike her own), she immediately began her campaign to win his heart. Bob was truly smitten; and before long, they decided to elope. Chris and Nancy couldn't believe that the same thing had happened twice in their family! Once again, they started annulment proceedings, this time to have Bob and Lisa's marriage annulled. Unfortunately for the elder Hugheses, however, Lisa was pregnant — the annulment could not be granted. So, they decided instead to invite their son and new daughter-in-law to live with them while Bob continued medical school.

Several months later, after the baby (Tom) was born, Bob and Lisa started to have serious marital problems. Bob was working much of the time and Lisa felt bored, neglected and unhappy. She virtually ignored little Tom, and left him in Nancy's care most of the time while she continued to go to school. Later, she started to have an affair with a wealthy entrepreneur named Bruce Elliott, thinking he could give her a better life than the one she had. She asked Bob for a divorce, while planning that Bruce would marry her. Bruce was not at all interested in marriage, however. As soon as he found out that Lisa had divorced Bob, he bolted out of Oakdale. Lisa, feeling somewhat sheepish about the entire matter, came back to the Hughes family and asked for their understanding. They refused to

FIGURE 11

Prominent Families on AS THE WORLD TURNS (1960)

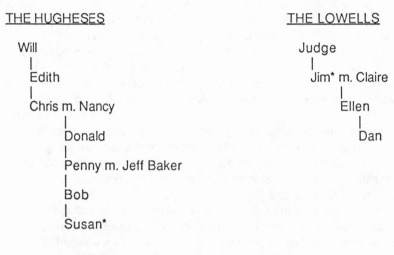

THE HUGHESES

Will
|
Edith
|
Chris m. Nancy
|
Donald
|
Penny m. Jeff Baker
|
Bob
|
Susan*

THE LOWELLS

Judge
|
Jim* m. Claire
|
Ellen
|
Dan

* indicates deceased

reconcile with her; so she ended up leaving baby Tom with Chris and Nancy, and ran off to Chicago. While in Chicago, though, Lisa met, married and divorced a very wealthy man. She later returned to Oakdale with the money and prestige she had always desired.

Elsewhere in the Hughes family, Bob's sister, Penny, was having her own romantic problems. Her marriage to Jeff Baker had begun happily, even though she had discovered that she was infertile shortly after the wedding. However, before long, tragedy struck: Jeff was killed in an auto accident. Penny, overwhelmed with grief at his death, sought solace from a former physician. His name was Neil Wade. Penny and Neil ultimately fell in love, and were married. But, just as their life began to settle down, Neil (who was going blind) was killed by a car while crossing the street. Penny was totally devastated after her second loss; she left Oakdale, and settled in England (returning only for a family reunion thirty years later).

In the Lowell family, things were changing as well. Claire Lowell, Jim's widow, remarried a doctor named Doug Cassen. Unfortunately, like Jim, Doug died after a short time. Claire continued to look for happiness through marriage; she later married a much younger man, Dr. Michael Shea. Michael was only interested in Claire for the money and power she would give him, though; he continued to flirt with other women.

Ellen Lowell, Claire's daughter, could not help her mother with her problems. She herself was in the depths of another exasperating situation. It seemed that Ellen, who was beginning to have enormous guilt knowing that her son was living with adoptive parents (Betty and David Stewart), decided to sue for custody. After a tiring legal battle, though, she decided to drop her case, since Dan seemed very happy where he was. Unfortunately, soon after she decided to leave the Stewarts alone, Betty Stewart (and, coincidentally, Tim Cole) died. David, a single father, did not know quite what to do with a small boy. He finally decided to consult Ellen; they later fell in love and planned to be married. But David had one major stumbling block: his extremely jealous housekeeper, Franny Brennan, who wanted him for herself. Franny would stop at nothing to drive a wedge between David and Ellen — even blackmail. One day, she called Ellen and threatened to tell Dan he was illegitimate if the marriage ever took place. After arguing over her vindictive schemes, Ellen and Franny began to fight; Franny was killed in the struggle; and Ellen was ultimately found guilty of murder. She spent some time in prison after her conviction; but after she was released, Dan and Ellen were wed.

Such was how life had evolved in Oakdale ten years after the story had begun (see Figure 12). By the mid-sixties, many of the now-established characters had large followings. These characters continued to figure strongly in the storylines, along with several new town residents, such as the expanding Stewart family. By this time, the Stewarts had grown enormously, now including David and Ellen; David's son, Paul; Ellen's real and David's adopted son, Dan; and David and Ellen's two daughters, Carol Ann ("Annie") and Dawn ("Dee").

As far as the established characters were concerned, Lisa Miller Hughes became most prominent by causing trouble after she returned from Chicago. Upon re-entering Oakdale, Lisa met Michael Shea (Claire's new husband), and they were attracted to each other immediately. Naturally, when they became involved in a torrid love affair, Lisa became pregnant. When she told Michael about the baby, however, he was furious; he did not want to lose his solid meal ticket with Claire. Despite her pleas, Michael kept Lisa's pregnancy a secret — for awhile, at least. Claire ultimately found out about the baby and divorced Michael. Later, she was killed in a car accident.

Michael, with Claire out of the picture, began to enjoy the company of Lisa and his new son, Chuck. He finally decided to marry her. But when he proposed, Lisa turned him down. Not about to be dismissed, Michael plotted and schemed to find a way for her to accept. He finally succeeded when he discovered that her other son, Tom, had become addicted to drugs in Vietnam, and was robbing Michael's medicine cabinet for supplies. Michael took this information to Lisa, who subsequently agreed to marry him in exchange for his keeping Tom's drug problem a secret. But the

FIGURE 12

Prominent Families on AS THE WORLD TURNS (mid 1960's)

THE HUGHESES

Will
|
Edith
|
Chris m. Nancy
    |
    Don
    |
    Penny m. Jeff Baker (1)* m. Neil Wade (2)*
    |
    Susan*
    |
    Bob m. Lisa Miller
      |
      Tom

THE LOWELLS

Judge
 |
 Jim* m. Claire (1)
     |
     | m. Doug Cassen (2)*
     |
     | m. Michael Shea (3)
     |
     Ellen m. David Stewart (widowed from Betty)
       | |
       | Paul
       |
       Dan
       |
       Carol Ann (Annie)
       |
       Dawn (Dee)

* indicates deceased

marriage was unhappy from the beginning. Michael and Lisa continued to torture each other with threats and subversion. Lisa finally left for awhile, taking Chuck with her. However, when she returned, she found that Michael had been murdered and Tom was on trial as the prime suspect. Ultimately, Tom was acquitted because it was discovered that Michael was murdered by a former lover. For a while, at least, Tom and Lisa's lives returned to normal. Tom even found romance with a nice girl named Carol Deming, whom he later married.

Unlike Tom, Bob Hughes was experiencing marital woes. Shortly after his divorce from Lisa, Bob met and married a woman named Sandy McGuire. The marriage was not solid; Sandy really only wanted security for herself and her little boy, Jimmy. Before long, Sandy divorced Bob, and went to New York to pursue a modeling career.

At the Stewart household (which, by now, had replaced the Lowell family as a prominent Oakdale fixture), things were just as active. Like Tom Hughes, the Stewart boys had grown up quickly and were facing some very adult problems. Dan had become a successful doctor and had a lovely wife named Susan. Despite the appearances of family happiness, however, Dan felt incomplete. After realizing his dilemma, he fell in love and had an affair with a young woman named Elizabeth Talbot. For awhile, Dan was able to be discreet about his extramarital venture. But Liz became pregnant, and Susan wouldn't give Dan a divorce to marry Liz. Instead, Dan's adopted brother, Paul, who was also in love with Liz, offered to marry her, and Liz consented. Meanwhile, Susan was also pregnant by Dan. Liz gave birth first, naming the baby girl Betsy.

Liz's marriage to Paul soon dissipated, and they divorced; shortly afterwards, Paul died of a brain tumor. (His death signalled one of the many changes in the early 1970s; see Figure 13.) Susan gave birth to a girl, Emily ("Emmie"). Finally, Susan realized that her marriage to Dan was empty, and she decided to divorce Dan so they both could be free to marry others. Susan soon married another doctor, and, at long last, Dan and Liz were finally wed. Shortly after the ceremony, however, Liz fell down the stairs and died. Dan, totally bereft, moved away from Oakdale with his daughters, Emmie and Betsy.

Meanwhile, Lisa Miller Hughes Shea, after marrying badly several more times, decided that her first love, Bob Hughes, was the only man who had made her truly happy. Thus, she set about to win him back. Bob, on the other hand, was in love with a surgeon named Jennifer Ryan; he refused Lisa's advances. Lisa then turned to Bob's brother, Don, who'd had his own share of bad marriages. But, as Lisa soon discovered, Don was not the same man as Bob. She eventually discussed her unhappiness with Don (who was not very happy living in his brother's shadow, either) and they decided to part company. Each of them turned to other people.

Bob and Jennifer Ryan were later married but predictably, things were

FIGURE 13

Prominent families on AS THE WORLD TURNS (1970)

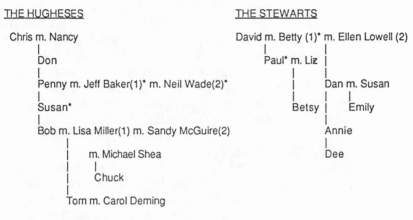

THE HUGHESES

Chris m. Nancy
|
Don
|
Penny m. Jeff Baker(1)* m. Neil Wade(2)*
|
Susan*
|
Bob m. Lisa Miller(1) m. Sandy McGuire(2)
|　　　|
|　　　m. Michael Shea
|　　　|
|　　　Chuck
|
Tom m. Carol Deming

THE STEWARTS

David m. Betty (1)* m. Ellen Lowell (2)
|　　　　　|
Paul* m. Liz　|
|　　　　　|
|　　Dan m. Susan
|　　　|　　|
Betsy　|　Emily
　　　|
　　Annie
　　　|
　　Dee

* indicates deceased

not happy. Jennifer's son from a former marriage, Rick, resented Bob and interfered with him and Jennifer constantly. Jennifer, unable to handle the conflict, left Oakdale for awhile; when she returned, it was because she had discovered she was pregnant. Upon coming back to tell Bob he was about to become a father, she found that her sister, Kim Reynolds, was also pregnant. What she didn't know, though, was that Kim was also carrying Bob's child. And to make matters worse, a devious newcomer, Dr. John Dixon, found out about Kim's pregnancy and the baby's father. John was an ambitious man, and felt that Kim could provide his passage for social success. He decided to blackmail her into marriage. Kim finally agreed, feeling that her life could not become much worse. It did.

After her marriage to John, Kim carried Bob's baby to term, but it was delivered stillborn. Bob found out that Jennifer was dying from a rare neurological illness. Overcome by guilt, Kim and Bob confessed their indiscretion to her. Unbeknownst to them, however, Jennifer had suspected it all along; she immediately forgave them both. (Jennifer, by the way, did not succumb to her illness; instead, she died in an auto accident some time later.) Kim believed she was free at last — from her past sins and John's blackmail. But John was not about to lose Kim at any cost. One day, when running after her, John fell and injured himself severely. Kim knew she couldn't leave him at this point, so she agreed to stay until he recovered. John, of course, played this for all it was worth. However, while John was faking his lack of recovery, Kim found a new love: Dr. Dan Stewart.

John ultimately found out about Kim's feelings for Dan through Dan's ex-wife, Susan. Susan, who was despondent after (presumably) losing Emmie in a fatal car accident, told John (an alcoholic himself) about Kim and Dan's love affair when she was in a drunken stupor. Kim asked John for a divorce, but he was able to forestall her once more. Kim then decided to get away for awhile. However, while she was away, she was hit on the head and developed amnesia. She returned to Oakdale, not knowing whom she loved. John convinced her it was he; and by the time her memory returned, she was pregnant with John's child. She could not divorce him now.

As for Lisa, she turned away from the Hughes family, and found love with a newcomer instead. His name was Grant Colman. Grant seemed to bring a security to Lisa that she had not known before. And Lisa would have married him in an instant, but for the fact that he was already wed. And Grant's wife, Joyce, was a real problem. At every opportunity, she tried to win Grant back. Finally, after months of conflict, Joyce gave him a divorce. Lisa was ecstatic, for she knew they could finally be married. However, Joyce had one more trick up her sleeve: On Lisa's wedding day, Joyce told Grant that he had had a son he never knew about. He left Lisa shortly after the ceremony to see if Joyce's story was true. This time it was.

Grant discovered that his little boy was now three years old. His name was Teddy and he had been adopted by a young couple, Brian and Mary Ellison. Grant liked the Ellisons, and felt that they had provided his son with a good home; he was content to let the arrangement remain the same. However, Joyce was less reasonable; she tried to sue for custody, but later failed. After losing her battle, Joyce got drunk and became injured in a car accident. Grant rushed to her side once again.

By this time, Lisa was so disturbed by Grant's attentions to Joyce, she threw him out of their apartment, and rekindled affairs with some of her old flames. Later, Grant reconciled with her. But Joyce was still prominent in their marital picture, because Mary Ellison, recently widowed, had come to live in Oakdale with little Teddy. Joyce was still determined to get the boy back, so Grant spent many hours helping Mary to keep Joyce away from him. Needless to say, Lisa had had more than enough of Joyce Colman.

Elsewhere, Lisa's son, Tom, was also having a troubled marriage with Carol. Tom was working day and night with a client named Natalie Bannon. Carol mistook this for an affair, and asked him for a divorce. Shortly after, Carol married Jay Stallings; Tom, alone and unhappy, turned to Natalie for comfort. Natalie was not as much in love with Tom as he was with her. She left him once, but then returned and married him, much to Lisa's chagrin. Lisa was convinced that marriage to Natalie would only cause trouble for Tom. Indeed it did.

Looking back through the early seventies in Oakdale, the Hugheses

FIGURE 14

Prominent Families on AS THE WORLD TURNS (mid-1970's)

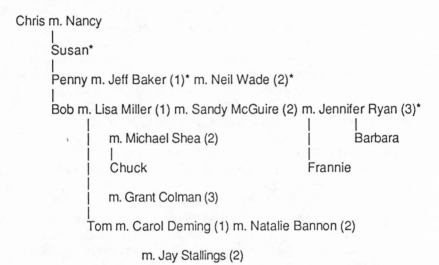

THE HUGHESES

Chris m. Nancy
|
Susan*
|
Penny m. Jeff Baker (1)* m. Neil Wade (2)*
|
Bob m. Lisa Miller (1) m. Sandy McGuire (2) m. Jennifer Ryan (3)*
| | | |
| m. Michael Shea (2) | Barbara
| | Frannie
| Chuck
|
| m. Grant Colman (3)
|
Tom m. Carol Deming (1) m. Natalie Bannon (2)

                m. Jay Stallings (2)

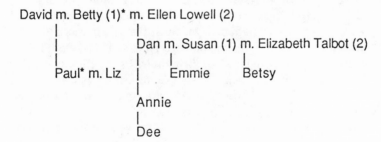

THE STEWARTS

David m. Betty (1)* m. Ellen Lowell (2)
| |
| Dan m. Susan (1) m. Elizabeth Talbot (2)
| | | |
Paul* m. Liz | Emmie   Betsy
                    |
                    Annie
                    |
                    Dee

* indicates deceased

and Stewarts were plagued with bad marriages and unplanned pregnancies. By the mid–1970s (see Figure 14), their families had changed greatly.

In the Tom Hughes household, Natalie was very bored and unhappy. She decided to seek an extramarital affair, and chose Jay Stallings as her consort. Stallings was attracted at first; he even became involved enough to make Natalie pregnant. However, Jay still loved Carol, and wanted to keep his marriage together; he told Natalie to get out of his life. Unfortunately, Carol found out about Jay's affair and filed for divorce. She was now free to see Tom's attempts to win her back. Despite his efforts, though, Carol and Jay later reconciled. They eventually became even happier, when Natalie left Jay's baby at their doorstep on her way out of Oakdale. Carol and Jay named their new baby Amy.

Amy was only one of two young additions to Oakdale; the other was little Andrew Dixon, Kim and John's son. Kim was delighted with her new baby, but her marriage to John had gone from bad to worse. Since Kim had finally straightened out her differences with Dan, she again planned to divorce John and marry him. John, though, having recently become a father, was even more obsessed with keeping the marriage together. He finally resorted to kidnapping little Andrew one day; but his plot was soon uncovered and Andrew was found. Kim finally divorced John and married Dan.

Kim and Dan's marriage was rocky at first, for they had a myriad of problems to address (including Dan's impotence and subsequent affair with ex-wife Susan, Betsy's true parentage, and John's constant interference with Andrew). After awhile, however, they finally started to be very happy ... until misfortune struck once again. Dan became afflicted with a fatal blood disease and died. Kim, along with Betsy, David and Ellen Stewart, mourned him terribly, as they had mourned Dan's brother, Paul, just a few years before.

Over at the Hugheses', Donald continued to marry the wrong women. His latest choice was Joyce Colman (Grant's ex-wife), who demanded a large house, costly furnishings and lots of spending money. As a result, Don worked overtime to make ends meet. While he was busy, Joyce hunted for men with whom to have affairs. One such paramour was a wealthy realtor named Ralph Mitchell. Ralph, however, met and liked Don; he told Joyce to confront Don with the truth of their affair. Joyce refused, and then plotted to kill Ralph. She accidentally shot Don instead, paralyzing him permanently. Later, Ralph exposed Joyce's plot and she ran away from Oakdale. She was ultimately killed in an auto accident.

Finally, the late seventies ushered in a new generation of Stewart adults: Annie and Dee Stewart had now become college students. They had always been close while growing up, but adulthood complications had begun to challenge their strong bond. This conflict was most dramatic when they both fell in love with the same man, Beau Spencer. Annie was first to realize this rather embarrassing situation, so she tried to hide her feelings from Dee. But Dee later found out, and after awhile realized that Annie, not she, should marry Beau. As it turned out, Dee was only half right: Beau should not have married either one of them. After he had several extramarital affairs, Annie finally divorced him, and the young Stewart women went on to other men.

By 1980, Annie and Dee (as well as the rest of the people of Oakdale) became involved with a whole new cast of characters (see Figure 15). In the first of many new character introductions, the Stewarts met Brad and Eric Hollister. The Hollisters had come to town because Brad, a talented geologist, wanted to mine silver on some land that the Hughes and Stewart families owned jointly. With them, they brought a silver refiner named James Stenbeck, and before long, these three turned the lives of several Oakdale women around. Dee Stewart met and fell in love with Brad Hollister; however, she was desperately afraid of sex (having had a bad experience some months earlier). After awhile, Brad became so frustrated at her frigidity that he turned instead to Annie. They were soon married. Dee, on the other hand, found comfort with John Dixon, who, as a doctor, understood her medical problem; as a friend, he wanted her. Dee became so emotionally dependent on John that he convinced her to marry him. However, Dee was still in love with Brad, and John, aware of that fact, frequently had outbursts of jealousy. One night, John went so far as to rape Dee. She responded by having him arrested and put on trial.

At the trial, John was defended by a crackerjack attorney named Maggie Crawford. Maggie was part of the Montgomery family, a new middle-class family who had come to town. John had known the Montgomerys because he had once had an affair with Maggie's older sister, Lyla; he was sure that they were among the few people in Oakdale that would support him. In any case, during the long, gut-wrenching trial, two major pieces of information surfaced, causing hurt and harm to several people: the admission by Dee that the only time she had made love to John, she was thinking only of Brad Hollister; and the declaration by Lyla Montgomery that John Dixon had fathered her young daughter, Margo. John was freed, but Dee subsequently divorced him; Annie left Brad; and Lyla was dumped by her current fiance, Bob Hughes.

Annie later married a young doctor named Jeff Ward; they had quadruplets and left town. Dee also left after several more encounters with John. As for Bob Hughes, he ultimately married Kim Reynolds Dixon Stewart.

Before Bob married Kim, however, she went through several changes. In the early eighties, a Greek family, the Andropouloses, moved into town. Kim fell in love with Nick, and they eventually wed after a series of family conflicts, including Nick's wild brother, Steve. Steve seemed to be in trouble perennially; he slept with Nick's first wife, stole precious jewelry, and, in general, became the Oakdale bad boy before marrying Carol Deming Hughes Stallings (and later, Betsy Hughes). After clearing up these conflicts, Kim and Nick wed. But one day, Nick died of a heart attack. Kim vowed never to marry again, although she was courted by several men. She

FIGURE 15

Prominent Families on AS THE WORLD TURNS (1980)

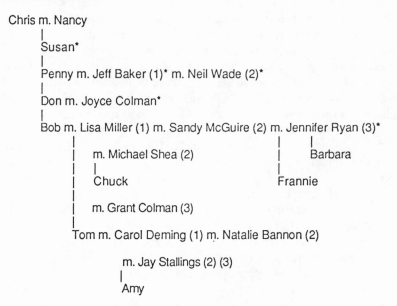

THE HUGHESES

Chris m. Nancy
|
Susan*
|
Penny m. Jeff Baker (1)* m. Neil Wade (2)*
|
Don m. Joyce Colman*
|
Bob m. Lisa Miller (1) m. Sandy McGuire (2) m. Jennifer Ryan (3)*
   | | |
   | m. Michael Shea (2) | Barbara
   | | Frannie
   | Chuck
   |
   | m. Grant Colman (3)
   |
Tom m. Carol Deming (1) m. Natalie Bannon (2)

         m. Jay Stallings (2) (3)
         |
         Amy

THE STEWARTS

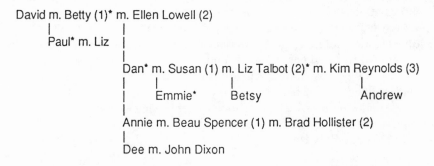

David m. Betty (1)* m. Ellen Lowell (2)
| |
Paul* m. Liz |
             |
             Dan* m. Susan (1) m. Liz Talbot (2)* m. Kim Reynolds (3)
             | | | |
             | Emmie*   Betsy   Andrew
             |
             Annie m. Beau Spencer (1) m. Brad Hollister (2)
             |
             Dee m. John Dixon

* indicates deceased

---

changed her mind, however, when she finally rediscovered Bob Hughes. Bob was exhausted himself, after another bad marriage—this time to Miranda Marlowe. Kim and Bob married and were happy, living with Frannie, Andy and their expected child.

Lisa had been in Europe during much of this time. When she returned to Oakdale, though, she was married to a man named Whit McColl. She seemed truly happy at last. Unfortunately, this did not last long; for one night soon after their marriage, Whit was brutally murdered in his home. Lisa and Whit's sons, Brian and Kirk, spent months trying to find the true murderer. They finally discovered that the housekeeper, Dorothy Connors, was the culprit—she had been in love with Whit for years; mothered an illegitimate son (Kirk); and was hoping they'd marry, until he wed Lisa. After uncovering the murderess, Lisa settled into business with Barbara Ryan Stenbeck.

Barbara had decided to marry James Stenbeck after a bizarre courtship. She had been engaged to Tom Hughes when James moved into town with the Hollister brothers. However, she soon left Tom for James, because, as Oakdale discovered later, she and James had been involved once before. From the prior relationship, Barbara had born a child named Paul, whom James had kept away from her. Upon seeing James again, Barbara succeeded in reconciling with him, and they finally decided to live as a family.

But the Stenbeck marriage was not a happy one. James soon started his wayward womanizing habits and Barbara mistrusted his rather shady business practices. She subsequently divorced him and married his "cousin" Gunnar. Then, James learned he wasn't really a Stenbeck. Having lost his name, his "family" money and his wife, he decided to fight for the one thing he had left: his son. He stopped at nothing to keep Paul, and later died in the attempt. With James gone, Barbara, Gunnar and Paul were a true family at last. However, not long after James' death, Gunnar discovered he had a terminal illness. He divorced Barbara and left Oakdale. Later, Barbara fell in love with the young publisher, Brian McColl; but he soon grew tired of her family problems with Paul. Brian decided to leave Barbara for someone else. Barbara retaliated by trying to break up many of the more solid marriages of Oakdale.

One of her victims was Tom Hughes. Despite his previous marital mistakes, Tom had found happiness with Margo Montgomery. They each had demanding careers, but they seemed to be able to work things out . . . until Margo started getting special assignments outside of town. Barbara saw this weakness and capitalized upon it by drugging Tom and then claiming he'd made love to her. Tom remembered nothing, so he could not deny the charge when Margo confronted him. They were separated soon after.

Finally, a new, lower-class rural family moved to Oakdale in the mideighties. They were the Snyders, and included mother Emma, Iva (the secret mother of Lily Walsh—a young socialite), Holden (Lily's would-be boyfriend), Meg (who wanted Lily's current boyfriend, Dusty Donovan) and Seth (who was attracted to Bob Hughes' daughter, Frannie). In a short while, they had become an important focal point for the residents of Oakdale.

When last reviewed in the mid-eighties, the family structures in *As the*

FIGURE 16

Prominent Families on AS THE WORLD TURNS (mid-1980's)

THE HUGHESES

Chris* m. Nancy
|
Susan*
|
Penny m. Jeff Baker (1)* m. Neil Wade (2)*
|
Don m. Joyce Colman (1) m. Mary Ellison (Brian Ellison's widow) (2)
|
Teddy
|
Bob m. Lisa Miller (1) m. S. McGuire (2) m. J. Ryan (3)* m. M. Marlowe (4) m. Kim Reynolds (5)
| |
| Andrew
m. Michael Shea (2)
|
Chuck

m. Grant Colman (3)

m. Whit McColl (4)*
|
Brian
|
Kirk

Barbara m. James Stenbeck*
|
Paul

Tom m. Carol Deming (1) m. Natalie Bannon (2) m. Margo Montgomery (3)

m. Jay Stallings

Amy

m. Steve Andropoulos

m. Norman Frazier

THE STEWARTS

David m. Betty (1)* m. Ellen Lowell (2)

Paul* m. Liz

Dan* m. Susan (1) m. Liz Talbot (2)* m. Kim Reynolds (3)

Emmie*

Andrew

Betsy m. Craig Montgomery (1)

m. Steve Andropoulos (2)

Danielle

Annie m. Beau Spencer (1) m. Brad Hollister (2) m. Jeff Ward (3)

Dee m. John Dixon

quadruplets

* indicates deceased

World Turns had undergone major revisions once more (see Figure 16). Based on these changes as well as the patterns which have emerged over the last thirty years, some predictions can be made about future plotlines and family structures:

1. The Snyder family is certain to be around for awhile. They've only been introduced recently, and already are in the middle of several romantic triangles.

2. Chances are very good that a long, lost relative (maybe even one who was previously thought dead) will emerge from either the Hughes, Stewart, Montgomery or Walsh family. *As the World Turns* is famous for keeping many of its characters in a nebulous state so that they may return at any time.

3. Romance, marriage and babies will continue as major themes. They have been the bases for Oakdale storylines since the beginning and are likely to remain as such. Other, more contemporary issues, such as drug abuse and political upheavals, will enter into the plot structure occasionally, but *As the World Turns* has achieved much of its popularity by staying traditional.

Capitol
First Broadcast: March 26, 1982 (CBS)

Capitol began as daytime television's answer to the classic romance of Romeo and Juliet, set in the political arena of Washington, D.C. The two conflicting families in this case were the Cleggs and the McCandlesses (see Figure 17). From these homes, most of the dramatic action occurred.

Julie Clegg, daughter of former Senator Sam and Myrna Clegg, was very much in love with a young Air Force captain named Tyler McCandless. Unfortunately, their star-crossed love was hindered at every turn by Julie's family, for the Cleggs were bitter enemies of the McCandlesses. This antagonism had gone on for many years, and now two generations had cause for battle.

On the one hand, Myrna had harbored a long-standing hatred for Clarissa McCandless because Clarissa had married Myrna's true love, Baxter. Myrna had never gotten over her jealousy of Clarissa's good fortune, although Myrna had herself married a wealthy, powerful political leader and had had several children by him. Clarissa McCandless, widowed for many years and with four sons to raise alone, suffered from Myrna's venom everywhere she went — this in full view of the Washington gossipmongers and the voting public.

As for the second generation of Cleggs and McCandlesses, young Tyler McCandless, a military hero, had decided to run for political office; so did young Samuel Clegg III ("Trey"). And, fueled by the fire begun by

FIGURE 17

Prominent Families on CAPITOL (1982)

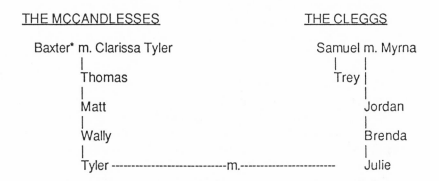

THE MCCANDLESSES   THE CLEGGS

Baxter* m. Clarissa Tyler   Samuel m. Myrna

* indicates deceased

their parents, their political ambitions went far beyond the political office. Both generations of Cleggs would now stop at nothing to see the McCandlesses fall politically and socially.

In the midst of these warring families, Julie and Tyler had fallen in love, and decided to be married. Myrna did everything she could to prevent the wedding. However, despite her unceasing trouble, the ceremony actually took place. Eventually, the young Cleggs (Trey, Jordy and Brenda) as well as Sam accepted Tyler and Julie's marriage. Myrna was forced by them to leave the newlyweds alone. She complied, but never really warmed up to Tyler.

Myrna was not the only stumbling block in Tyler and Julie's marriage, though. After they survived Myrna's meddling, Julie found out that she could not bear children. Feeling badly that she was denying Tyler the pleasure of fatherhood, she distanced herself from him and found friendship with a restaurant owner named Zed Diamond. Tyler, confused about Julie's actions, finally confronted her and they reunited. Zed was happy that Julie and Tyler were together again, but he was upset that he had grown so attached to Julie. This was because she had reminded him of his dead wife, Jenny.

After the young McCandlesses had reconciled, they decided to privately adopt a toddler named Scotty. Julie and Tyler were absolutely elated with this charming little boy . . . until they discovered that he was actually Trey's son.

Trey was unaware at that time that Scotty was his son; in fact he didn't even know he was a father. Trey was happily married to a young journalist named Sloane Denning (the daughter of Senator Mark Denning and his estranged wife, Paula). Trey and Sloane had come together after unhappy affairs: Sloane, who was in love with Tyler, had lost him to Julie; and Trey had fallen in love with a hooker named Kelly Harper (Scotty's mother), who left him because she would ruin his chances for political success. In any case, Trey and Sloane were happy until Trey found out about Scotty and the fact that Kelly had never left Washington. He tracked her down, fell in love with her again, divorced Sloane and moved in with Kelly and Scotty. Tyler and Julie were distressed to lose Scotty, but they ultimately adopted a beautiful baby girl named Alison.

Back at the Clegg household, Brenda Clegg became especially friendly with the McCandlesses, much to Myrna's chagrin. In addition to liking her new brother-in-law, Tyler, Brenda also developed a crush on his brother, Wally. Through a series of incidents, Brenda and Wally were soon drawn together, and before long, they, too, wanted to be married. In fact, they actually ran off to elope at one point — but they were caught eventually, and returned to their parents' homes.

Myrna did not accept Brenda and Wally's relationship any better than she had that of Julie and Tyler. So, once again, she set about to destroy the new Clegg-McCandless couple. This time, she stopped at nothing: sending Brenda away, encouraging other young men to date her, and enticing Wally to renew his former gambling habit. As a result, Wally and Brenda broke their engagement. Their love for each other, however, was still not broken.

Unlike Brenda and Julie, Jordy was not in love with any of the McCandlesses. He was having equally severe romantic problems, though. A confirmed playboy, Jordy had at one time seduced many beautiful women, including Lizbeth Bachman (Thomas McCandless' fiancee). But he soon tired of his womanizing habits when he fell in love with a young woman named Lee Anne Foster. Unfortunately, however, Lee Anne had a serious blood disorder and needed a marrow transplant from a close relative or she would die. And the only close relative who was alive, her sister, actress Kate Wells, refused to help because she blamed Lee Anne for the death of their parents years before. Despite all of Jordy's pleas, Kate ignored Lee Anne's needs . . . until she discovered that Jordy's father was wealthy and prominent. She decided immediately to come to Washington to help her sister, and herself as well.

Meanwhile, the McCandless home had other problems besides the Cleggs. Clarissa, presumably widowed after Baxter was lost at sea, fell in love with Senator Mark Denning. Mark had been separated from his wife, Paula, for years, but he had never divorced her because she was mentally unstable. Paula really wasn't as bad as Mark was led to believe; she simply behaved badly, knowing it was a successful way to keep their marriage

FIGURE 18

Prominent Families on CAPITOL (1986)

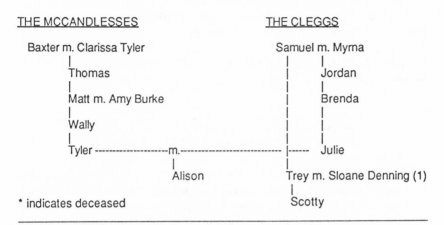

THE MCCANDLESSES

Baxter m. Clarissa Tyler
Thomas
Matt m. Amy Burke
Wally
Tyler -------------------m.-------------------
Alison
* indicates deceased

THE CLEGGS

Samuel m. Myrna
Jordan
Brenda
|----- Julie
Trey m. Sloane Denning (1)
Scotty

intact. In any case, after awhile, Mark decided he could do no more for Paula. He wanted to divorce her so he could marry Clarissa.

Mark did receive his divorce; unfortunately, though, he never was able to marry Clarissa. On his wedding day, Mark was accidentally shot — by Jenny Diamond, who, it developed, had not died after all. While Mark was in a coma as a result of the shooting, Paula had him kidnapped so that she could convince him to reconcile with her. By the time Mark was found, another person had "returned" from the dead — Baxter McCandless. Clarissa and Baxter later remarried.

The other McCandlesses had dramas of their own. Matt, one of Clarissa and Baxter's sons, fell in love with a beautiful girl named Amy Burke. She soon discovered that she was going blind, however, so she ran away. Matt finally tracked her down in Europe. He decided to remain with her there.

Meanwhile, Thomas, another son, was successful in medicine (despite a physical handicap) but unlucky in love. His many relations included Lizbeth Bachman and Kelly Harper. Each time, unfortunately, he was viewed as a better friend than lover. In spite of his losses, though, Thomas kept searching — he vowed he would find the right woman to marry.

By 1986, the McCandlesses and Cleggs had shown the results of four dramatic years (see Figure 18). And from the appearance of some interesting relationships, their situations are likely to change again soon.

The following are predictions for *Capitol:*

1. Producers seem to be spending much more money on this soap than they have on shows in the past. This trend is likely to continue for ratings'

purposes. As a result, look for more travel to exotic locations, action/adventure plots, international intrigue and celebrity cameo appearances.

2. Look for certain characters to return, especially Matt McCandless. After his three brothers have played out all their options, he's likely to return, so that writers can create new ones.

3. The animosity between the Cleggs and McCandlesses will continue because it is one of the basic premises of the story. Also likely to continue are the romantic triangles (or, in some cases, rectangles) of: Kelly-Trey-Sloane; Julie-Tyler-Zed; and Paula-Mark-Clarissa-Baxter. Other, newer romantic triangles will emerge as well.

Days of Our Lives
First Broadcast: November 8, 1965 (NBC)

For over twenty years, MacDonald Carey has invited viewers to join his Salem friends and relatives as they live through the *Days of Our Lives*. In 1965, his invitation began very simply when he introduced the Horton clan — a large, professional, upper-middle-class family recognized as one of the town's finest. Dr. Tom Horton was a respected physician and served as the Chief of Internal Medicine at University Hospital. Together with his wife, Alice, Tom had raised five children: Tommy (who was thought to be MIA while fighting in the Korean Conflict); his twin sister, Addie; Mickey (an attorney); Bill (a surgeon); and Marie (see Figure 19).

When the story opened, Addie, now married to a banker named Ben Olson, had just left for Europe. She planned to live there with her husband and son, Steve. However, she decided that her daughter, Julie, would be best off in Salem, so she put her in the care of Tom and Alice. They were absolutely delighted at the prospect of raising their grandchild, but Julie was not pleased at all. She felt abandoned and unloved by her parents and responded to her unhappiness by looking for affection from people outside of her family. Two such people who filled Julie's needs at this time were her secret fiance, David Martin, and her best friend, Susan Hunter.

But it was not long before Julie's fragile security was shattered by the people she had trusted most. Just as she began planning for her marriage, Julie discovered that Susan had become pregnant with David's baby. She felt terribly betrayed. Still, she valiantly agreed to step aside so that Susan and David could be wed. In return, the couple agreed to divorce after their infant had been given a legitimate name. This would leave David free to marry Julie. Julie kept her part of the bargain; in fact, she even served as Susan's maid of honor at the ceremony. Unfortunately, though, after the birth of Susan's little boy, Richard, she refused to divorce David. Julie was enraged, and the two young women quickly became bitter rivals for David's love.

FIGURE 19

Prominent Families on DAYS OF OUR LIVES (1965)

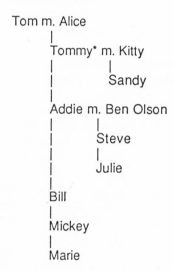

THE HORTONS

Tom m. Alice
│
Tommy* m. Kitty
│   │
│   Sandy
│
Addie m. Ben Olson
│   │
│   Steve
│   │
│   Julie
│
Bill
│
Mickey
│
Marie

* indicates deceased

Needless to say, the Martin marriage was not a happy one; Susan's only real hold on David was his little son, Richard. So David continued to see Julie secretly, who later became pregnant as well. As if things were not bad enough, one day young Richard fell off a swing while playing with his dad. He died shortly thereafter. Susan, out of her mind with grief and anger at the death of her baby, later shot and killed David for his negligence.

Julie was despondent over David's tragic death, and the infant son to whom she had just given birth served as a constant reminder of her loss. Julie then decided to give her baby up for adoption to a young couple, Scott and Janet Banning. Julie now felt that her painful past with Susan and David could be ended.

Unfortunately, such was not the case. It seemed that Susan was a friend and neighbor of the Bannings. When Scott and Janet brought little Brad home, Susan (who did not know Brad was Julie's son) became a regular babysitter and lavished incredible amounts of attention on him. Susan obviously had substituted the Banning baby for young Richard; she treated him as her own son. This, of course, made Julie furious. And she became even more angry when Janet Banning died of a brain tumor and Susan began to act as Brad's adopted mother.

Susan and Scott, after Janet's death, had been drawn together because they were both concerned over little Brad's care. As they spent more time with each other, their feelings turned into love, and there was little doubt that they would soon marry. Upon discovering Susan and Scott's relationship, however, Julie was not about to lose a second time. She sued for custody of Brad, renamed him David, and then ultimately married Scott (who couldn't bear to be away from his son) just to spite Susan.

Julie's was not the only dramatic story at the Hortons', though. There was also the romantic triangle involving Bill, Mickey, and a psychiatrist named Laura Spencer, as well as Tommy Horton's "return from the dead."

Bill Horton, an ambitious young surgeon, had met and fallen in love with another intern, Laura Spencer. They later decided to be married. But not long after their announced engagement, Bill became afflicted with an unknown illness and was unable to use his hands fully. Feeling that his career would soon end, he fled from Salem . . . and Laura. Unfortunately, Laura was unaware of Bill's medical problem; she could not understand why he had left her. She decided to try to forget him by plunging herself into her work.

Much of Laura's workload at this time involved Susan Hunter Martin's murder trial. Laura was Susan's psychiatrist, so she spent many long hours with her defense attorney, Mickey Horton. Eventually, Laura and Mickey were able to have Susan acquitted of murder due to temporary insanity. In the meantime, they also fell in love and married.

When Bill finally returned to Salem, he discovered that Laura was now married to his brother, Mickey. Overcome by his loss as well as his guilt for letting it happen, Bill decided (as Laura had) to devote himself to his work and other friends, especially a young doctor named Mark Brooks. Bill had met Mark while he was away from Salem. Later, he felt particularly protective towards him when he found out that Mark had been burned and tortured during the Korean Conflict, and subsequently had faced plastic surgery, amnesia and shell shock. As a result, Bill felt Mark needed the support of a family; he then introduced him to the Hortons.

As expected, Bill's family welcomed Mark and became very attached to him in a short time. But no one could predict the immediate love that sprang up between Mark and young Marie Horton. They had a wonderful courtship, too . . . until Mark's memory returned and he discovered he was actually Tommy Horton. Everyone was shocked, but no one was more devastated than Marie. She saw no other course than to leave Salem and become a nun. She was not heard from again until much later. Tommy, on the other hand, tried to fit the pieces of his life back together again; this process included a reunion with his troublemaker wife, Kitty, and their daughter, Sandy.

In the meantime, Bill was still obsessed with his love for Laura. Despite his grueling workload, he could not escape the fact that his brother had married the woman he wanted. One night, when he could stand it no longer, he raped Laura at the hospital. She then became pregnant — and as Dr. Tom soon discovered, it was with Bill's child. Mickey, however, was unaware that the child was not his. But there was no doubt about the baby's true parentage because Mickey, unknowingly, was sterile. In any case, Bill, Laura, and Dr. Tom decided to keep the baby's true father a secret. And, when little Michael Horton was born, no one was prouder than Mickey.

Unfortunately, the Hortons' secret was not as safely hidden as everyone had thought. One night, while Bill and Laura were discussing Michael's parental background, Tommy's wife, Kitty, taped the conversation and then tried to blackmail Bill. As he struggled to get the incriminating tape from her, though, Kitty had a heart attack and died. Bill was then arrested for murder. During his trial, Bill managed to keep the secret, but he was eventually found guilty of manslaughter. He then went to prison for a six-month term.

With Bill in jail, the Hortons found themselves very depressed during the early seventies. While it was true that their family had expanded (see Figure 20), they also had lost some members as well. As more time passed, however, new people and events created a different environment in Salem. Before long, after Bill was released from prison, the family moved on to other crises.

One of the new characters who came to Salem during this time was Doug Williams, a handsome con man who had been in prison with Bill. Doug had followed Bill to his hometown because he had heard that Susan Martin had inherited a huge sum of money upon David's death. Doug's plan was to romance Susan, relieve her of her inheritance, and then leave Salem. His plan did not turn out the way he'd originally thought, though; Susan was not attracted to him because she was hopelessly in love with Scott Banning (now married to Julie). Doug and Susan did become friends, however, and after hearing about his original plot, Susan offered him an alternative: She would pay him handsomely if he lured Julie away from Scott. After seeing Julie, Doug was only too happy to comply with Susan's wishes. The two of them fell in love immediately, and Julie finally believed she had met the man of her dreams. Just as she began to plan her divorce from Scott and remarriage to Doug, however, her mother, Addie, returned to Salem and caused more trouble.

Addie's husband, Ben Olson, had recently died of a heart attack in Paris. She decided that the best way to adjust to her newfound widowhood was to come back home. And so she did (although Steve remained in Paris to complete his education). Upon her return, Julie was suspicious and

FIGURE 20

Prominent Families on DAYS OF OUR LIVES   (1970)

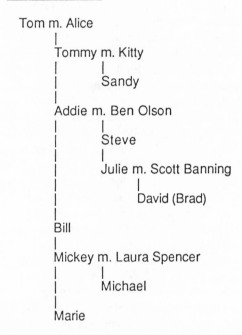

THE HORTONS

Tom m. Alice
|
Tommy m. Kitty
| |
| Sandy
|
Addie m. Ben Olson
| |
| Steve
| |
| Julie m. Scott Banning
| |
| David (Brad)
|
Bill
|
Mickey m. Laura Spencer
| |
| Michael
|
Marie

hateful; she had never forgiven her mother for leaving her in Salem and later rejecting her pleas for help when she had been pregnant with David. As a result, Julie made all the aspects of her life secret — especially her relationship with Doug. However, Julie's evasiveness only succeeded in piquing Addie's curiosity. She responded by hiring a private detective to investigate Julie's activities. Most interesting to her was Doug Williams.

At first, Addie disliked Doug's playboy manner, but after several nasty encounters, she found that she was very much attracted to him. One night, she impulsively asked him to marry her, and Doug, having just had an argument with Julie, agreed. They ran away and eloped. And despite the "quick engagement," they found that they were very happy as a married couple. Doug still felt guilty about Julie, however; between her unrequited love for him and her hatred for her mother, she seemed to stop at nothing to try to ruin Doug and Addie's marriage. Addie retaliated by showering Doug with love, expensive gifts like the nightclub he had always wanted, and finally, her pregnancy.

Julie continued her unhappy marriage with Scott Banning, but after a while, she realized that she was putting them both through hell for little reason. She finally decided to get a divorce. However, before the papers were submitted, Scott died tragically at a construction site. Julie was forced to portray a bereaved widow, with no one knowing that she had never loved Scott in the first place. She was soon "comforted" by several men, including her attorney, Don Craig, and Scott's boss, Bob Anderson: but she was still hopeful that she would end up with Doug.

Doug was unaware of Julie's intentions at this point. He and Addie had grown happier every day and were anticipating the birth of their child when Addie discovered she had leukemia. Despite her declining health, she succeeded in giving birth to a beautiful baby girl. They decided to name her Hope. After Hope's birth, Addie, not wanting to die without reconciling with her elder daughter, summoned Julie to her hospital room. She told Julie that she was sorry for her past mistakes, but that Doug and she had been truly happy. She then made Julie promise to take care of Hope when she died. Julie agreed enthusiastically, for at last she would be with Doug, and at the request of her mother!

Julie waited for Addie's health to deteriorate further; she even broke her engagement to Don Craig in anticipation of Addie's death. However, much to everyone's surprise, Addie went into remission, and she recovered dramatically. Julie, once again disappointed, turned her attentions to the then-married Bob Anderson. He promptly divorced his wife, Phyllis, and married Julie instead. Not much time had elapsed, though, before fate cheated Julie once again: Shortly after Julie's marriage to Bob, Addie was killed by a truck as she crossed the street. Doug was terribly grief-stricken by her death, and at the time, he could think of nothing but his loss. Later, when he had recovered somewhat, Doug remembered Julie's promise to Addie. But by then, he found out, Julie was pregnant with Bob Anderson's child. Doug decided to lie to her, saying he didn't love her, so that she would not divorce Bob. He then left Hope in the care of Grandma Alice and Dr. Tom Horton.

Meanwhile, Susan Martin had never remarried after David's death and Scott Banning's unavailability. Instead, she devoted herself to the free clinic she'd built with David's money. At the clinic, she became especially close to a young doctor named Greg Peters; and for the first time since Scott's death, she fell in love. Unfortunately, on her way to the clinic one day, Susan was raped in the park (and became pregnant). As it turned out, her attacker was Greg's brother, Eric. This shocking discovery caused a series of problems, but in the end, Greg decided to marry Susan and be a father to her baby. Unfortunately, the rape was not easy to forget, and Susan and Greg began having marital problems almost immediately. The pressure drove Greg further into his work, and shortly thereafter, he met and fell in love with a young woman named Amanda Howard, who was having problems in her own relationship with Dr. Neil Curtis.

Back at the Hortons', the romantic triangle of Bill, Laura and Mickey continued to resurface. After Bill returned from prison, he told Laura why he had refused to give a reason for being at Kitty's house. Laura was overwhelmed with compassion and love at the thought that Bill had sacrificed his reputation for her. While very much in love, though, they decided to keep things as they were and not to tell Mickey their secret. Despite their discretion, Mickey suspected they were having an affair; so to get back at them, he had an affair with his secretary, Linda Patterson. Upon discovering their romance, Laura threatened to divorce Mickey. She later had to change those plans, however, when Michael, overhearing his mother and "Uncle Bill" talking, ran away and was gravely injured in a car accident. Also, in the meantime, Mickey had developed a serious heart condition; he later suffered a devastating attack when he and Michael argued over Michael's discovery of his affair.

After Mickey's coronary attack, Bill performed a triple bypass on him, and ultimately saved his life. Still, Mickey was not happy, and the stress of feeling himself not to be a "complete" man physically caused him to have a stroke and lose his memory. He wandered away from Salem one day, and found himself on a farm with a beautiful girl named Maggie Simmons. Completely unaware of his past, Mickey gave himself the name Marty Hansen. He later wed Maggie, not knowing he was already married to Laura.

Such was the family picture of the Hortons in the mid-seventies (see Figure 21). And, as Salem moved into the late seventies, even more dramatic action occurred. Much of this came from the Horton grandchildren, who were growing up quickly.

Michael Horton, feeling confused and upset with his father's refusal to return to Salem and his mother's marriage to "Uncle Bill," found friends outside of his family. Most important among them was Trish Clayton, who had a troubled mother (Jeri) and an "overly interested" stepfather (Jack). Neither Mike nor Trish was happy at home, so they decided to live together (platonically) in a small apartment.

David Banning, on the other hand, had decided to live outside of Salem for several months. Like Mike and Trish, he was none too pleased with his home situation, and he felt that the only person who'd ever truly loved him was his dead adoptive father, Scott. One night, after having adjusted to living with his new stepfather, Bob Anderson, David overheard Doug and Julie professing their love for each other. He ran out the door, took Doug's car and ran it over a bridge. While no one found his body, he was presumed dead. David did nothing to change this misconception and chose, instead, to live with a kind black family, the Grants. David had been

FIGURE 21

Prominent Families on DAYS OF OUR LIVES   (mid 1970's)

THE HORTONS

```
Tom m. Alice
  |
  Tommy m. Kitty*
  |       |
  |       Sandy
  |
  Marie
  |.
  Mickey m. Laura Spencer (1) m. Maggie Simmons (2)
  |       |
  |       Michael
  |
  Addie* m. Ben Olson(1)* m. Doug Williams (2)
  |       |                |
  |       Steve            Hope
  |       |
  |       Julie m. Scott Banning (1)* m. Bob Anderson (2)
  |              |
  |              David
  |
  Bill
```

* indicates deceased

---

good friends with Danny Grant; but when he met Danny's sister, Valerie, he fell in love immediately. Their interracial romance was not acceptable to anyone. Soon, Mr. Grant told David it was best for him to leave.

When David returned to Salem, he had nowhere to go but to the Hortons. Julie, upon hearing that her son was alive, rushed to see him. But in her hurry to get there, she fell down the stairs and lost her baby. Despite her grief at miscarrying, she was now free to divorce Bob and marry Doug. Doug, however, was not as free because a former wife (from a former life), Kim Douglas, came to town as Doug and Julie were planning their wedding. She bothered them for several months until Doug was finally able to secure his divorce. Then, at long last, Julie and Doug were wed! They continued to have some problems after their marriage, but overall, their love was enough to surmount the difficulties.

As for David, Doug and Julie's marriage was somewhat hard for him to take. He reacted by drinking heavily and then seducing Trish Clayton. Actually, Trish was very much in love with Michael, but neither was able to resolve the sexual difficulties they both experienced. When David came on the scene, Trish slept with him to relieve her sexual tension; unfortunately, this encounter resulted in a pregnancy. Michael, feeling betrayed by his parents (who by now he had discovered to be Bill and Laura), could not take another rejection, so he ran off to be a mechanic. Trish had a breakdown, but later married David so that their son, Scotty, could have a name. For a long while, Trish felt she still really loved Mike; but in the end, she and David stayed together. A few years after their marriage, David, Trish and Scotty moved away from Salem.

As for the other Hortons, Mickey finally regained his memory and stayed married to Maggie. But Linda Patterson Phillips was still in love with him, and stopped at nothing to get him back. First, she claimed that her young daughter (Melissa) was Mickey's child; then she left her new husband (Jim Phillips) to die after a seizure, hoping this would free her to marry Mickey. In the end, Linda gave up and married Bob Anderson. Mickey and Maggie were happy at last, and continued to look for ways to have a family.

While Mickey and Maggie may have won in the Linda Patterson Phillips battle, Bob Anderson became the big loser by marrying her. Immediately after their marriage, Linda began battling with Bob's daughter, Mary. In addition, she started an affair with Dr. Neil Curtis. Bob became disenchanted with her behavior within a short while; he later divorced her, and reconciled with his ex-wife, Phyllis. However, Bob and Phyllis' reconciliation did not occur until after Phyllis cut off her romance with the new con man in town, Alex Marshall.

Alex had met Phyllis Anderson outside of Salem while she was grieving over her divorce from Bob. Within a short while, they became engaged. Of course, Alex did not love Phyllis; he was only interested in her money. When they returned to Salem to be married, Alex quickly decided it was more to his liking (and equally profitable) to be involved with Phyllis' daughter, Mary. Heartbroken, Phyllis finally gave in to the inevitable and allowed Mary to wed Alex; and later she reconciled with Bob (shortly before he died).

Alex, it was later revealed, had known more people than the Andersons in Salem. It seemed that at one time, long ago, he had had a relationship with Marie Horton. The outcome of this romance had been a young girl, whom they later discovered was living in town. Her name was Jessica. After finding out that Jessica existed, Marie decided to leave the convent and marry Alex. However, at least two people objected to this plan: Mary, who was not about to lose Alex to Marie; and Jessica, who became schizophrenic when she learned who her true parents were. Needless to say,

Alex and Marie's wedding plans never materialized. Marie and Jessie finally left town, but Alex stayed on to prey on other unsuspecting people.

Meanwhile, at the Hortons', Bill and Laura had begun to have marital problems. Their differences revolved largely around work. Laura was laboring day and night as well as helping friends like Dr. Marlena Evans with their psychological difficulties. Bill felt ignored, so he started working long hours himself. In the process, Bill became involved with another doctor, Kate Winograd. Kate later left, but the Hortons' problems continued as Laura began to have psychological difficulties about her childhood. Her mental illness became so intense that Bill had her committed to a sanitarium and left Salem to be with her. She was released after many months, but the Bill Hortons never returned. Instead, they had a happy life outside of Salem with their young daughter, Jennifer Rose.

As evidenced by Figure 22, the Horton family had once again undergone a metamorphosis by 1980. However, it is also significant to note that during this time, several of the original Hortons had either died or left town. The new storylines of the eighties began to involve either Horton grandchildren or completely new characters like the Brady family.

The Brady family became central to the plotlines in *Days of Our Lives* when Roman Brady, a police investigator, tracked down a criminal known as the "Salem Strangler." At the same time, he began a romance with Marlena Evans Craig. He later married her, and they had twins. According to the story, Roman and his family had always lived in Salem; however, they were lower-middle-class and had lived in the poorer section of town. The Bradys were a large group, including Shawn and Caroline (the parents), sons Roman and Bo, and daughters Kimberly and Kayla. Before long, most of the action in Salem revolved around them — and the Hortons had taken a back seat, for the most part.

Roman was the focal point of the group in the early eighties. He and partner Abe Carver soon became the leading crime fighters of Salem, cracking local cases such as the Salem Strangler as well as international syndicates with leaders like Stefano DiMera and Kellam Chandler. At home, Roman was the family rock — giving big-brotherly advice to Kimberly (who had been a prostitute, among other things) and Bo (a wild and carefree young man who was in trouble more often than not). Together with Marlena, his daughter from a previous marriage (Carrie) and the twins, Roman portrayed the epitome of solid citizenship in Salem. As such, it came as little surprise that several people would be deeply affected when they thought he died in an attempt to fight yet another battle.

Bo was most directly stricken, for he had held Roman in his arms before he had died. More importantly, however, Roman had become a close friend after many years of sibling fights. He helped Bo to straighten himself out; encouraged him to go into private detective work; and was delighted when he finally married Hope Williams, Doug and Addie's

FIGURE 22

Prominent Families on DAYS OF OUR LIVES　(1980)

THE HORTONS

```
Tom m. Alice
    |
    Tommy m. Kitty*
    |       |
    |       Sandy
    |
    Marie
    |   |
    |   Jessica
    |
    Mickey m. Laura (1) m. Maggie Simmons (2)
    |           |       |
    |           |       Melissa
    |           |
    |           Michael m. Margo Andermann*
    |
    Addie* m. Ben Olson (1)* m. Doug Williams (2)
    |           |           |
    |           Steve       Hope
    |           |
    |           Julie m.Scott Banning (1)*m.Bob Anderson(2)m.Doug Williams (3)
    |                       |
    |                       David m. Trisha Clayton
    |                               |
    |                               Scotty
    |
    Bill m. Laura Spencer
        |
        Jennifer Rose
```

* indicates deceased

daughter. After Roman's death, Bo was determined to pick up the banner he'd dropped, and destroy the syndicate that had destroyed Roman.

Together with his sister Kimberly and an international agent named Shane Donovan (with whom Kim later fell in love), Bo and Hope traveled from city to city and country to country to track down the evil syndicate that had killed Roman. They ended their travels by focusing on Victor Kiriakis, a prominent Salemite, and spent most of their time trying to put him in prison.

Victor was not easy to convict, though; he would cover his tracks well, and could destroy or pay off any other witnesses who might testify against him. Also, he had shown a mysteriously deep interest in the Brady family.

Bo and Kimberly would continually lose their battles to capture him, but they wouldn't lose their lives. Given Victor's reputation, this latter point was most perplexing to everyone until they discovered that Victor had once had an affair with Caroline Brady. Caroline had subsequently become pregnant and had a child. She named him Bo, and never told Shawn he wasn't the father. Needless to say, the Brady family was devastated by the news.

Roman's death also sent tremors in other places. Marlena was so grief-stricken that she left Carrie with Roman's first wife, Anna, and took the twins to Denver. She later returned, but was continually victimized by psychotic patients and romantic suitors. Also, she kept feeling Roman's presence wherever she went. She began to wonder about her own mental stability when she noticed that one of her patients, John Black, bore some amazing likenesses to Roman. Indeed, it was Roman. He had lived through his ordeal, but had lost his memory and become a pawn for the evil Stefano DiMera and Victor Kiriakis.

On the other side of town, only a few Hortons remained active in the Salem news. Alice and Tom continued to provide stability for their friends and grandchildren. Mickey, the only Horton child remaining in town, had survived a separation from his wife, Maggie; they reconciled and now lived happily as the adoptive parents of Melissa Anderson.

Melissa, Mickey's daughter, had had some difficulties while growing up, but she eventually married her true love, Pete Jannings, and began to pursue a dance career. Unfortunately, however, the marriage was not as stable as it might have been. Between Melissa's other suitors, Pete's desire to buy things for her that he could not afford, and Pete's child, Charley, a strong marital future for Pete and Melissa seemed unlikely.

The other Horton grandchildren in Salem (besides Hope, who had married Bo Brady) were Michael and Jennifer Rose, Bill and Laura's kids. Jennifer Rose, a teenager, looked to be more trouble than she was worth when she first came to Salem. But she seemed to have some good qualities also. In any case, her ascent into adulthood was likely to be filled with drama. Mike, on the other hand, was now a resident at University Hospital. He had never remarried after losing his wife, Margo; but most recently, he had begun a romantic interest in a young surgeon named Robin Jacobs.

By 1986, it was obvious that the characters and storylines of *Days of Our Lives* had changed drastically from years before (see Figure 23). As mentioned in Chapter 3, this soap opera has become very unique by attracting both a younger, newer audience as well as the older, more traditional one. And chances are the writers will continue this winning formula as long as it spells success. More specifically:

1. Alice and Tom Horton represent the thread of continuity for *Days of Our Lives*. They are likely to stay (although not very actively) because they attract the viewers who have been with them for many years. Their

FIGURE 23

Prominent Families on DAYS OF OUR LIVES (1986)

THE HORTONS

Tom m. Alice
|
Marie
| |
| Jessica
|
Tommy m. Kitty*
| |
| Sandy
|
Bill m. Laura Spencer
| |
| Michael m. Margo Andermann*
| |
| Jennifer Rose
|
Mickey m. Laura Spencer (1) m. Maggie Simmons (2) (3)
| |
| Melissa m. Pete Jannings
| |
| Charley
|
Addie* m. Ben Olson (1)* m. Doug Williams (2)
| |
| Steve   Hope m. Bo Brady (see below)
|
Julie m. Scott Banning (1)* m. Bob Anderson (2)* m. Doug Williams (3)
|
David m. Trisha Clayton
|
Scotty

THE BRADYS

Shawn m. Caroline
| |
| Bo m. Hope (see above)
|
Roman m. Anna (1) m. Marlena Evans Craig (2)
| | |
| Carrie   Twins
|
Kimberly
| |
| Andrew
|
Kayla

* indicates deceased

presence is most especially felt during holiday times such as Thanksgiving or Christmas, when they remember past years of family traditions.

2. The Bradys are an extremely popular family and are likely to be the center of most storylines for the next several years. Roman and Bo are particularly in demand because they are among the hottest sex symbols of daytime television. Also, Roman, Bo, Hope, Kimberly and Shane provide the action and adventure that appeal to the show's large male audience. After they've finished with Victor Kiriakis, they are likely to move on to other international villains.

3. In 1986, *Days of Our Lives* tried to bring back two of their previously popular characters, Doug Williams and Robert LeClaire. So far, the audience reception to their return has been lukewarm. But depending on the final audience response, other characters may also return ... or they may drop the notion of "friends and relatives" of the past altogether.

General Hospital
First Broadcast: April 1, 1963 (ABC)

As the program title implies, major characters in the first years of *General Hospital* were not members of one or two prominent families in Port Charles. Rather, they were the doctors and nurses of the busy medical center in that city. For example, Jessie, a nurse working in the seventh floor internal medicine division, was often the central figure in the early action of *General Hospital*. As the story began, Jessie had fallen in love with a handsome intern seven years younger than herself named Phil Brewer. After they married, she worked many overtime hours to support his career dream of becoming a cardiologist. Phil loved Jessie very much, but the age difference caused problems soon after they married, as did Phil's constant need to have an extramarital affair. Jessie tolerated Phil's infidelity for awhile; however, she later refused to condone his behavior and filed for divorce.

Phil was not happy with Jessie's decision to divorce him. As a result, he began to drink heavily and badger her for a reconciliation. On one particular night, he actually went to her home and raped her. Jessie subsequently became pregnant and had a baby. Unfortunately, though, the baby soon died because of a serious heart problem. Jessie and Phil, overcome with grief, mutually agreed to divorce and prevent any further harm to each other.

Jessie and Phil were not destined to stay apart forever, however. They were reunited when Jessie was placed on trial for the murder of her second husband, Dr. John Prentice (who, by the way, had actually committed suicide). Eventually, she was acquitted, and Jessie and Phil remarried. But shortly after the reconciliation, Phil, accused of murdering his former paramour, Polly Prentice, ran away from Port Charles and was reportedly killed in a plane crash.

Jessie was shattered over Phil's death, so she sought solace from her many friends at the hospital. Among them was her best pal, Dr. Steve Hardy (who was a brilliant physician but as unlucky in love as Jessie) and Dr. Peter Taylor, a psychiatrist whom she later married. Peter was the kind and loving husband Jessie had always desired, and she felt that she had finally entered into a long, happy marriage. She probably would have been right . . . if not for the fact that Dr. Phil Brewer was still alive and well. Phil had returned to Port Charles to find that his wife had unwittingly committed bigamy. He still loved her and didn't want to hurt her, though, so he dreamed up a false identity, "Harold Williamson," and washed dishes at a restaurant near the hospital to be close to her. His good intentions were short-lived in any case, for he soon became attracted to a waitress named Diana Maynard, and had an affair with her.

Shortly after Phil became involved with Diana, though, Jessie discovered his true identity and fell back in love with him. She arranged to have her marriage to Peter annulled, and she reunited once more with Phil. Phil was delighted to be back with Jessie again, and almost forgot about Diana . . . until he found out that she was carrying his son and had married Peter Taylor to give him a legitimate name. Phil went wild when he heard that Diana had given birth to his child because he had always believed he was sterile. He decided to break up with Jessie and marry Diana. He was terribly upset, however, when he learned that Diana actually *loved* Peter and was not interested in divorcing him for Phil. He reacted to her declaration by forcibly entering her apartment one night and raping her. Diana was now carrying a second child who was not Peter's.

Jessie and Phil Brewer and Diana and Peter Taylor were not the only people with problems in Port Charles during the mid- and late sixties, though. Jessie's friend Dr. Steve Hardy was also in the midst of a romantic roller coaster ride. Steve had fallen in love with a beautiful flight attendant named Audrey March (the sister of senior nurse Lucille). The feeling seemed to be mutual, too, for Audrey had grown tired of the swinging lifestyle of an airline hostess and wanted to settle down to raise a family. Accordingly, Steve and Audrey married shortly after they met. Unfortunately, however, the marriage soon faltered. Audrey's wish to become pregnant was not fulfilled, and she thought (mistakenly) that Steve was sterile. She later decided to be artificially inseminated; but this, too, failed when she and Steve were in an auto accident and she miscarried the unborn baby.

Audrey's obsession with children became worse after her accident, and she never forgave Steve for "killing her baby." Overcome with grief, she divorced him and went to Vietnam to help take care of war orphans. After a short while, though, Audrey returned to General Hospital as a nurse. She still loved Steve, but she couldn't bring herself to admit it, so she ignored him and married another doctor, Tom Baldwin, instead.

Audrey didn't love Tom, and the relationship soured quickly. However, Audrey, on the brink of a divorce, realized she was pregnant. Not knowing quite what to do, she left town, had the baby, and returned to claim (falsely) that he had died. She now felt free to remarry Steve.

But remarriage for Steve and Audrey did not become a reality. Tom discovered that the baby (Tommy) was alive, and tried to blackmail her into staying with him for the sake of their infant. Tom, however, recognized his vulnerability, and knew that the blackmail threat could not last forever. So, he chose to kidnap young Tommy instead, and he ran away from Port Charles with his son and the babysitter, Florence Andrews.

Needless to say, by the early seventies, the lives of several people on the medical staff of General Hospital had become intertwined and extremely complicated. And as the story progressed, they continued to change, along with the lives of some new characters.

Among the more established favorites, Jessie Brewer was still the subject for unhappy love. After divorcing Phil, she found another handsome man, this time a newspaper reporter named Teddy Holmes. Like Phil, he was young and bright; and also like Phil, he was interested in a meal ticket (he wanted to write independently). Teddy met Jessie while in the hospital with hepatitis. After he was released, she invited him to stay with her while he continued his recovery.

Jessie was most vulnerable during this time; in addition to dealing with Phil's countless infidelities, she had suffered the loss of her widowed brother and was obliged to take care of his children, Carol and Kent Murray. Because of her loneliness, she decided to have them move in with her (along with Teddy). But little did she know that her kindnesses to Teddy, Carol and Kent would explode in her face when her niece and nephew came to live with her. Teddy had discovered that Carol Murray was due to inherit a large sum of money on her eighteenth birthday, so he quickly turned his attentions away from Jessie and toward Carol. He finally told Carol that she, not Jessie, was the love of his life, and convinced her to run away with him. As if his betrayal were not bad enough, Teddy also took with him the $25,000 Jessie had loaned him. She was left alone again, but this time she was deeply in debt. She then turned to her friend Lee Baldwin for help.

Lee, the brother of Tom Baldwin, had once been in love with Jessie; but after losing her to Phil, he married a young nurse named Meg Clinton instead. Meg was a wonderful person, but the years she had spent as a single parent to her small son, Scotty, and the problems she had with her troublesome stepdaughter, Brooke, eventually took their toll. Meg first suffered a bout with breast cancer, and then had a mental breakdown after having a mastectomy. She was committed to a mental hospital for a while and then was released, only to find out she had a severe blood pressure problem. For this ailment, she was treated by a new doctor named Lesley Williams. But despite Dr. Williams' attempts, Meg could not recover. She finally died, leaving Lee a widower with a small stepson to raise.

Meanwhile, Lee's sister-in-law, Audrey, was still waiting for Tom to come to his senses and return little Tommy to her. Before his kidnapping, Tommy had been scheduled for surgery to repair his defective heart; Audrey had no idea how badly his condition had deteriorated since then. She found comfort in Tommy's surgeon, Dr. James Hobart, who by now had come to think of their relationship as more than professional. Tommy was eventually found after his father was reported killed in Mexico. Soon after his surgery, James and Audrey were married. The marriage was not perfect, however, for Audrey was not really in love with James. She merely felt sorry for him because he had had an auto accident and had damaged his hands in the process. She wanted to support him because of his earlier kindnesses to her; but the marriage, begun so shakily, seemed destined to fail. James later left her for a younger woman.

As for Diana Taylor, she now had two children (a boy and a girl) by Phil Brewer; and, of course, Peter was unaware that he had not fathered either one. Phil continually harassed Diana, telling her to leave Peter and marry him; but she always declined because of her love of her husband. However, one day, Peter discovered Diana's awful secret, and wanted nothing more to do with her. Phil, by this time, had left Port Charles once more because of Diana's constant rejection. Alone and depressed, Diana finally decided to divorce Peter; however, since they both really loved each other, the divorce was delayed by several reconciliations along the way. Ultimately, they reconciled, but not before high drama from General Hospital rocked Port Charles.

The focal point of this drama was the mystery surrounding Phil Brewer's death. Phil had been traveling around the world after leaving town, due to Diana's rejection. Yet he continued to keep informed of Diana's activities through (what he thought to be) a mutual friend, Augusta McLeod. Actually, Augusta was more interested in snaring Peter Taylor; so she told Phil that she was carrying Peter's baby, and he came back immediately. Shortly after his return, Phil was found dead by his ex-wife, Jessie. Jessie was arrested for his murder, but was released when Diana "confessed" to his murder. She was then convicted and sentenced to a long prison term. Actually, Diana was not the true murderess; she had claimed responsibility because she thought Peter had done it. When Peter realized the depth of her love, he tried frantically to find the true killer. He finally did — it was Augusta McLeod, who had accidentally murdered Phil during an argument. Diana was subsequently released, and Peter and she were once again reunited.

Back at the Baldwin household, things had also become quite different since Audrey and Jim Hobart's marital break-up. Dr. Steve Hardy had befriended Audrey during her ordeal with Jim; after her divorce, they renewed their romance and decided to be remarried. Shortly after their wedding, however, they discovered that Tom Baldwin had never really died in Mexico. They worried that upon his return, Tom would upset their happy household. Fortunately, Tom was not interested in keeping his marital commitment to Audrey (despite son Tommy's demands); so Steve and Audrey finally were able to settle into the married life they had started long ago.

At this same time, some new characters became important to the daily happenings of Port Charles. Among them was Terri Webber Arnett, whose father, Dr. Lars Webber, was a friend and colleague of Steve Hardy. Unfortunately, Lars and his wife were killed in a car accident, leaving Terri to take care of her brothers, Rick and Jeff. When first introduced, Terri had already been married and widowed by a psychiatrist named David Arnett. Her brother, Rick, had been engaged to intern Monica Bard, but had disappeared on a trip to Africa and was presumed dead. On the day the Webbers found out about Rick's ill-fated voyage, Monica also received a letter from him. His letter, however, was more depressing to her because he wanted to break their engagement. Out of loneliness and desperation, Monica rebounded to Rick's brother, Jeff. They married soon after.

Jeff Webber was also an intern, so his marriage to Monica was tedious at best. Between conflicting work schedules, career pressures, and Jeff's long-standing feelings of inferiority to big brother Rick, the environment was always open for conflict. Things began to settle down a bit after Jeff became more confident; but his new personality was short-lived when he discovered that Rick was actually alive. Monica also changed with Rick's return. She stopped at nothing to win him back, even causing Jeff's self-destruction. When Rick discovered Monica's motives, he quickly acted to end all relationships with her. Monica was not easily discouraged, however; she continued to plague the lives of the Webber brothers.

Jeff was most deeply victimized by Monica's deceitful behavior. He reacted to her abuse by taking drugs; one night, in drug-induced despair, he accidentally shot himself. Jeff survived the injury thanks to Dr. Mark Dante (who, incidentally, fell in love with Jeff's sister, Terri), but his psychological well-being was not so stable. Between dealing with Monica and falling prey to another hustler named Heather Grant, Jeff could not escape being hurt by women. He finally divorced Monica after much pain, and married Heather thinking she had had his baby and lost it. (Actually, Heather's baby, P.J., was alive and well, living with his adoptive parents, Diana and Peter Taylor.)

In the meantime, Dr. Lesley Williams was having romantic problems, too, which were constantly getting in the way of her professional life. It all started with her newest patient, Florence Gray, who was suffering from severe ulcers, the cause of which she claimed was her husband's indifference to her. Fearing a psychosomatic problem, Lesley turned the case over to Peter Taylor, who discovered that Florence's husband, Gordon, had indeed loved another woman long ago. In fact, the woman had actually had a child by Gordon, although it died shortly after birth. The other woman, unfortunately, had been Lesley. When she found out that Gordon had never forgotten her, she transferred Florence's case to another doctor and asked Gordon to leave her alone. Gordon finally reunited with his wife, and Lesley felt secure . . . for a little while at least.

Next, Lesley fell in love with another doctor named Joel Stratton. They seemed to be an ideal couple, and the attraction was certainly mutual, but Joel never asked Lesley to marry him. Despite her attempts to be loved, Joel always managed to keep her at arm's length. She finally turned away from him and became attracted to a rich patient, Cameron Faulkner. Lesley's affection for Cam devastated Joel, however, because he truly loved her; he had rejected her only because of a serious heart condition which he felt would imperil their marriage. Finally, when Cam and Lesley's relationship culminated in marriage, Joel left town. He couldn't stand the thought of his love in another man's arms.

Lesley's marriage to Cam was not happy for very long, though. Soon after their wedding, she discovered that the child from her relationship with Gordon had never died, so she set about to find her young daughter and eventually gain custody of her. Lesley ultimately found the girl, who was named Laura; she lived with Barbara and Jason Vining. Lesley's obsession with Laura truly jeopardized her marriage, for she no longer paid much attention to Cam. He later resorted to desperate measures by planning to bribe the Vinings into leaving Port Charles, thereby forcing Lesley to spend more time with him. In one of his more drastic attempts, Cam actually assaulted Lesley on the way to their cabin. She resisted him in the car, but in the struggle, they were in an accident. Cam later died; and Lesley discovered that she was carrying his child.

After clearing up the investigation into Cam's death, Lesley once again tried to locate her daughter, Laura. This time, however, she was joined by another doctor friend, Rick Webber. Rick stood by her as she discovered the awful news that Laura was living in a Charles Manson–type commune in Canada. They finally rescued Laura, and ultimately fell in love. Rick's ex-fiancee, Monica, was not happy with their relationship, and she tried to break them up. Unfortunately, Lesley miscarried in the process of Monica's revenge. Finally, after causing much pain, Monica gave up her fight and Lesley and Rick were married. They settled into a happy life with Laura.

By the late seventies, the story of Rick and Lesley Webber and Lesley's daughter, Laura, became one of the major focal points of *General Hospital*. Together with the Quartermaine family, the Webbers became one of the most prominent families in Port Charles (see Figure 24). And

FIGURE 24

Prominent Families on GENERAL HOSPITAL (late !970's)

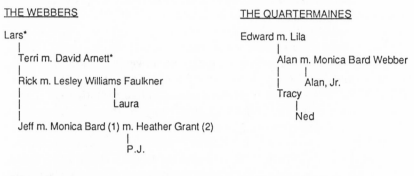

THE WEBBERS

Lars*
|
Terri m. David Arnett*
|
Rick m. Lesley Williams Faulkner
| |
| Laura
|
Jeff m. Monica Bard (1) m. Heather Grant (2)
                |
                P.J.

THE QUARTERMAINES

Edward m. Lila
|
Alan m. Monica Bard Webber
| |
| Alan, Jr.
Tracy
|
Ned

* indicates deceased

while some of the storyline action still took place at the medical center, most of the important plotlines involved these families and the political and criminal happenings of the town.

The Quartermaines were one of the wealthiest families in the community, but they were hardly considered the most trustworthy or morally upstanding. Dr. Alan Quartermaine, son of Edward and Lila, was employed at General Hospital and was married to Monica Bard Webber. He was very jealous of Rick Webber both personally and professionally because he knew that he was well respected as a doctor and that Monica still loved him. As a result, Alan tried continuously to wreck Rick's career and marriage. Actually, causing trouble between Rick and Lesley was relatively easy — the Webbers' marriage was already strained due to Lesley's frigidity.

Lesley had begun having sexual difficulties shortly after she had falsely confessed to murdering Rick's old college pal, David Hamilton. David was a snake who had moved in with the Webbers, and then moved in on Lesley to pay Rick back for having had a relationship with his wife. Lesley rebuffed him; but Laura gave in to his charms. She fell in love with him, and was understandably shattered when he told her it was all a sham. Laura then flew into a rage, killed David, and then blocked out the entire incident by running away to New York.

Lesley, protective of her daughter's reputation, "confessed" to killing David herself. She was then sentenced to prison and was not released until Laura returned to Port Charles and admitted her crime. Laura was then put on probation and was confined to Lesley's protective custody. Needless to say, the aftermath of the David Hamilton murder greatly impaired the Webbers' marriage as well as Lesley's relationship with Laura.

Laura was terribly upset about being held prisoner in her own home. She resented her parents and rebelled by renewing her relationship with her boyfriend, Scotty Baldwin. Scotty had always loved Laura, but since Laura had jilted him for David Hamilton, he had begun seeing a provocative student nurse named Bobbie Spencer. Bobbie was not pleased when Scotty tried to break off their romance to return to Laura, so she asked her brother, Luke, to woo Laura away from him.

Luke Spencer was a young hood with underworld connections; but he genuinely loved his family. Thus, he did not hesitate to seduce Laura for his sister. As time went on, however, Luke actually fell in love with Laura, and consequently was terribly upset when he heard that she was going to marry Scotty Baldwin anyway.

Indeed, Laura did get married to Scotty; but not long afterwards, she found that she really preferred Luke and his friends to her dull life with Scotty. She then decided to take a waitressing job at the disco where Luke was manager. They became close friends at first. However, before long, Luke found that he could not resist his passion for Laura. One night, he finally admitted that he loved her; then he raped her on the dance floor. Surprisingly, Laura did not report him to the authorities. She didn't even identify him to her husband, although she said she couldn't make love to Scotty because of the rape.

Scotty ultimately found out about Luke when he read a letter Laura had written about her rape. Outraged, he sought after Luke, found him on a yacht, and tried to kill him. In the fight than ensued, Luke fell off the boat and was presumed dead. Later, Laura found him washed ashore, and the two ran away from Port Charles.

Unfortunately, however, Luke could not easily escape his underworld connections. On the day of his fight with Scotty, Luke had been about to marry — under pressure — the daughter of syndicate kingpin Frank Smith. When he ran off with Laura, he managed to grab Smith's black book of criminal records. Smith was livid when he discovered it missing, so he hired hit men to kill the young lovers. Ultimately, Smith was caught; but the trials and tribulations of Luke and Laura's romance continued until they married some time later. Between Smith's death and their wedding, they endured international intrigue through the Cassidine brothers' scheme to develop synthetic diamonds as well as risking death and destruction when they helped Luke's friend, investigator Robert Scorpio, track down the sinister duo.

Freed at last (or so they thought) from Luke's mob connections and Laura's marriage to Scotty (who was now living in Mexico and had finally agreed to a divorce), the young couple had a beautiful storybook wedding ceremony. However, not long after they married, Laura disappeared from sight. Luke was devastated at the thought that she was murdered, so he devoted all his energies to finding her. The search was exhausting, and after awhile, he heard she had been killed by an underworld figure. Luke decided to put his life back together and find a new love.

The new woman in Luke's life after Laura was Holly Sutton. Originally, Holly was sent by the mob to find out about Luke's business on the yacht. However, they soon fell in love, and she abandoned her plans to betray him. They truly began to enjoy each other's company. Then Luke went away for a short skiing vacation. Holly, who by now had become pregnant with Luke's baby, waited for his return, but then she heard that he had been killed. Overwhelmed by her grief, she turned to Robert Scorpio, Luke's best friend, who promised to marry her for the sake of the baby.

After their marriage, Holly actually began to fall in love with Robert, despite the fact that she had miscarried. As they began to settle into their new relationship, however, Holly received word that Luke had not really died — he had become paralyzed in a skiing accident and had arranged the lie so that she would not feel compelled to live with an invalid. Luke had not stayed an invalid, though; he received therapy and was almost fully recovered. When he returned to Port Charles to find Holly married to his best friend, he fell apart. But he later understood Holly and Robert's love, and decided to let them be. Shortly after he reconciled his loss of Holly, Laura returned, having not been killed, but held prisoner by the underworld in Greece. Luke and Laura then left Port Charles to live in marital bliss. Robert and Holly ultimately moved away also, settling in Australia, Robert's native country.

Back at the Quartermaines, Monica Webber Quartermaine was still trying to win Rick back. And, because of Lesley's abhorrence of sex, he turned to her for comfort more than once. Soon after the affair had begun, Monica became pregnant and claimed that Rick was the father. Lesley could take no more of Rick's feelings for Monica, so she decided to divorce him. Rick loved Lesley, but wanted to have his child with Monica, so he finally asked her to marry him.

Alan Quartermaine would have no part of Monica's plan to marry Rick, although his sister, Tracy, was only too happy to see Alan's marriage dissolve. This was because she wanted her son, Ned, to inherit the Quartermaine fortune instead of Alan, Jr. Thus, she set about to "prove" that Alan, Jr., was actually Rick Webber's son. Unfortunately for both Monica and Tracy, however, Alan, Jr., was actually proven to be Alan's son. And after all this time, Rick finally realized Monica's powers of deception. He promptly left her and reconciled again with Lesley. They lived contentedly for a long while afterwards until Lesley was tragically killed in an automobile accident.

Elsewhere in Port Charles, the Taylor household was in disarray because of Heather Grant Webber's repeated attempts to get her son, P.J., back from Diana and Peter. And Heather stopped at nothing, including trying to drive Diana insane. To curb her wild ploys, Diana hired a private investigator named Joe Kelly to track her day and night. Heather was evasive, but she finally did herself in by mistakenly ingesting some of the LSD she had put in a drink intended for Diana. As a result, Heather was committed to a sanitarium for schizophrenic behavior. However, she was later released, and renewed her relentless attack on her favorite victim. This time, she was even more committed – for Peter Taylor had died of a heart attack, and after his death, Diana decided to pursue Jeff so that she could keep P.J.

By now, everyone was aware of Heather's hatred of Diana, so it came as no surprise that she was a prime suspect when Diana was murdered. In fact, Heather had intended to kill Diana the very night she was found dead; however, she was unable to remember actually shooting the gun. To most folks, this made little difference. But Joe Kelly, who by now had fallen in love with Heather, vowed to find the true killer. Indeed, it was not Heather; instead, her mother, Alice Grant, finally admitted that she had fired the fatal shot when she saw that Diana had a gun and intended to harm her daughter. After Alice Grant's admission, the judge set her free and sentenced Heather to six months' probation for attempted murder. Later, Heather left Port Charles, as did Joe Kelly, who fell out of love with her and moved to Albany.

Toward the mid-1980s, another Quartermaine emerged in Port Charles. Her name was Celia and she was the rich second cousin of Alan Quartermaine. Celia had come to town shortly after Jimmy Lee Holt, Edward Quartermaine's illegitimate son, showed up to claim his rightful place in the family (and his share of the fortune). When he first met Celia, Jimmy Lee fell deeply in love; however, Celia did not reciprocate immediately because she was engaged to marry her childhood sweetheart, Grant Putnam. Before long, though, the chemistry between Jimmy Lee and Celia was undeniable. In fact, Jimmy Lee pursued her every day, but she finally married Grant (over her better judgment). Her marriage to Grant did not stop Jimmy Lee, however; nor did it stop Celia's doubts about the wisdom of her choice. As it turned out, she was right to have doubts.

"Grant Putnam" was actually a Russian spy sent to the United States to steal a secret formula. He had been trained since childhood to be an "American," and his physical appearance was altered to duplicate the Grant Celia had fallen in love with many years before. Celia was completely fooled by the switch. However, during the course of his "mission," Grant's double fell in love with Celia and the American way of life. He ended up wanting to defect, but was almost killed by his Russian "bosses" in the process.

"Grant" was ultimately given asylum in the United States, after he had proven that he was anxious to become a loyal citizen. Meanwhile, the *real*

Grant Putnam showed up in Port Charles. He had been placed in a mental institution by the Russians several years before.

But life had grown more complicated during this time—especially for Celia. After his amazing reappearance, she was torn between the *real* Grant and her husband, Grant (now known as Grant Andrews). At first, she chose to be with Grant Putnam; but she discovered eventually that he was really a devious murderer, who really *belonged* in a mental institution. She then went back to Grant Andrews. However, their marriage was never quite the same after Celia had lived with Grant Putnam. They eventually divorced, and Celia finally gave in to her long-suppressed feelings for Jimmy Lee and married him ... but only after he had managed to claim twenty million dollars from the Quartermaine fortune. As for Grant Andrews, he got involved with a medical ship and eventually left Port Charles to oversee the project.

Celia and Jimmy Lee's marriage lasted just a short time because it was really only based on physical attraction and greed. Several months after the wedding, Celia suspected that Jimmy was having an affair with a South American woman (during a business trip). She subsequently divorced him and left town.

While the Quartermaines were dealing with their complex family problems, some new characters came onto the scene in Port Charles. Two such additions were the Jones brothers: Anthony, a doctor, and Frisco, a rock star.

Frisco came to town as a patient at General Hospital. When first introduced, he was recovering in the hospital after having been beaten up by some thugs because he wouldn't sign a record contract drawn up by the local syndicate. At first, he and his brother Tony were estranged from each other; but soon after Frisco's arrival in town, they worked out their childhood differences and became very close friends. Tony subsequently married the hospital's speech therapist, Tania, and they were very happy as they awaited the birth of their first child.

Frisco, on the other hand, had a more adventuresome romance before he settled into marriage. During a party, he met a princess named Felicia Cummings. Felicia was disguised as a boy because, unbeknownst to Frisco, she had come to Port Charles to steal back a family heirloom ring that had been taken from her grandmother. Frisco fell in love with her, but Felicia was not interested in romance—her only goal was to find the ring.

Not to be discouraged, Frisco decided to help her in her search, along with Robert Scorpio; his old WSB friend, Shawn Donnelly; and Luke Spencer (who returned to the show for a thirteen-week segment). Eventually, they discovered that the ring was a clue to an ancient Aztec treasure hidden in Mexico, and that the entire heist had been engineered by Shawn Donnelly, who had sold his soul to greed. Felicia subsequently retrieved her ring, fell in love with Frisco, and was later married to him.

Since the mystery of the Aztec ring, the residents of Port Charles have seen numerous mysteries, romances and new characters. One of their most intriguing new residents was Duke Lavery, a Scottish immigrant who owned several nightclubs on the waterfront. Unfortunately, he was also involved with the syndicate, which threatened his business reputation as well as his romance with Robert Scorpio's ex-wife, Anna DeVane.

Looking back on the history of *General Hospital,* its evolution of characters and plotlines is astonishing. While Jessie still works on the seventh floor of the hospital, the action has totally shifted from medical stories to action and adventure plots. This new approach is likely to continue, with more romantic mysteries involving established audience favorites as well as new characters. However, many viewers have lately become disenchanted with *General Hospital,* claiming that it is too slowly paced and unbelievable. As a result, fans of *General Hospital* may expect the following:

1. Within the next two years, writers may conduct a massive overhaul in characterization and plots. And since *General Hospital* has never been dependent on one or two particular families, this transition will be easier than in most of the other daytime dramas.

2. Plotlines will move more quickly and be less fantasy-oriented than in the past. When producers discover that they have gone beyond the audience threshold of credibility, they will have to modify their scripts to maintain the soap opera's popularity.

The Guiding Light
First Radio Broadcast: January 25, 1937 (NBC)
First Television Broadcast: June 30, 1952 (CBS)

The Guiding Light lays claim to being the longest continually running soap opera in broadcast history. Originally begun as a fifteen-minute radio serial in 1937, this daytime drama has survived the transition into television, the expansion to an hour-long format, and stiff competition against *General Hospital* to become one of the most popular and critically acclaimed soaps today.

The first episodes of *The Guiding Light* took place in Five Points, a fictional town in the Midwest, and centered on the life of Dr. John Rutledge, his family, and the parishioners of his church. In fact, the program was initially very religious in nature, using its title to signify the evangelistic sermons delivered by Dr. Rutledge each weekday. Later, the show changed its focus to a more general family orientation, featuring the Bauers with all their trials and tribulations.

The Bauers were a first-generation family of German-Americans who had come to seek a better life in America. They originally settled in Five

FIGURE 25

Prominent Families on THE GUIDING LIGHT (late 1940's)

THE BAUERS

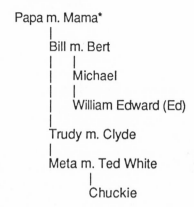

* indicates deceased

Points, but later moved to Selby Flats (a fictional Los Angeles suburb), and then to Springfield—as they moved, the radio show moved along with them. During the late forties, the clan was comprised of Papa and Mama Bauer and their three children, Bill (originally called Willie), Meta and Trudy. Most of the storylines revolved around these three young people and their marital problems (see Figure 25).

In the radio version, Bill had married Bert shortly before Mama Bauer died. During the early days of their marriage, Bert was a demanding, selfish young wife. She nagged Bill incessantly, forcing him to buy things they couldn't afford. She was a very materialistic woman who was never satisfied with her middle-class status. Bill's sister, Trudy, married a man named Clyde, but shortly after their wedding, she moved to New York. She was rarely featured from that point on. Finally, Meta Bauer, Papa and Mama's third child, was the most rebellious of the group. She was the major storyline character in the beginning, and her adventures were a key element in the Bauers' successful transition from radio to television.

In one of her escapades, Meta ran off to become a model; in her travels, she met a mean, devious man named Ted White. After having an affair with him, Meta became pregnant, and they subsequently married so that the baby would have a legitimate name. After Chuckie was born, however, they divorced, with Ted having partial custody of their son. Meta was not happy with the arrangement because she felt that Ted had such a heavily machismo attitude that Chuckie would suffer while growing up with him. Indeed, she was right. One day, she found out that Ted had been forcing Chuckie to learn to box. Chuckie was apprehensive, but obeyed his father anyway. Then, in a freak accident, Chuckie was killed. Meta, out of her mind with grief, went after Ted and fatally shot him. Eventually, she was acquitted because of temporary insanity; in the meantime, she met a kind newspaperman, Joe Roberts. Joe had helped Meta with her acquittal, and while fighting for justice, they had fallen in love. After Meta was freed, she and Joe were married; at last (Papa Bauer thought) she had finally settled down.

In fact, Meta and Joe did have a strong marriage, although it showed some strain from Joe's worries about his grown daughter, Kathy. Kathy had been married to Bob Lang, but their marriage was tragically shortened when Bob was killed in a car accident. Kathy was devastated by her loss, especially after she discovered that she was pregnant. Anxious for her baby to have a father, she impulsively married a doctor named Dick Grant, and let her young daughter, Robin, grow up thinking he was her true father. Ultimately, however, after the marriage had floundered, she was persuaded to seek an annulment and tell Robin the truth. Dick accepted their marital fate, but continued to be in love with her, anyway.

Kathy's unhappiness was a continual concern for Joe Roberts, and until he died (of cancer), Joe kept trying to help her deal with the tragedies of her life. Kathy accepted her father's wisdom, but after he died, she resented Meta's attempts to substitute for Joe's involvement. They argued constantly, and fought over everything ... especially a handsome businessman, Mark Holden. Eventually, Mark married Kathy and adopted her daughter, Robin (who by now had become a rambunctious teenager). They lived happily for awhile, but then Kathy was in an automobile accident, became paralyzed and finally died after a long convalescence. Meta and Mark were reunited briefly because of their mutual dedication to Robin; however, Meta ultimately became Robin's guardian and she married a doctor named Bruce Banning. They had a long, happy marriage together.

Meanwhile, Bill and Bert Bauer continued their stormy marriage in much the same way as before. However, the consequences by now had become more troublesome. For one thing, Bert, after all these years, had still kept her materialistic attitude; but now, in retaliation, Bill frequently turned to alcohol to drown his sorrows. Also, Bill and Bert's sons, Michael and Ed, had grown into young adults. Their lives and loves had become much more complicated than before. Mike was the greatest problem at this point, for he had fallen in love with Robin Holden, much to Bert's chagrin. Robin enjoyed Mike's attention; she also enjoyed that of Karl Jannings, who was the son of the housekeeper her adopted father had married. Robin continually encouraged competition from her two young suitors, but one

FIGURE 26

Prominent Families on THE GUIDING LIGHT (late 1950's)

THE BAUERS

```
Papa m. Mama*
|
Bill m. Bert
|   |
|   Michael m. Robin Holden (see below)
|   |
|   Ed
|
Trudy m. Clyde
|
Meta m. Ted White (1)* m. Joe Roberts (2)* m. Bruce Banning (3)
     |                    |
     Chuckie*             Kathy* m. Bob Lang (1)* m. Mark Holden (2)
                          |                        |
                          Joey                     Robin
```

* indicates deceased

day, the situation got out of hand. Mike and Karl, in the midst of an argument over Robin, got into a fight and Karl fell to his death. Mike was arrested for murder, but was acquitted later. As for Robin, Mike married her, but Bert ultimately forced an annulment. The Bauer household had begun its long history of change (see Figure 26).

By the early sixties, the younger generation of the Bauer clan began to settle into their adult lives. Mike, no longer married to Robin (who, incidentally, had happily married a young doctor named Paul Fletcher), began to study law seriously. He clerked under a respectable attorney, George Hayes, and soon became well acquainted with legal procedures ... as well as with George's secretary, Julie Conrad. Bert was quite happy with Mike's romantic interest in Julie and so did not discourage his association with her. In fact, when they discovered she was pregnant, both Bert and Bill encouraged Mike to marry her. After the marriage and birth of little Hope, however, Julie suffered a mental breakdown and later committed suicide in the sanitarium where she was sent. Bert took over the maternal duties of raising Hope, but she was compulsive and domineering. Mike felt that the situation could become unhealthy for the entire Bauer family, so he decided to move Hope away from Springfield. He took her to Bay City, where he set up a law practice. Along the way, he started an ill-fated romance with a married woman named Pat Randolph (see *Another World* summary). Mike later returned to Springfield and his family with Hope.

In Mike's absence, Bill and Bert's marriage deteriorated even more rapidly than it had before. Bill, disgusted by Bert's obsession with Hope, resumed drinking heavily and had an affair with his secretary, Maggie Scott. Maggie was married, but like Bill, her relationship was strained at best with husband Ben. Later, however, Ben tried to reconcile with Maggie and their daughter, Peggy. They settled into a happy life again, until Peggy discovered that her mother had had an affair with Bill Bauer. She became so angry with Maggie's indiscretion that she rebelled by having her own affair with Paul Fletcher's son, Johnny. And Ben Scott became so upset by Peggy's behavior that he had a heart attack and died. Overcome by the guilt of being responsible for her father's death, Peggy stayed away from Johnny and reconciled with her mother and the Bauers. In fact, after Maggie Scott died, Peggy moved into the Bauer home under the loving care of Bert and Bill until she married Johnny. By now, Bert had grown into the warm, friendly leadership figure fans had come to love. Thus, it was not unbelievable that Peggy would experience a good family environment by living with the Bauers.

The Bauers' other son, Ed, had grown up quickly amongst all this turmoil. He had always loved medicine, so he went to school to become a doctor. While there, he became friends with a cad named Joe Werner. Ed and Joe played as hard as they worked, but when they finished school and came to practice medicine at Cedars Hospital in Springfield, both seemed to mellow considerably. Joe met and fell in love with another doctor, Sara MacIntyre; Ed, meanwhile, began to work diligently under the watchful eye of his mentor, Dr. Steve Jackson.

Ed worshipped Steve Jackson . . . and the feeling was mutual. In fact, Dr. Jackson, a widower, could think of no young man better suited than Ed to marry his daughter, Leslie. Ed and Leslie were not romantically suited to each other, but both were eager to conform to Steve's wishes. After a while, they were married. Predictably, however, the marriage was not stable, and it deteriorated even more when Leslie demanded to have a baby. Ed, out of frustration and pressure, became an alcoholic, and started beating her during his drunken fits.

While Ed was growing more unhappy and insecure, Mike had finally decided he was stable enough to return to Springfield. He brought Hope with him and ironed out his previous problems with his mother. Unfortunately, though, his sense of well-being did not last very long; soon after he came back to Springfield, he fell in love with another married woman — Ed's wife, Leslie! Torn between love and loyalty, Leslie and Mike tried to stay away from each other. But Ed's drinking and extramarital affairs made it almost impossible for Leslie to stop thinking about Mike. One day, just as Leslie was about to divorce Ed, she discovered she was pregnant. Mike could not stand this new turn of events, so he got out of Leslie's life and married the conniving Charlotte Waring instead. Leslie, destroyed by Mike's actions, decided she had had enough of the Bauer sons, so after her son Frederick (named after Papa Bauer) was born, she left Ed for good, got a divorce and quickly married the wealthy Stanley Norris.

Stanley Norris was new to the storyline, but he had apparently been a fixture in Springfield for some time. Stanley was a power-hungry business magnate who loved fast money deals and fast women. He had married Barbara and had three children, Andrew, Holly and Ken. However, Barbara eventually found she could not tolerate Stanley's lack of ethics, so she divorced him, settled in a modest home with her children, and wrote a cooking column for the local newspaper.

Ken and Holly Norris grew up in the shadow of a famous father whom they rarely saw and hardly knew. As a result, they both seemed to have trouble handling their own romantic relationships. Ken, an attorney, fell in love with Janet Mason (an old paramour of Ed Bauer's); but he never seemed to trust her, even after they were married. Holly, Ken's sister, was a flaky, immature adult who rarely went beneath surface relationships. When she met and fell in love with playboy Roger Thorpe (an employee of her father's), Holly was convinced that having an affair with him would make him want to marry her. Roger, a calculating young man, saw through Holly from the start, but he played along with her so that he could see the woman he really wanted — Janet Mason Norris. Janet, of course, was not interested; but Ken could not be convinced that she had refused Roger. Thus, Ken left Janet after a few short months. Holly, distraught after seeing Roger with Janet, became seriously injured when she ran into a street filled with oncoming traffic.

Roger Thorpe was a truly evil young man, but his father, Adam, was very good and decent. He had originally come to the Norrises to apologize for Roger's behavior; as he spent more time there, he fell in love with Barbara. Barbara was also beguiled by Adam, so they began a warm romance. Everyone seemed pleased that Barbara had finally found happiness with Adam — that is, everyone, but Stanley Norris. Even though he had remarried, Stanley was not anxious to see Barbara with another man. He started to harass the couple, but his attempts ended abruptly when he was found murdered in his home.

The early seventies on *The Guiding Light* began with the investigation into Stanley Norris' murder, for in a short while, the Norrises had become one of the prominent families in Springfield (see Figure 27). Leslie was the prime suspect in Stanley's death because her fingerprints were found on the murder weapon. However, Stanley had made enough enemies to allow the trial to go on for weeks. Mike became Leslie's defense attorney, and the

---

FIGURE 27

Prominent Families on THE GUIDING LIGHT (late 1960's)

THE BAUERS

Bill m. Bert
|
　Mike m. Robin Holden (1) m. Julie Conrad (2)* m. Charlotte Waring (3)
　|　　　　　　　　　　　　　|
　|　　　　　　　　　　　　Hope
　|
　Ed m. Leslie Jackson (1)
　　|
　　|　　　m.Stanley Norris (2)* (see below)
　　|
　　Frederick

THE NORRISES

Stanley* m. Barbara (1) m. Leslie Jackson Bauer (2)
　　|
　　|　　　m. Adam Thorpe (2)
　　|
　　Ken m. Janet Jackson
　　|
　　Holly
　　|
　　Andrew

* indicates deceased

---

constant contact allowed them to be more in love than ever. After Leslie's acquittal (they ultimately discovered that Stanley's secretary's mother had murdered him), she decided to leave town because she could no longer bear being in love with another woman's man. But Mike had learned during the trial that Charlotte didn't really love him; she was more interested in the status of being an attorney's wife. Mike then set about to divorce Charlotte. However, with Leslie gone, he wasn't as enthusiastic as he might have been. Only after a freak accident which seriously wounded Mike did Leslie return. When he recovered, they had to live through Charlotte's vicious attacks during the divorce and Steve Jackson's apprehensions about Leslie marrying another Bauer. However, after all the trauma, Leslie and Mike were married at long last.

Charlotte, Mike's ex-wife, was terribly upset by the divorce — not because she loved Mike, but because she'd lost the status for which she'd worked so hard in Springfield. Not long after the papers were finalized, though, Charlotte went after Joe Werner. Joe loved his wife, Sara, very much, but he found it impossible to resist Charlotte's seductive charms. Thus, for a short time, they had an affair. Sara was unaware of Joe's infidelity, but Kit Vested, a mentally unbalanced hospital volunteer who had a crush on him, was all too cognizant of what was going on. Kit was hurt deeply by Joe's behavior; she was even more disturbed by Charlotte, whom she had considered to be a friend and confidante. She then decided to have revenge on them both. First, Kit invited Charlotte over for a drink that she had laced with sleeping pills. Next, she phoned Joe and told him that Charlotte had passed out after a fall. When he arrived at Kit's house, he treated Charlotte for a simple concussion. Little did he know that she had overdosed on barbiturates. When the coroner's report was released, Joe was cited for negligence. He was relieved of his job as Chief of Staff at Cedars, turned to drinking, and then left Sara.

Kit was overjoyed when Joe left Springfield; she later found him holed up in a shabby motel suffering from pneumonia. Kit began to take care of Joe, and, thinking her fantasies would finally come true, stopped all his letters from reaching Sara. Joe, of course, was convinced by Sara's "lack of communication" that she no longer loved him, so he filed for a divorce. Sara, upon receiving word of his intentions, declared that she would do nothing until she saw Joe. Kit was not prepared for this turn of events, so she schemed to kill Sara in much the same way as she had Charlotte. This time, however, Joe found Sara in time, saved her life, and then killed Kit in the midst of a struggle. Joe and Sara were finally reunited and lived happily with a son (T.J.) they later adopted until Joe's sudden death from a heart attack several years later.

Back at the Bauers, Ed was still licking his wounds from his bad marriage to Leslie when he was asked to treat Holly Norris at Cedars. Holly, deeply hurt from her betrayal by Roger Thorpe, became extremely attached to Ed. And Ed, feeling sorry that he had lost his wife to his brother, began to return Holly's affections. In fact, one night, Ed married Holly and spent the night in Las Vegas on a drunken spree. When he awakened the next morning, Holly falsely claimed that they had consummated the marriage, so he felt forced to live with his mistake. It turned out to be disastrous for both of them.

Ed discovered (much too late) that Holly was entirely too immature to live the life of a doctor's wife. Holly, on the other hand, had never really gotten over her attraction for Roger. Thus, when he came back into her life in Springfield, she did little to rebuff him. In fact, Holly was so starved for affection (since she and Ed no longer shared the same bedroom) that she welcomed Roger with open arms. Soon after, Holly became pregnant. Obviously, the baby was Roger's, but Holly did not want Ed to discover her extramarital affair. Consequently, one night, she seduced him in her bedroom and later claimed that the baby was his.

Roger, needless to say, was not interested in Holly for anything but sex. However, he did fall for young Peggy Scott Fletcher, and tried to be a good person for her. He might have succeeded, too, had Holly not continued to chase after him. Roger worried that Holly would destroy the only love he'd ever known, so he discouraged her at each turn. Finally, when she gave birth to "Ed's" daughter, Christina, Roger felt things would settle down. Little did he know, though, that the baby's true parentage could not remain a secret forever. One night, Christina became critically ill and needed a blood transfusion. It was soon discovered that Roger was the only one who could give it to her. Ed was torn apart; he left Holly and turned once again to drinking. As for Peggy, she was hurt but still convinced that Roger really loved her. She ultimately married him. Holly was left to raise Christina alone.

While Ed was having his marital woes, brother Mike and Leslie were enjoying the marital happiness that had been denied them for so long. Despite some of the romantic misadventures of Mike's daughter, Hope, they really began to enjoy their newfound family life. Their happiness proved very temporary, however, when a psychotic man (whom Mike was investigating) accidentally ran Leslie over with his car. After waiting so long to be married, Mike and Leslie had had only two years together as man and wife. Mike, overcome by grief, plunged himself into his work.

After Ed divorced Holly, he, too, went through several periods of despondency. And if it were not for the care and understanding of a pretty fourth floor nurse, Rita Stapleton, he might not have made it through his ordeal. Before long, the two of them fell in love. In the meantime, Holly finally realized how much she really loved Ed, so she tried to woo him away from Rita. By now, however, Ed was committed to making Rita his next wife. Despite Holly's attempts, Ed really loved Rita . . . and this was never more evident than during her trial for murder.

Rita was considered a suspect in a murder that had been committed in Abilene years before. Mike offered to serve as her attorney, but he was virtually helpless in her defense because she refused to divulge much of her past in Abilene. Later, everyone found out that it was because she had had an affair there with Roger Thorpe long ago. Then Roger, in a surprising character twist, actually testified on her behalf. As expected, though, his motivations were not entirely altruisitic; he wanted to become involved with Rita once again.

But Rita was not interested in Roger; she truly loved Ed. After Rita's trial, they became engaged. Unfortunately, however, Roger was not easily dissuaded from Rita. One night, he actually forced himself upon her. Rita survived the assault and later decided not to tell anyone. Rita and Ed were married subsequently, and Roger was left to prey upon someone else.

Roger certainly kept busy with his antics at this time. His own wife, Peggy, finally decided to divorce him because she felt she could no longer trust him. She left Springfield shortly after her divorce. Barbara Norris Thorpe was another indirect victim of Roger's behavior. After blaming Roger for Holly and Ed's marital breakup, Barbara began to cause a constant strain in her own marriage to Adam. They were divorced some time later.

As for Holly, she could never truly rid herself of her fixation on Roger. However, her once deep love for him had become twisted after many years. He finally proposed to her (to give Christina his name), and Holly accepted, but she couldn't bring herself to trust him. In fact, after their marriage, Holly refused to have sex with him. Outraged at her refusal, Roger felt that she was holding out for Ed Bauer. He then raped her. But unlike Rita, Holly refused to keep silent, and she had him arrested. Roger was defended by a new lawyer in town named Ross Marler. Ross was somewhat unscrupulous at the time, stopping at nothing to win a court case. In one dramatic attempt, he brought up Ed Bauer's relationship with Holly. Ed later confronted Roger and Roger drew a gun on him. Holly walked in on the scuffle and grabbed the gun, shooting Roger in the process. Roger was said to be dead, but instead, he had escaped to Puerto Rico. He later returned and tried to kidnap Christina, but he finally was killed while trying to escape from Ed and Mike.

The pressure of Roger's behavior and Ed's protective attitude towards Holly and Christina began to weaken Ed and Rita's marriage. Rita began to feel lonely and unloved with Ed's preoccupation with Holly; she resented even more his expectation that she take care of little Christina while Holly was going through her trauma. As a result, Rita began to look at other men. Before long, Ed realized that another marriage had failed. He subsequently divorced Rita and she left town, along with her sister, Eve, and mother, Viola.

By the late 1970s, the Bauer family had changed enormously. In addition to Mike and Ed's hapless marriages, Bert and her clan suffered the loss of Papa Bauer as well as going through the pain of discovering an illegitimate daughter of Bill Bauer's (conceived while he was leading a double life), Hillary. With the further addition of two new families, the Spauldings and the Marlers, the world of Springfield (as well as the lives of the Bauers) grew wildly in its complexity (see Figure 28).

Dr. Justin Marler was a handsome new surgeon at Cedars Hospital. He had been married to the former Jackie Scott (the daughter of his mentor, Dr. Emmett Scott) but had always loved Dr. Sara McIntyre. While they

FIGURE 28

Prominent Families on THE GUIDING LIGHT (late 1970's)

THE BAUERS

Bill m. Bert
```
|— Mike m. Robin Holden (1) m. Julie Conrad (2)* m. Charlotte Waring (3)* m. Leslie Jackson (4)*
|                                                               |— Hope
|— Ed m. Leslie Jackson (1)* m. Holly Norris (2) m. Rita Stapleton (3)
|                               |— Christina
|        |— Frederick (Rick)
|— Hillary
```

THE MARLERS

Ross m. Carrie Todd

Justin m. Jackie Scott (1) m. Sara McIntyre (2)

THE SPAULDINGS

Alan m. Elizabeth (1) m. Jackie Scott (2)
```
            |——|——|
                  |— Phillip
```

* indicates deceased

were interns in Chicago, Justin and Sara had actually been engaged to be married; but Justin, realizing that Jackie Scott had more social status and money than Sara, had dumped her for the security of Jackie's purse. As could be predicted in such a situation, however, Justin and Jackie's marriage soon ended in divorce. During the many years between his divorce and joining Cedars, Justin yearned to be reunited with Sara.

When Justin arrived in Springfield, so did his brother, Ross, and Justin's ex-wife, Jackie. After Jackie came into town, Mike Bauer became attracted to her and they started a romantic relationship. Jackie was bright, beautiful, and especially close to the wealthy Spaulding family. The latter characteristic disturbed Mike; he couldn't understand her total devotion to the family, especially to young Phillip (Alan and Elizabeth's son). As it turned out, Phillip was actually Jackie and Justin's son who had been adopted by Alan at birth. It seemed that both Elizabeth Spaulding and Jackie Marler had been pregnant at the same time. The Spauldings were anxiously awaiting the glorious event, while Jackie was going through her pregnancy alone (Justin had already divorced her and was unaware of her condition). Elizabeth's child, however, was stillborn; and Alan, fearful that his wife might have a mental breakdown, made a deal with Jackie for her baby. The secret had been well kept for many years, but when it was finally exposed, most of Springfield felt the tremors of the Spaulding family's shock. Ultimately, Elizabeth divorced Alan and left town; Jackie married Alan; Justin married Sara; and Phillip tried to adjust to the new facts about his birth. Mike, once again, was alone and unloved.

Phillip's true parentage was only one of the episodes involving the Spaulding family. By the early eighties, they, along with the Chamberlains, Reardons and Lewises, became the central forces from which most of the plotlines evolved (see Figure 29). The Bauers were still an important force in Springfield, but most of their stories focused on Ed and his family. Mike, Bill, Meta and Hillary had been written out, and the actress who had played Bert masterfully for many years (Charita Bauer) passed away and was not replaced.

These families (the Spauldings, Lewises, Chamberlains, Reardons and Bauers) all became intertwined within a short while. As the Phillip Marler/Spaulding storyline grew in popularity, more Spauldings were introduced to Springfield. Alan's father, Brandon, was presented as a ruthless businessman who cared mainly for Spaulding Enterprises rather than his family. Thus, it came as a surprise when, upon his "death," he mysteriously left a part of his fortune to a woman named Lucille Wexler. Lucille had a "daughter," Amanda, and the two seemed very removed from the Spaulding dynasty. Later, however, it was discovered that Lucille Wexler had been a mistress of Brandon's and, even more surprisingly, Amanda had been Alan's illegitimate daughter by a woman named Jennifer Stafford. For years, most of Springfield's secrets revolved around Brandon's fake death

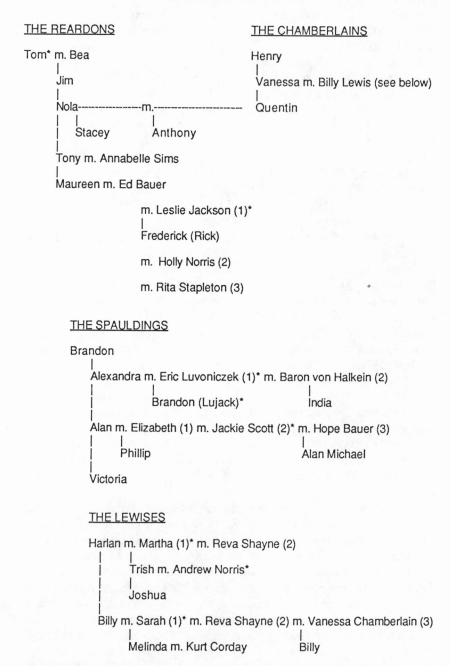

FIGURE 29

Prominent Families on THE GUIDING LIGHT (1986)

THE REARDONS

```
Tom* m. Bea
  |
  Jim
  |
  Nola-----------------m.--------------------- Quentin
  |   |              |
  |   Stacey         Anthony
  |
  Tony m. Annabelle Sims
  |
  Maureen m. Ed Bauer
```

THE CHAMBERLAINS

```
Henry
  |
  Vanessa m. Billy Lewis (see below)
  |
  Quentin
```

```
        m. Leslie Jackson (1)*
          |
          Frederick (Rick)

        m.  Holly Norris (2)

        m. Rita Stapleton (3)
```

THE SPAULDINGS

```
Brandon
  |
  Alexandra m. Eric Luvoniczek (1)* m. Baron von Halkein (2)
  |              |                        |
  |              Brandon (Lujack)*        India
  |
  Alan m. Elizabeth (1) m. Jackie Scott (2)* m. Hope Bauer (3)
  |     |                                     |
  |     Phillip                               Alan Michael
  |
  Victoria
```

THE LEWISES

```
Harlan m. Martha (1)* m. Reva Shayne (2)
  |       |
  |       Trish m. Andrew Norris*
  |       |
  |       Joshua
  |
  Billy m. Sarah (1)* m. Reva Shayne (2) m. Vanessa Chamberlain (3)
  |                                          |
  |     Melinda m. Kurt Corday                Billy
```

* indicates deceased

and second life (with Lucille as well as with a Bahaman woman named Sharina); Amanda's adjustment to her newly discovered mother and father; and Jennifer Stafford Richards' appearance in town with Amanda's half-sister, Morgan.

Morgan Richards was a rebellious teenager who seemed to be in trouble more than she was out of it. Her most complicated relationship was with handsome Kelly Nelson (Ed Bauer's godson), who had previously become involved with Hillary Bauer and Nola Reardon. Ultimately, Kelly and Morgan settled into marriage; but before long, problems ensued between them as they tried to balance their personal happiness with each other's career goals. They were later divorced.

As mentioned earlier, Kelly Nelson was a very desirable young man, but he was also very naive. His relationship with Nola Reardon (before Morgan) became a real trial for him because Nola was intent on marrying him under any circumstances. Kelly liked Nola, even trusted her. However, he was never in love with her. But Kelly's resistance only served to encourage Nola even more. One night, she staged a seduction scene and later claimed that Kelly had impregnated her. Actually, Nola had duped the young man who really loved her, Floyd Parker, into impregnating her, and then lied about Kelly's fatherhood. Later, Nola's scheme was revealed, and she and her young daugher, Kelly Louise (later renamed Stacey), lived in the Reardon boardinghouse until she married Quentin (McCord) Chamberlain.

Nola was only one member of the large Reardon family, who lived in the lower-class part of Springfield. The rest of the family included Bea, the widowed mother; Maureen; Tony, a street kid who later straightened himself out and started his own business; and Jim, a doctor, seemingly surrounded by a cloud of mystery. Each of the Reardons became deeply involved with one or more of the other prominent families in Springfield. Bea was courted by the wealthy Henry Chamberlain; Tony was involved with Vanessa Chamberlain (before he married Annabelle Sims and Vanessa married Billy Lewis); Jim fell in love with Hillary Bauer before she died; and Maureen met and married Dr. Ed Bauer. Their lives and loves provided a strong framework for many of the Springfield happenings.

Back at the Spaulding household, new family members kept the drama high in that area of town also. After Amanda, Jennifer and Morgan left town, Alan married Hope Bauer (against Mike's wishes) and they had a young son, Alan Michael, before they divorced and Alan presumably died. Next, Alan's heretofore unknown sister, Alexandra, came to town, causing several other mysterious characters to emerge, like her ex-stepdaughter, India von Halkein, son Brandon Luvoniczek (Lujak) and mystery man Simon Hall. Alexandra and Alan were never fond of each other; in fact, they sparred continuously for control of Spaulding Enterprises. After Alan's "death," however, Alexandra felt she had finally won. Little did she know that Alan was alive and well, and planning her ultimate demise.

Spaulding Enterprises was one of several large corporations dominating Springfield. The others included the Lewis and Sampson Corporations, which were comprised of a bizarrely interwoven family structure. Harlan B. Lewis, the patriarch, had been married to lovely Miss Martha. Together, they had raised two sons, Billy and Josh, and one daughter, Trish. However, H.B. had also been long-time friends with a former madam named Sally Gleason. Sally had borne a son, Kyle Sampson, who was a venomous competitor of the Lewises until he discovered that Billy was actually his half-brother. In addition to the family connection, H.B., Billy, Josh and Kyle had one other thing in common: They had all fallen in love with Reva Shayne. Reva was an amazing woman—passionate, seductive and beautiful, yet, honest, trustworthy and capable of friendship. While all of the Lewis and Sampson men had loved and lost her at one time or another, they still turned to her in times of trouble. In truth, the Sampsons and Lewises were bonded by blood, love for one woman, and the common competitive need to bankrupt Spaulding Enterprises.

The Guiding Light has certainly experienced its high and low points in the course of its long history. However, the soap has survived admirably, due to its strict attention to audience desires as well as other outside trends. Most probably, the trends already established in the past several years will continue for a while longer, for they have proven to be successful. More specifically:

1. The Bauer family seems to be on its way out. At present, Ed, Maureen, and Rick Bauer are the only remnants of the once dominant clan. While Hope Bauer Spaulding may return for a brief time (due to the reappearance of Alan Spaulding), chances are that the most significant action will center on the Spaulding-Lewis conflict.

2. Since *The Guiding Light* has had a long history of viewer popularity, its audience is comprised of many older, more traditional fans. However, like *Days of Our Lives,* this soap opera has made a grand effort to attract younger viewers by introducing more investigation-oriented stories. Because of their past success, these storylines are likely to continue as well as the plots with older, more established characters. In addition, fantasy-like themes will stay prominent to attract a more diverse audience. Some caution should be exercised in this area, though, for soap opera writers have learned that beyond a certain point, fantasy can be detrimental to viewer satisfaction in daytime drama.

Loving
First Broadcast: June 26, 1983 (ABC)

When *Loving* premiered (in a two-hour Sunday night made-for-television-movie), ABC was confident that the daytime soap opera would

FIGURE 30

Prominent Families on LOVING (1983)

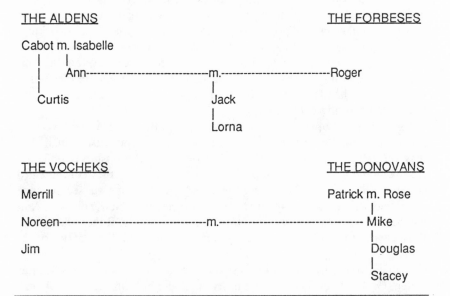

soon find itself in a high ratings placement like *All My Children* and *General Hospital.* Its co-creators, Agnes Nixon and Douglas Marland, were proven hitmakers, and the basic story premise seemed to guarantee that the young college audience would be interested, just as the network wanted.

Taking place in Corinth, a small university town, *Loving* focused initially on four families: The Forbeses, the Aldens, the Vocheks and the Donovans (see Figure 30). Roger Forbes was Alden University's president. He had married Ann Alden (the daughter of wealthy socialites Cabot and Isabelle) years before, and they had two children: Jack (their adopted son), a college sophomore and popular athlete; and Lorna, a wild, rambunctious teenager who planned to enter Alden as a freshman before long.

Despite the apparent success of the Forbes marriage, Roger had never loved Ann; he had married her simply for political reasons. The Aldens had founded the University, and Cabot was chairman of the board. Thus, Roger felt that the only real chance he had to realize his ambition as Alden University president was to marry the "boss's" daughter. In truth, Roger loved Merrill Vochek, a news anchorwoman for the local TV station. She was also in love with him. But Cabot Alden rarely questioned Roger's fidelity to his daughter, Ann—he was too busy trying to raise his impetuous grandson, Curtis, who seemed to be in trouble all the time.

Merrill Vochek's family was as interesting as the Forbes and Alden clans. Though not as wealthy as the Aldens, the Vocheks were highly regarded in the town of Corinth; they were seen as community-oriented people because Jim, Merrill's brother, was a priest, and her sister, Noreen, was a very devoted nurse doing AIDS research. Noreen, incidentally, was married to Mike Donovan, a Vietnam veteran who had returned home to become a policeman. Mike was only one of several Donovans — working-class citizens committed to Corinth and Alden University.

Patrick Donovan, Mike's father and a retired policeman, ran the campus police at the university. His wife, Rose, was a seamstress. Besides Mike, the Donovans had two other children: Douglas, a professor of drama, and Stacey, an aspiring student.

As the story opened, Roger Forbes's love affair with Merrill Vochek was in full force, although no one knew about it ... at least, that's what they thought. As Merrill carried on a romantic relationship with Doug Donovan and a close friendship with Roger's wife, Ann, they continued to see each other secretly. They were convinced that the affair was secret, since Doug had actually asked Roger to look after Merrill in New York and Ann had begun to use Merrill as a confidante. Unfortunately, Roger's daughter, Lorna, suspected her father's affair and began to hint about it to her friends.

One of the people most interested in Lorna's suspicions was a dean at Alden, Garth Slater. Garth was a nasty man who beat and sexually abused his wife and daughter, and aspired to ruin Roger Forbes's career so that he could improve upon his own. Garth was unable to carry out his plans, however. By the time he told Ann about her husband's affair, she and Cabot already knew about it from Lorna. Cabot fired Roger from the university (as well as Merrill from the TV station), and Ann planned to divorce him (although they later reconciled for political reasons).

As for Garth, he had other problems besides his career aspirations. Roger's son, Jack, had fallen in love with Garth's daughter, Lily, and had vowed to protect her from her father's incestuous behavior. Garth found himself out of control both professionally and personally.

Garth's violent treatment of Lily had begun to take a terrible toll on her. But in addition to her father's abuse, she also worried about her mother, June, who couldn't seem to cope with Garth's behavior either. As a way to adjust to her sad life, June became an alcoholic; and instead of helping his wife with her problem, Garth used it to blackmail her into submission. For example, Garth told June that if she continued to allow Lily to see Jack, he would see to it that she was institutionalized. June knew that Jack was probably the best thing to ever happen to Lily, but since she was powerless with Garth, she escaped her guilt about her daughter by drinking. After seeing her mother's behavior, Lily, now physically and mentally abused, became schizophrenic. The "good" Lily decided her love for Jack was not worth the pain it caused, so she broke up with him. The "bad" Lily, however, was delighted at the breakup, so she could seek other men, like Curtis Alden and Tony Pirelli (a new addition to Corinth). Unfortunately, the real Lily still loved Jack, and could barely remember her alter ego behavior.

Jack also loved Lily — even with her severe emotional problems — so he set about to release her from Garth's control. Despite his efforts, though, he seemed to be stopped at every turn, either by Garth's ability to evade retribution or by Curtis Alden's continuous attempts to cause trouble for him. One day, Garth was found murdered, and although other people were certainly listed as suspects (including Roger Forbes), Jack's feelings about Garth were known well enough to arrest him as the killer. While Jack languished in the courtroom, Lily's alter ego continued to take control of her. Even after he was acquitted of the crime — June finally admitted to murdering her husband — Lily continued to associate with Curtis rather than him. After much trauma, however, Lily decided to leave Corinth and spend time in a sanitarium. She subsequently left town and Jack was left alone and unloved. He sought no permanent relationships for awhile, but later became involved with Stacey Donovan. Unfortunately, before falling in love with Stacey, Jack had slept with Ava Rescott (a fortune hunter from the other side of town). Ava later told Jack she was pregnant with his child, and he felt obliged to marry her. Actually, Ava had lost Jack's baby, but wanted to marry him so badly that she claimed her sister's baby was Jack's just to keep him with her.

Needless to say, Jack's life had become most unstable since he'd been the star football player at Alden University. However, he was certainly not alone in his troubles. His adoptive father, Roger, had been killed in a plane crash. Ann Alden subsequently married Jack's real father, Dane Hammond. Dane was a real snake. He had worked in one of Cabot Alden's companies, but was constantly embezzling money or blackmailing someone in Corinth to get ahead. Most often he chose Shana, who was Cabot's illegitimate daughter (though no one knew it). Dane found out about their secret . . . as well as Shana's former love affair with Father Jim Donovan. He then blackmailed her for desirable real estate holdings of Cabot's. After awhile, Shana could not handle Dane's pressure, so she left town. She did return later, however, and married Fr. Jim's brother, Mike. Mike had been divorced from Noreen (Vochek) because of his refusal to seek help for his constant, violent Vietnam flashbacks. He also had had an affair with Ann Alden during the same time. But after Ann's marriage to Dane, Mike began to settle down. He sought help for his personal problems, and after much time, finally married Shana.

Elsewhere in the Alden/Forbes household, Lorna continued her wild, impetuous behavior — sleeping with men, plotting to keep them, and becoming pregnant because of her behavior. Her first real love was Tony

Pirelli (a prep school friend of Jack's) by whom she became pregnant and later contemplated an abortion. Next was Jonathon Matalaine, a devious man who stopped at nothing, including murder, to get a piece of Cabot Alden's fortune. And later, Lorna found herself in love with Linc Beecham, who loved Lorna, but also loved her economic status. Together with Dane Hammond, Linc plotted to gain more control of Alden Enterprises. Each time Lorna found out about the Machiavellian natures of her lovers, she vowed never to make the mistake again. However, she seemed to be unlucky in love.

By 1986, the writers at *Loving* seemed to have exhausted all the possibilities of love triangles between the Aldens and other families in Corinth. In fact, the mating-marriage-baby-affair cycle happened so often that all the romances in Corinth were too numerous to mention here. Despite the action, however, *Loving* has not performed very well in the Nielsens or Arbitrons. As a result, most of the original characters have died off or moved away, the university focus has lessened, and new plotlines of business crime and corruption have emerged. At this writing, it is difficult to predict the future success of such a massive facelift. Some serials, such as *Another World,* have survived because of such revisions. However, *Loving*'s need to revise so strongly after such a short time in daytime television does not look positive for long-term success.

One Life to Live
First Broadcast: July 15, 1968 (ABC)

One Life to Live has been recorded in broadcast history as one of the most unique soap operas of all time. Under Agnes Nixon's superb leadership, this drama was the first to include various ethnic groups in its cast of central characters as well as addressing social problems in a meaningful, realistic way.

Taking place in Llanview, the story originally focused on the prominent Lord family (see Figure 31). Victor Lord, a widower, was the owner of the local newspaper, the *Banner,* and was the proud father of two daughters, Victoria and Meredith. However, he had always wanted a son to carry on the family name and the inheritance that went along with it. Because he had no son, he ultimately chose Victoria to continue his legacy. He nurtured and trained her for many years until she became the strong young business executive he'd always hoped for. Despite her strength at the conference table, though, Vicky had unfortunately acquired a false sense of her stability in other areas. As she tried to manage a personal and professional balance in her life, she found that she was woefully ill-equipped for the latter. As a result, Vicky developed a schizophrenic personality: At certain times, she was the cool, calm newspaper executive everyone had always

FIGURE 31

Prominent Families on ONE LIFE TO LIVE (1968)

THE LORDS

Victor
|
Victoria m. Joe Riley
|
Meredith m. Larry Wolek

known; but during other periods, she became "Nikki" — a vulnerable young woman who chased love wherever she could find it.

One of the men to whom Vicky became attracted was a compulsive Irish journalist named Joe Riley. Joe was one of the *Banner's* most talented writers, and he and Vicky had often competed for stories while she trained as a reporter. Their "friendly competition" later turned into love. However, as their romance heated up, so did the battle between Vicky's dual personalities. She found that she became "Nikki" more often as she fell more deeply in love with Joe. Finally, she sought psychiatric help from Dr. Marcus Polk, and was able to resolve her schizophrenic dilemma. She then married Joe, and they lived happily until he was "killed" tragically in an automobile accident. Devastated by her loss, Vicky sought comfort from another colleague at the *Banner,* Steven Burke. They later married.

Meredith Lord, Vicky's sister, was shaping her future during this time also. She had always been much more fragile than Vicky, having suffered from a chronic blood disorder as a small child; but she seemed to have a good sense of who she was through it all, and often put her feelings above material gain. Thus, it came as no surprise when she fell in love with Larry Wolek, a Polish-American doctor whose family had lived in the very poorest section of town. At first, Victor Lord opposed his daughter's love, feeling that she would never be happy with a man who was not acquainted with the finer aspects of life. Later, after he saw the depth of their feelings, he relented, and invited Meredith and Larry to live in his mansion. Larry refused the mansion invitation at first, but after awhile, he and his wife agreed to live in a garage apartment on the estate. They then settled down to enjoy a happy, independent life together.

Larry Wolek's strength of character in standing up to his father-in-law was only one of several admirable characteristics of the Woleks. All the family members enjoyed the reputation of becoming successful because of good, hard work. In addition to Larry, there was Vince Wolek, who had saved enough money to buy his own company (B&W Trucking). And Anna, the only Wolek daughter, eventually followed in Larry's footsteps by becoming a respected part of Llanview society when she married Dr. James Craig and helped him to raise his troublesome teenage daughter, Cathy.

Meredith and Dr. Larry Wolek enjoyed the relative simplicity of their married life for a time, but after awhile, they decided to start a family. Due to Meredith's physical condition, her doctor advised against it. Despite his wishes, however, Meredith became pregnant. She later delivered twins; but only one (Danny) survived. Depressed by the death of one of her babies as well as her doctor's warning that she not become pregnant again, Meredith became mentally unstable. Soon after she realized her problems, though, she sought counseling from Dr. Joyce Brothers. She was subsequently treated successfully, but later died of a cerebral hemorrhage after a burglar scare. Larry was truly devastated; he then went (with Danny) to live with his sister, Anna, and her family.

Back at the Burke household, Vicky and Steve made the most of their life together, and seemed very content . . . until Joe Riley came back to Llanview. It seemed that he had not died in the car crash after all; instead, he had sustained a head injury which had left him with temporary amnesia. After wandering around for several days, he went to a restaurant and met a cute waitress named Wanda Webb. Wanda and Joe had subsequently fallen in love. And, while neither of them had known his true identity until he collapsed at the restaurant one day and was rushed to the hospital, they soon discovered that his life was complicated by his marriage to Vicky.

Vicky was even more distressed, for she didn't know whom she loved more — Joe or Steve. Initially, she planned to stay with Steve, but soon after Joe rejoined the *Banner* (and they saw each other every day), she decided to divorce Steve and remarry Joe. Wanda Webb was upset at first, but she later fell in love with Vince Wolek. They were happily married months later, and remained so until Vince's death many years after.

Wanda was not the only other woman in Joe Riley's life, however. During one of his more depressing periods, Joe had run off to New York with Cathy Craig (Dr. Jim Craig's daughter) and allowed her to seduce him. He really hadn't thought much about it (since the affair had ended months before), but when he announced joyfully that he was going to remarry Vicky Lord Riley Burke, Cathy told him the news of her pregnancy. Joe, torn between love and obligation, finally broke down and offered to marry Cathy for the sake of the baby. At first, Cathy refused; but later, after she had considered her other options, she decided to accept his proposal. Unfortunately for her, though, she made her second decision too late, for Joe had already run off to remarry Vicky.

After Joe's marriage, Cathy gave birth to a beautiful little girl, Megan Craig Riley. She started out to be a healthy baby, but after a short time, she began to grow frail. The doctors later determined that she had a congenital heart defect and did not have long to live. As a result, Joe spent long hours with Megan and Cathy and began to neglect his relationship with Vicky.

While his daughters were suffering the pains of life and death, Victor Lord was on his own mission of self-discovery; it seemed that he had fathered an illegitimate son years before. Immediately upon coming across this new information, Victor began to scour the country to find his son. As it turned out, at least two people had known about his existence before Victor. They were Mark Toland, a doctor at Llanview Hospital; and his lover, Dr. Dorian Cramer (also at Llanview Hospital). Earlier, Mark and Dorian had unwittingly become involved in a patient's death, and Mark had fled town after being convicted of manslaughter. While hiding out in San Francisco, he found out that Victor had been searching for his long-lost son. Quite by accident, Mark met a woman named Dorothy Randolph, who later claimed to be the mother of Victor's son, Tony. However, Mark was murdered before he could sell the information to Victor.

Dorian knew about Tony's parentage via Mark, but she was not anxious to acknowledge his true identity, for she had her own plans in mind for Victor Lord. Victor had suffered a heart attack in the search for his son. While caring for him at the hospital, Dorian decided she wanted to share his money and power. So she conspired with another doctor friend, Matt McAllister, to make Victor dependent on her for his health ... and ultimately marry her.

Dorian's plan worked for the most part. She conned Victor into marrying her, and, for a while at least, she kept Tony (who by now had come to Llanview) at arm's length from his true father. However, before long, Tony persevered with his search and discovered that Victor was his dad. Dorian was apprehensive about their meeting, so she filled Tony's head with lies about Victor. As it turned out, Dorian's quick thinking made her a wealthy widow; by the time Tony and Victor were able to iron out their differences, Victor had suffered a massive stroke, and was unable to alter his will to acknowledge Tony.

By the mid-seventies, the Lord family had undergone some extensive changes (see Figure 32). However, theirs was not the only drama in Llanview at this time. Another popular storyline involved Vince Wolek's black friend, Lt. Ed Hall, who fell in love with Dr. Jim Craig's secretary, Carla Gray. Carla was a very light-skinned Negro who had tried to "pass for white" many times in her young life. In fact, Carla had once rejected her mother in her attempts to run away from being black. She had also had love affairs with both Jim Craig and a black intern, Price Trainor. However, Carla's attitude changed completely after she married Ed Hall. She soon became proud about being black, especially after adopting a young ghetto youth named Joshua West. Together, Ed, Carla and Joshua became a happy family.

FIGURE 32

Prominent Families on ONE LIFE TO LIVE (mid 1970's)

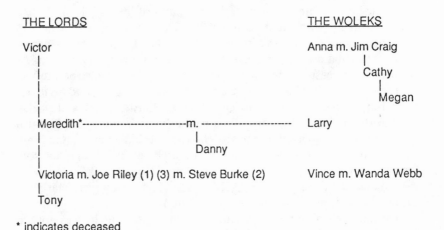

THE LORDS   THE WOLEKS

Victor   Anna m. Jim Craig
| |
| Cathy
| |
| Megan
|
Meredith*---------------------------m. ------------------------ Larry
| |
| Danny
|
Victoria m. Joe Riley (1) (3) m. Steve Burke (2)   Vince m. Wanda Webb
|
Tony

* indicates deceased

Elsewhere, things began to heat up in the Wolek family when a young cousin, Jenny Wolek, came to Llanview to take courses in nursing. Jenny was a novitiate nun who had not yet taken her final vows. Needless to say, Vince, Anna and Larry were extremely proud of her past achievements and future ambitions. Unfortunately, Jenny was not so sure about her vocational aspirations . . . especially after she met young Tim Siegel (Joe Riley's sister's son). Tim had fallen deeply in love with Jenny, too, and the young couple's romance sent tremors through much of Llanview. Tim's mother was most vehemently opposed to his relationship with Jenny because she felt that it had been the reason Tim had dropped out of law school. The Woleks were equally upset, feeling that Jenny should not have swayed from her commitment to God.

Jenny spent a great deal of time searching for a solution to her dilemma between Tim and the convent before she finally decided to marry him. Vince Wolek was livid about her final decision, however. One night, he confronted Tim, and they had a violent argument, resulting in Tim's accidental fall down a stairway at Llanview Hospital. Tim incurred a serious head injury from the fall, but he and Jenny were married anyway . . . shortly before he died from the accident. Jenny later married a man named Brad Vernon, who caused her extreme pain by constantly having affairs with other women.

Back at the Lords, Tony was reunited with a former lover when Pat Kendall moved to Llanview with her son, Brian. Unbeknownst to Tony, however, Brian was his son also—a fact that Pat struggled to keep from him because she feared that her estranged husband (a fugitive from justice) would ultimately reappear and cause trouble. Tony could not understand Pat's strange attitude towards him. At times, he felt she had encouraged a relationship; but just as he began to feel comfortable with her, she became cold and indifferent. As a result, he turned to Cathy Craig for solace, and later married her.

Unfortunately, Tony did not know that Cathy had become mentally unstable since he had first met her. Beginning with her discovery of baby Megan's health problems, Cathy had begun a downward spiral of depression, mood swings and extreme anxiety. But her condition worsened dramatically after Megan was tragically killed in a car crash. It seemed that Megan was suffering from a severe respiratory infection on the night of her death. Vicky Lord Riley, concerned for her welfare, had decided to drive her to Llanview Hospital. On the way there, she had an automobile accident which killed Megan and put Vicky into a deep coma. Despite the fact that no one else blamed Vicky for the crash, Cathy never forgave her. And, given Cathy's previous mental problems (caused by drug addiction), this terrible accident only served as an impetus for more bizarre psychopathic behaviors.

After several months, Vicky came out of her coma and discovered that she was pregnant with Joe's baby. Under normal circumstances, she would have viewed this as joyous news; however, she knew that Megan's heart problem had been traced to Joe (although he was unaware of it). She then had to decide between aborting a potentially unhealthy baby or keeping her precious child no matter what its fate. Ultimately, Vicky chose to have the baby, even though the event was marred by vicious attacks from Dorian and Cathy.

Dorian had never forgiven Vicky for her lack of support in Dorian's ill-fated marriage to Victor. Thus, she set about to gain revenge by causing friction in Vicky's marriage. Actually, she had quite an easy time of it – all she had to do was inform Joe that Vicky had known all along about Megan's heart problems being traceable to him. Joe was devastated by the knowledge of his congenital heart condition as well as Vicky's suppression of the truth. Needless to say, Dorian had achieved her goal: Vicky's marriage had indeed become troubled.

As for Cathy, her psychotic state worsened day by day. By the time Vicky gave birth to her frail son, Kevin, Cathy had convinced herself that the baby was hers. Shortly after his birth, Cathy kidnapped Kevin, and their departure left most of Llanview panic-stricken. Eventually, however, Kevin and Cathy were found, Kevin was returned to his grateful parents, and Cathy was treated by psychiatrist Will Vernon. She later recovered, divorced Tony (who was still in love with Pat Kendall), and moved out west.

Vicky and Joe Riley seemed happy at last. After little Kevin's recovery, they reconciled their differences, and lived a contented life together. In fact, Vicky became pregnant shortly after their reconciliation and both were overjoyed at their good fortune ... until they discovered that Joe had an inoperable brain tumor. He died soon after the discovery, shortly before Vicky gave birth to their second son. She named him Joey after his brave father.

Meanwhile, at the Woleks, Larry found himself falling in love with Karen Wolek (Jenny's sister and a distant cousin). He married her after a short while and, in his haste, neglected to find out much about her. As it turned out, Karen was more interested in Larry's money than in his love. And when his physician's salary proved too small for her extravagant whims, she became a part-time prostitute to earn extra money. Larry, of course, was unaware of everything. However, it wasn't long before Karen's secret was out—and several people in Llanview were hurt in the process.

The tragic chain of events began when Marco Dane came into town. Marco was Karen's former lover; he was also a professional pimp and pornographer. After his arrival, it did not take long before he discovered Karen's sexual moonlighting adventures. He then coerced her into becoming one of his prostitutes. She tried to refuse at first, but later accepted reluctantly.

As it turned out, Karen was not Marco's only prey in Llanview. Vicky Lord Riley's young godchild, Tina Clayton, had arrived in town in recent months; and one day, she unwittingly accepted Marco's offer to make her a "model" (against Vicky's wishes). After he photographed several legitimate shots of Tina, he superimposed her head on an obscenely nude body. His purpose, of course, was to blackmail Vicky with the photos. For awhile, Vicky considered paying him off, but then decided to refuse the threat. When she went to his studio to tell him of her plans, however, she found him murdered. She later was arrested for the crime and underwent a long, grueling trial.

After several weeks, Vicky was acquitted, but not until Llanview discovered Marco's true killer as well as Karen Wolek's "other" life. Marco had been murdered by a man named Talbot Huddleston (one of Karen's johns). One day, Talbot was speeding away from Marco's studio (with Karen beside him). In his haste to get to their rendezvous, he accidentally hit and killed Pat Kendall's son, Brian. He then sped off without reporting the accident. Marco had discovered his crime and was blackmailing him, so Talbot had eventually killed him off. (Actually, Talbot had killed Marco's lookalike brother, but no one knew that until years later.)

After Talbot's admission, Vicky was freed from the murder charge, but Llanview would never be the same. Karen and Larry divorced shortly after the trial. And Pat Kendall and Tony Lord were still not reunited, even over the grief for their son. It seemed that on the day of the tragedy, young

Brian had found out that Tony, not Paul Kendall, was his true father. In a fit of anger and confusion, Brian had run out of the house and into the street — where he had been fatally struck by Talbot's car. Tony was overcome by guilt when Pat told him the sad story. He later left Llanview and only returned for a short while before leaving again. He did not return for several years.

It was in this context that viewers of *One Life to Live* began to see the prominence of the Lord family diminish in Llanview. The Lords were subsequently replaced in the late seventies by the Buchanans — Texan transplants that took the small town by storm. It all began when Clint Buchanan came to town to replace Joe Riley as owner of the *Banner*. Clint was handsome, sexy and very attractive to most of the local women — especially to Pat Ashley (who was known before as Pat Kendall, but had reverted to her maiden name after divorcing Paul Kendall).

Shortly after Clint's arrival, Pat began to see him romantically. She admired his tough sense of independence as well as his ability to succeed in his quest to become publisher of the *Banner*. Pat did not know much about Clint's past, however, until his estranged father, Asa, and brother Bo moved into town to renew their relationships with him. After Clint's relatives came to Llanview, Clint became moody and less confident about himself. Pat later discovered that this was because Asa Buchanan was a willful, autocratic father. Her discovery led Clint to distance himself from her even more.

But Clint's father was not the only factor in the failure of Pat and Clint's romance. More important to their demise was the arrival of Pat's twin sister, Maggie, who was extremely envious of Pat's personal and professional life. In fact, Maggie became so jealous of her sister that one night, she actually kidnapped Pat, locked her in the cellar, and then disguised herself as Pat so that she could win Clint's love. Clint became suspicious after awhile, however, and Maggie felt the only option left was to kill her sister. Unfortunately for Maggie, though, she was the one killed. Pat had been saved, but Maggie' death had driven a permanent wedge between her and Clint. She later broke up with him and dated his younger brother, Bo.

Asa Buchanan did not want Pat Ashley in either of his son's lives, so he set about to discourage Bo and Pat at every turn. After several of his failed attempts, however, the couple decided to run away to Paris. There, they met an interesting woman named Nicole Bernard, who (they later discovered) was actually Olympia Buchanan, Asa's wife and Bo and Clint's mother. It seemed that Olympia had had a lover years before and had accidentally killed him in an argument over her newfound pregnancy (although Asa was actually the father). After discovering Olympia's infidelity as well as her lover's (Yancy Ralston's) death, Asa had exiled Olympia to France. He supported her financially but cut off any other ties to her.

Bo's reunion with his mother was so heartwarming, Olympia decided to come to Llanview and become reacquainted with her other son, Clint. While she knew she would risk Asa's ire, she felt the potential rewards were worth the risk. As soon as she arrived, however, Asa kidnapped her and placed her under his own "house arrest," using his nephew, Rafe Garrison, to guard against her escape. Asa, meanwhile, was preparing for his upcoming marriage to Samantha Vernon (Brad Vernon's sister and Dr. Will Vernon's daughter).

After their wedding, Asa and Sam threw a masquerade party to celebrate their union. By now, Olympia had become mentally deranged due to her imprisonment; so she convinced the sympathetic Rafe to let her out for awhile and prepared to kill Sam. After finding her at the party, Olympia tried to push Samantha over a balcony, but she fell to her own death instead. Bo, grief-stricken by her death and falsely informed that Yancy Ralston was his real father, "avenged" his mother's death by changing his last name to "Ralston," and getting to know his "father's" family, which included Euphemia, Delilah and Drew. He also broke up with Pat Ashley (who later married Tony Lord when he moved back to town) and started a new career managing the singing stardom of his friend Becky Lee Abbott. Later, however, he discovered that Asa was his real father after all. He scrambled about to pick up the pieces of his twice-shattered life, but things seemed more complicated than ever.

For one thing, Bo's relationship with Asa was tenuous at best during this time. However, it soon became highly flammable when Bo, upon discovering his true parentage, decided he wanted to romance Delilah Ralston. By the time he decided to declare his love, however, Delilah had married Asa instead. She later divorced Asa to marry Bo, but by then, he had become involved with Becky Abbott. He finally left Becky to marry Delilah. Soon after that marriage, though, Becky discovered she was pregnant with Bo's child. Asa then decided to marry her as a way of giving the baby a name as well as getting revenge on Bo. Asa's love-hate relationship with Bo continued through the birth of little Drew as well as Bo's troubled marriage to Delilah. In fact, it seemed as though Asa and Bo would always be competing with each other in matters of money and love.

As for Clint, he had begun to fall in love with Vicky Lord Riley shortly after he had become publisher of the *Banner*. Vicky certainly was attracted to him, but she was still mourning Joe, so discouraged his advances. However, after he helped her with her godchild Tina's troubles, she began to consider him as a serious marital choice.

Tina had been kidnapped shortly after Joe's death and held for a ransom of $500,000. But Clint Buchanan rescued Tina as well as the money, and after his heroism and obvious dedication in this terror-filled situation, Vicky decided she would accept his proposal of marriage. However, not long after they began their courtship, Tina's father (Ted Clayton) came into

FIGURE 33

Prominent Families on ONE LIFE TO LIVE (mid 1980's)

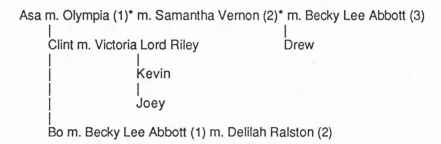

THE BUCHANANS

Asa m. Olympia (1)* m. Samantha Vernon (2)* m. Becky Lee Abbott (3)

Clint m. Victoria Lord Riley   Drew

Kevin

Joey

Bo m. Becky Lee Abbott (1) m. Delilah Ralston (2)

* indicates deceased

town. Ted knew that Vicky could be a substantial meal ticket for him, so he induced her with drugs to make her forget about Clint and turn to him instead. Clint was aware of Ted's deviousness, but he was unable to convince Vicky that he was a snake. Finally, after a series of murders and other crimes, Ted was eventually apprehended; Vicky, convinced of Clint's love for her, then accepted his marriage proposal a second time.

Vicky's marriage to Clint was never easy, however. For one thing, Tina Clayton (who had left town after her father's convictions) kept reappearing in Vicky's life, causing more trouble with each visit. Before long, the stress forced Vicky to readopt her dual personality, and she found herself awakening in the mornings with no recollection of what she had done the night before. Also, Clint was haunted by the memory of a past love named Giselle. He was forced to relive the pain of her death when her children, Echo and Giles, came to Llanview to make him pay for their loss (though it was actually their father who killed Giselle).

Elsewhere, Dorian Cramer Lord moved from lover to lover after Victor Lord's death. However, she ultimately married a district attorney named Herb Callison, who agreed to adopt her illegitimate teenage daughter, Cassie Howard. The three of them endured some very shaky times, especially when Cassie's real father (David Reynolds) came to Llanview to claim his daughter (and blackmail Dorian in the process). After several years, though, Dorian finally realized that she and Herb really loved each other, and they began to settle into some stability . . . for a while, at least.

By the mid-eighties, the Buchanans strongly dominated the storylines of *One Life to Live* (see Figure 33), and Llanview had experienced a world of problems it had not known earlier, including the discovery of drug problems on the local football team (the Cougars), mafia crime, and international intrigue. Also, new characters like Mitch Laurence, the O'Neill family and Maxie McDermont joined the lives and loves of the older, more established characters (Dorian, Vicky, Danny, Tony, Rafe, Delilah, etc.). In short, *One Life to Live* continued to live up to its reputation of excitement, uniqueness and high ratings.

In the future, it seems that *One Life* will continue these same trends. The Buchanans and their influence on Llanview have proved successful; future stories, especially those involving the continuous conflict between Asa and Bo, seem imminent. Also, Victoria Lord Riley Buchanan and Dorian Cramer Lord Callison appear to be quite secure as viewer favorites. Thus, at this point in *One Life to Live's* evolution, the characters and plotlines seem to be enjoying a very stable popularity, and are likely to continue their high ratings with minimal dramatic formula adjustment.

Ryan's Hope
First Broadcast: July 7, 1975 (ABC)

When *Ryan's Hope* premiered in 1975, its creators, Claire Labine and Paul Avila Mayer, reintroduced many of the same elements found in the Irna Phillips soaps of the thirties. Taking place in the inner city of New York, this serial featured the Ryan family, the proprietors of a saloon. This large, lower-middle-class Irish-American clan took great pride in hard work and strong family values. Included among the Ryans (at that time) were parents Johnny and Maeve and their five grown children, Mary, Frank, Patrick, Cathleen and Siobhan (see Figure 34). The main storylines originally surrounded Mary, Frank and Pat.

As the story began, Johnny and Maeve's eldest son, Frank, a former policeman, had decided to run for city council. However, before his campaign had even gotten off the ground, Frank was found at the bottom of a stairway at Riverside Hospital with a broken neck. Everyone was aghast at the terrible tragedy; Frank was in a semi-comatose state and his total recovery was extremely doubtful. But equally important and no less immediate were the questions surrounding his accident. No one seemed to know who had pushed Frank, much less why the incident had occurred at all.

From time to time, Frank became conscious; whenever it happened, some family member was usually around to help sort things out. One night, he mumbled two important words—"Delia" and "pushed." The Ryans were totally confused by this "declaration" because Frank's wife, Delia, had seemed totally devoted to him. After awhile, though, when Frank regained

FIGURE 34

Prominent Families on RYAN'S HOPE (1975)

<u>THE RYANS</u>

Johnny m. Maeve
|
Frank m. Delia
|
Cathleen m. Art Thompson
| |
| Maura ("Katie")
|
Mary m. Jack Fenelli
|
Patrick
|
Siobhan

consciousness, some answers were finally given. It seemed that Frank, on the night of his "accident," had had $6500 with him to pay off some blackmailers and keep secret the fact that he'd been having an affair with an attractive attorney named Jillian Coleridge. Before he reached them, however, he ran into Delia and told her he wanted a divorce. Enraged by his betrayal, Delia had pushed him down the stairs and then run away. Jill's brother, Dr. Roger Coleridge, found Frank shortly after his fall, and decided to take his money so he could pay off some of his gambling debts.

Ultimately, Frank recovered physically, but his marriage was in more trouble than it had been before his fall. The Ryans, after hearing the terrible truth of his blackmail and illicit affair, told Frank that their religion would not allow him to divorce Delia. Frank also realized that his chances at winning the city council election would be diminished greatly by the news of an unhappy marriage. Thus, he and Delia decided to try a reconciliation, even though Frank was still in love with Jill. Jill tried to stay away from Frank as well. In fact, she often buried herself in work to avoid thinking about him.

One of Jill's more complicated legal cases at this time involved a doctor named Seneca Beaulac. He had been married to his wife, Nell, for several years before she discovered she had an incurable neurological disorder. Unfortunately, by the time Seneca was informed of the situation, Nell had already had several cerebral hemorrhages and was now being kept alive by life-support systems in a bed at Riverside Hospital.

Seneca knew Nell would never approve of that type of existence, so he fought with hospital administrators to disengage her from the life-support equipment. When they refused, he took the law into his own hands and pulled the plugs himself. Afterwards, he was arrested for murder; he subsequently hired Jill to plead his case. In the course of the trial, Seneca fell in love with Jill, She tried to return this love, but found that she could not forget Frank. Finally, after Seneca pleaded guilty for a reduced sentence, Jill broke off with him and tried to go back to Frank.

Frank, of course, was still trying to make his marriage to Delia work. By now, they weren't really in love with each other (in fact, Delia had actually been in love with Frank's brother, Pat, at the outset of their romance); but they tried to keep up appearances, anyway. Also, shortly after their "reconciliation," they had become the parents of a little boy, Johnny. Frank felt that for the baby's sake as well as his own political career, he and Delia should make every effort to make their marriage a success.

Delia wanted to be married to Frank, but wasn't as concerned about their agreement of marital fidelity as he. She soon became bored with their "arrangement," and allowed herself to be seduced by Roger Coleridge (who was only involving himself with her to gain revenge on Frank). Several months later, Frank discovered Delia's betrayal, and ultimately arranged to be divorced from her.

After their divorce, Delia moved on to other men, including young Patrick Ryan (who was then engaged to Faith Coleridge). She tried to get him to marry her by sleeping with him and becoming pregnant. Indeed, Delia did become pregnant—but not with Pat's baby. As it turned out, Roger Coleridge was the true father. He and Delia later married, but the baby died. Without the baby to keep them together, Delia lost interest in her marriage; not long after the baby's death, Roger and she were divorced.

Meanwhile, Jill Coleridge began to plan her marriage to Frank Ryan (against Maeve's wishes) when she found out that she, too, was pregnant. Unfortunately, the baby was Seneca's, not Frank's. Jill tried to deceive Frank into thinking he was the father for a while, but he discovered the truth just before marrying her. When he found out, Frank stipulated that Seneca was to have full custody of the unborn child if he were to marry Jill. Jill refused, and the couple went their separate ways.

Love had also come into the lives of the other Ryan children at this time. Frank's sister, Mary, had become his most avid campaign supporter, but she had also unwittingly fallen in love with one of his adversaries, reporter Jack Fenelli. Jack did not like Frank Ryan, and his newspaper articles about him were derogatory. Nevertheless, Mary was enamored of

Jack; and not long after their first meeting, the young couple fell in love and moved in together (much to the Ryans' chagrin). Mary was not completely happy with this arrangement, either; while she loved Jack, she regretted her family's unhappiness as well as her sins in the eyes of the Church. After awhile, she tried to talk Jack into marriage; but he, the victim of an unhappy childhood, was not secure enough to make a permanent commitment, so they broke up. Later, however, Jack realized that he loved Mary. The two of them ultimately reconciled their differences; got married; had a baby girl (named Ryan); and remained fairly happy until Mary was tragically murdered by the Mafia while she and Joe explored a story on organized crime. Jack, beside himself with grief, now devoted all his energies towards writing exposés on crime and corruption in New York City.

As for the other Ryans, Johnny and Maeve's youngest daughter, Siobhan, returned to New York and the family bar after having spent a few years in Europe. Siobhan had the reputation of being the rebellious one of the family; she often rejected her parents' "old-fashioned" ideas and liked to think of herself as a very independent woman. As soon as she arrived in New York, the Ryan clan was in for loads of excitement — as well as problems. First, Siobhan became attracted to Mary's husband, Jack. Later, when they decided that their relationship would be hurtful and unwise, she moved on to other men, including Joe Novak, a handsome (but mysterious) fisherman.

Unbeknownst to the Ryans, Joe's uncle, Tiso Novotny, was the head of a local syndicate operation; Joe was one of his many dope-smuggling employees. Unfortunately, when Mary Fenelli had caught on to his dealings, Tiso had her murdered (see above). After Mary's death, Jack Fenelli and Johnny Ryan became close companions, teaming up to find Mary's killers. In the end, they traced the murder to Joe Novak and his uncle. By then, Siobhan had already married Joe; but when she was confronted with proof that Joe had inherited his uncle's connections to the syndicate (after Tiso's death), she divorced him and left town. She returned later and took a job with the local police department. Despite Joe's mob dealings, he still loved Siobhan; so as soon as he discovered she was back in town, they began seeing each other again. Needless to say, however, Joe's mafia contacts and Siobhan's career as a law enforcement officer would continue to plague the love they shared.

By the late seventies, the Ryans had begun to address several long-term family problems. Besides having custody of Ryan Fenelli (Mary and Jack's daughter, who was motherless after Mary's death) and Johnny Ryan (Frank and his ex-wife Delia's son), Johnny and Maeve had to watch their own children go through more adult pain.

Jillian Coleridge had had her baby, a small son whom she had named Edmond. And despite the fact that she still loved Frank, she never had gotten over the pain of Frank's ultimatum for marriage: giving full custody of her baby to Seneca. In addition, Frank seemed to be interested in another woman, Rae Woodward, at the time of Edmond's birth. Consequently, Jill gave up on her former goal of marrying Frank, and decided instead to wed Seneca (who still loved her) and tried to forget the past. Unfortunately, though, Jill's fragile marriage was based completely on little Edmond; when he died tragically in a gas explosion, she had nothing left to do but divorce Seneca and leave town.

As she prepared to depart, however, she and Frank were trapped in an elevator, and they were forced to declare their love for each other. After Frank dealt with Rae's wrath, he and Jillian opened up their own law firm and became engaged. They did not marry right away, though, because complications seemed to occur at every turn. Finally, they overcame their difficulties and had a simple wedding. But Frank and Jill were not destined for simple happiness; every time they thought they had achieved it, something seemed to go wrong.

Frank and Jill saw their turbulent marriage go through several trials during the early- and mid-eighties. Their marriage faced its greatest threat, however, when Dakota Smith (Johnny's illegitimate son and Frank's half-brother) romanced Jill after she had run away from Frank and developed amnesia (calling herself "Sarah Jane"). When Jill regained her memory, she came back to New York . . . and Dakota followed, vowing to take her away from Frank.

The other Ryans were faced with serious dilemmas as well. Siobhan continued her rocky relationship with Joe Novak until it could go no further. She finally gave up on it and married an exotic entrepreneur named Max Dubujak, who seemed to have his finger on the pulse of certain international white collar crimes. Max also seemed to be well acquainted with Roger Coleridge, who was as devious and criminally minded as ever. One of Roger's grandest schemes was to marry Maggie Shelby (Jill's half-sister) because of her access to Max's international "business" secrets. Max found out about Roger's plan, however, and engineered his demise during Roger and Maggie's honeymoon getaway.

As for Patrick Ryan, he had become a fine doctor, and was always concerned about his parents' health as well as about his young niece, Ryan Fenelli. Johnny and Maeve had raised young Ryan because of Jack Fenelli's single-minded devotion to his work. As Ryan developed into a young woman, she fell in love with a high school drop-out named Rick Hyde. Jack disliked Rick because he didn't feel Rick was good enough for Ryan. However, Ryan fell in love with Rick anyway; and Rick finished his high school degree and trained as a policeman to show Ryan (and her father) that he cared a great deal for her. They ultimately ran away and were married (illegally). When they returned, they still lived as man and wife, but

FIGURE 35

Prominent Families on RYAN'S HOPE (mid 1980's)

THE RYANS

```
Johnny m. Maeve
   |   |
   |   Frank m. Delia (1) m. Jillian Coleridge Beaulac (2)
   |   |        |
   |   |     Johnny      Edmond*
   |   |
   |   Cathleen m. Art Thompson
   |   |        |
   |   |      Katie
   |   |
   |   Mary* m. Jack Fenelli
   |   |        |
   |   |      Ryan m. Rick Hyde
   |   |
   |   Siobhan m. Joe Novak (1) m. Max Dubujak (2)
   |   |
   |   Patrick
   |
Dakota                      * indicates deceased
```

the marriage was troubled due to Jack's constant interference and Rick's new job assignment as an undercover cop.

Figure 35 illustrates the evolution of the Ryan family over the last decade. There is no question that the storylines surrounding this clan have been rich and timely. Unfortunately, however, the ratings have never been very high for this well-written drama. As a result, it seems likely that several areas will probably change so that *Ryan's Hope* can attract more viewers. These include the following:

1. Some of the older, more established members of the Ryan household are likely to bow out of the more central storylines, leaving room for newer members to emerge as the focal points of the family saga. These newer characters will probably include grandchildren (like Ryan Fenelli Hyde) as well as previously unknown nieces, nephews and cousins who will show up on the Ryans' doorstep.

2. Crime and international intrigue have been very popular on daytime drama over the last few years; *Ryan's Hope,* like the other soaps, has included a heavy dosage of these types of stories in its program fare.

However, as producers of the show learned in the late seventies, too much crime and action/adventure can prove detrimental to the program's success. *Ryan's Hope* carries with it a strong family affiliation, and this is not likely to change.

Santa Barbara
First Broadcast: July 30, 1984 (NBC)

Santa Barbara has been NBC's latest attempt to win high ratings in the daytime television race. Taking place in Santa Barbara, California, this soap opera originally dealt with four families who spanned the economic spectrum of that small city. They included the aristocratic Lockridges, the nouveau riche and power-hungry Capwells, the middle-class Perkinses and the lower-class Hispanic Andrades family (see Figure 36). For the first several months of production, most of the serial's central storylines revolved around the interrelationships of characters within these complicated families; after a while, however, the major action settled on the Capwells and Lockridges and their insatiable lust for money and power.

C.C. Capwell was a wealthy autocrat who ran his family in much the same way as his businesses: He trusted no one and felt that money was the only means to happiness. C.C. had quite a large family by his second wife, Sophia, and he spent most of his time meddling in their lives. Channing, Jr., C.C.'s eldest son, had been murdered several years earlier after an argument with Joe Perkins, his sister Kelly's fiance. Channing's death sent shock waves throughout Santa Barbara when C.C. vowed revenge on Joe and the Perkins family for his loss. Only later did a Hispanic detective named Cruz Castillo discover that Joe was not Channing's killer; instead, Channing's mother and C.C.'s ex-wife, Sophia, was the actual murderess — she had accidentally shot her son while trying to scare off one of her old suitors, Lionel Lockridge. After Channing's murder was solved, Lionel continued to court Sophia; however, she soon realized that his prime motivation was not love. Lionel was obsessed with taking anything — and everything — from C.C. Sophia would only serve as his most triumphant conquest. And since she still loved C.C. despite all their problems, she soon rejected Lionel's proposals and decided instead to live as an independent woman in Santa Barbara.

Sophia later reconciled with C.C., but not until after several large complications in their relationship were resolved. The most significant of these was C.C.'s third marriage to Gina Demott, a conniving gold digger who stopped at nothing to weasel her way into the Capwell fortune. Gina had originally romanced C.C.'s younger son, Mason; however, she later realized that her best chance to become a wealthy matron was to marry C.C.

FIGURE 36

Prominent Families on SANTA BARBARA (1984)

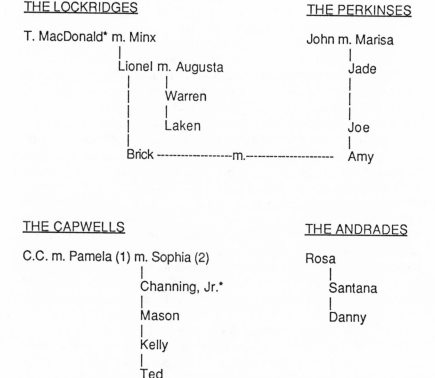

THE LOCKRIDGES

T. MacDonald* m. Minx
   |
   Lionel m. Augusta
   | |
   | Warren
   | |
   | Laken
   |
   Brick ----------------m.-------------------- Amy

THE PERKINSES

John m. Marisa
   |
   Jade
   |
   |
   |
   Joe
   |
   Amy

THE CAPWELLS

C.C. m. Pamela (1) m. Sophia (2)
   |
   Channing, Jr.*
   |
   Mason
   |
   Kelly
   |
   Ted
   |
   Eden

THE ANDRADES

Rosa
   |
   Santana
   |
   Danny

*indicates deceased

Mason and C.C. had never really gotten along, for each of them saw the other as a barrier to total power and control. Thus, it came as no surprise that C.C.'s success in "winning" Gina intensified their already heated rivalry. Gina did nothing to discourage the competition, either. She continued to flirt with Mason even after her marriage to C.C.; in fact, one night, things became so intense that C.C. threw Mason out of the Capwell mansion. He also punished Gina by making her a prisoner in her own home and giving custody of her adoptive son, Brandon, to his housekeeper Rosa Andrades' daughter, Santana (who was actually the boy's mother as a result of her affair with Channing, Jr.).

In the midst of C.C.'s retribution toward Gina and Mason, however, he suffered a debilitating stroke, leaving him helpless and comatose. For months, he lingered on the brink of life and death. But because of his past behavior, most of the Capwell family prayed for his demise instead of his recovery. Obviously, Gina and Mason were not anxious for C.C. to come out of his coma; for despite his many acts of terror, C.C. had not yet changed his will to eliminate them. Both Gina and Mason knew that if C.C. recovered they would lose everything for which they'd schemed.

Mason and Gina were not C.C.'s only detractors, however. Daughter Kelly had never quite forgiven him for blaming Joe Perkins for Channing's death. Even though Joe had since died and Kelly was now living with a freelance photographer named Nick Hartley, she had always believed that Joe's last few months would have been much happier if she had not been forced to choose between love and family loyalty. C.C.'s other daughter, Eden, had similar feelings toward her father. Eden had fallen deeply in love with Detective Cruz Castillo, a bright, articulate, honorable young Hispanic whom C.C. downgraded constantly because of his ethnic background and low economic status. C.C. disliked the idea of Cruz becoming his son-in-law so much that he plotted along with Santana Andrades (who also loved Cruz) to destroy Eden's romance with him. In addition to Santana's help, C.C. found unsolicited aid from Kirk Cranston, an ambitious young man who wanted to marry into the Capwell fortune himself. Together with Kirk and Santana, C.C. had succeeded in alienating Eden from Cruz shortly before C.C.'s attack.

Having made so many "enemies" within the Capwell family, it came as no surprise that one night C.C. was found with his life-support system turned off. For a time, it seemed that he would die, but C.C. miraculously began breathing on his own and later recovered fully. Needless to say, however, C.C. wondered about the identity of his potential assassin. Eden seemed to be the most likely candidate, since she had been the person last seen in the room before the support system had been unplugged. Several months later, though, Kirk discovered that Gina was the guilty one. She had disguised herself as Eden, and pulled C.C.'s oxygen supply plugs so that she would inherit the majority of the Capwell fortune. Kirk blackmailed Gina with his knowledge: He would say nothing about her crime if she promised to help him marry Eden. Gina agreed, and with her help, Kirk and Eden were subsequently married. But before long, the "secret" of Gina's assassination plot was uncovered (by Cruz). Gina was banished from the Capwell home, and Kirk lost Eden because of his betrayal. Mason was allowed to come back to the family on a trial basis. However, no one ever truly forgot the "crimes" that had been committed against them ... especially C.C.

C.C. Capwell was not totally corrupt, however. In fact, he became a most dedicated and trusted friend to two of his employees: Rosa Andrades, his housekeeper, and an ex-nun named Mary, who became his nurse. C.C. was sincerely interested in their welfare and that of their families, but even his good intentions led to harmful meddling. In Rosa's case, C.C. helped to engineer her daughter Santana's marriage to Cruz Castillo. Eden Capwell and Cruz were still very much in love, though, so Santana's marriage became tedious at best. As a result, she felt unloved and began to behave irrationally by seeking an affair with sleazy district attorney Keith Timmons (who only used her to show superiority to Cruz) and unwittingly taking drugs (which were supplied by Gina Demott Capwell).

As for Mary, C.C. sensed that she was falling in love with his estranged son, Mason. C.C. could not stand the thought of their potential marriage because he felt that Mason was too corrupt for Mary's gentle heart and virtuous ideals. Thus, he set about to ruin their romance by exiling Mason and encouraging another suitor, Dr. Mark McCormack.

Mark seemed to be a very likeable young man, but as time went on, he seemed to display some extremely unsavory qualities. One such characteristic was his uncontrollable jealousy, even after he and Mary were married. One night, when he could not control his rages any longer, Mark raped Mary. She then turned to Mason, who began to live up to her high standards of goodness and sensitivity. Unfortunately, however, Mary was tragically killed before she and Mason were wed. After her death, Mason was beside himself with grief. He blamed Mark and C.C. for his loss and vowed to get revenge on them both.

Mason was not the only unhappy Capwell in 1986. Eden was still yearning to be married to Cruz; Kelly had become mentally unstable after killing Nick's brother accidentally; and Ted Capwell, C.C.'s youngest son, had unwittingly become involved with Gina Demott and Capwell's niece, Hayley. Upon discovering Hayley's background, Ted felt he could no longer trust her, so he broke their engagement and ran around with other women. Despite his actions, however, Ted still loved Hayley.

At the Lockridge estate, Lionel had given up on Sophia and found himself falling in love again with his ex-wife, Augusta, a conniving but lovable woman. Augusta and Lionel were not able to go through a smooth reconciliation, however. Between their worries for their children and other relatives as well as their respective "get rich" schemes, the road to remarriage seemed bumpy at best.

Like the relationship of Augusta and Lionel Lockridge, the future success of *Santa Barbara* seems rocky. Despite massive recharacterizations (resulting from an earthquake and mass murder), this soap opera is not doing as well as NBC predicted it would two years ago. However, there are some very popular elements within the basic premise of the story. These include complex, likeable characters in romantic triangles as well as the action/adventure plotlines which have proven to be so successful in the past few years.

Perhaps *Santa Barbara's* major problem lies in the fact that its regularly scheduled network time is 3:00 p.m. (EST), which places the show in heavy competition with two more established hits, *General Hospital* and *The Guiding Light.* At present, the story formula on *Santa Barbara* seems sound; however, the show's time slot is not. This fact should be considered before any harsh judgments can be made about the overall success of the soap.

Search for Tomorrow
First Broadcast: September 3, 1951 (CBS)
Network Change: March 29, 1982 (NBC)

Search for Tomorrow is television's longest-running soap opera (having begun its broadcasts before *The Guiding Light* transferred from radio to TV in 1952). The central character in this serial was Joanne Gardner Barron ("Jo"), a young military housewife who tried to cope with the daily trials of raising a small daughter, Patti, while battling the seemingly never-ending interference from her meddlesome in-laws. She braved all the domestic storms valiantly while she awaited her husband Keith's return from overseas. However, shortly after he came back to their home in Henderson, Keith was fatally injured in an automobile accident. Consequently, Jo's problems went from bad to worse: As a new widow, she now faced the challenge of finding a job and being a single parent as well as maintaining her hard-earned independence from Keith's parents.

Jo ultimately found a job at the hospital in town, and while she did not earn a large salary, she felt that she had enough money to keep Keith's parents, Irene and Victor, from succeeding in their attempts to gain custody of little Patti. Irene was Jo's greatest enemy in this dispute. Patti's welfare had become an obsession with her. She was convinced that she was wealthy enough to provide "true" happiness for Patti, in contrast to Jo, who was poorer, but very loving to the little girl. Finally, the courts awarded custody of the child to Jo. Despite the ruling, however, Irene could not be discouraged in her attempts to keep Patti, and finally went so far as to kidnap the child. Luckily, Irene and Patti were later found, and Irene was forced to allow Jo to raise Patti without any further interference.

During the ordeal of Keith's death and Patti's subsequent custody battle, Jo found great comfort from her best friends, Stu and Marge Bergman. No matter how depressing Jo's situation became, the Bergmans were always able to help her understand the more optimistic side of things. And their children, Janet and Jimmy (and later Tommy), were excellent playmates for Patti. In fact, Janet and Patti became best friends from the start. After a while, Jo began to believe that her own life was not over after her husband died.

Jo and Patti enjoyed their newly found contentment, and in time, Jo also began to look for romance to enhance their already happy life. One of her suitors was Arthur Tate, with whom she owned a motel called Motor Haven. Jo and Arthur eventually married after a long and arduous courtship. Before they got to the altar, however, Arthur was greeted by a woman who claimed she was his dead wife, Hazel. As it turned out, the mysterious newcomer was actually Hazel's twin sister, Sue. She had been hired by the Mafia to pose as her dead sister, and thereby gain possession of Motor Haven. The mob then planned to use the motel as a front for dope smuggling.

Jo and Arthur found out about Sue's scheme before she and the mob succeeded. Unfortunately, though, Arthur was critically injured in the process. As a result of his injury, Arthur became an invalid. He then told Jo he wanted to cancel their wedding plans. Later, Jo convinced him to marry her, and despite his fragile health, they enjoyed a happy marriage.

Jo and Arthur's happiness was not always easy to maintain, however. Shortly after their wedding, Jo became pregnant and had a baby boy — just as Arthur began to encounter financial troubles at Motor Haven. Beset by the worry of having to support his growing family, he invited his wealthy aunt, Cornelia Simmons, to become an added partner in their business. Cornelia was interested in helping Arthur, but she did not want to become an inactive investor. So she decided to move to Henderson as an active business partner. Cornelia disliked Jo from the very first day she arrived. She later did everything she could to destroy their marriage.

In addition to Cornelia's antagonism, Jo experienced other difficulties during this time. For one thing, her small son, Duncan Eric, was killed one day when he ran into the path of an oncoming car. Next, Jo received word that her mother had also died. But the greatest trouble of all was yet to come ... when Jo's father, Frank, and her widowed sister, Eunice, turned up in Henderson to complicate Arthur and Jo's lives.

Eunice was a very self-serving woman. Before coming to town, she had promised herself she would remarry as soon as possible and at any cost. After arriving in Henderson, she was attracted immediately to Arthur; and, given Eunice's lack of family loyalty, it came as no surprise that she brazenly set about to seduce him. Unfortunately for Jo, Arthur gave in to Eunice's seductive attempts.

In time, Cornelia Simmons became aware of Arthur and Eunice's romance. She decided to use it to her advantage by convincing Arthur of his guilt in the extramarital affair, and then offering him an opportunity to get away from his marital pressures by taking a job at one of her many businesses in Puerto Rico. Arthur agreed enthusiastically, and Cornelia felt that she had finally destroyed any remaining vestiges of Jo and Arthur's tattered marriage. She then plotted to find her own marital partner. His name was Rex Twining, an attractive, virile, younger man. Little did Cornelia know, however, that Rex was extremely attracted to Eunice Gardner.

Several months later, Arthur came back to Henderson to reconcile with Jo. But during his absence, his aunt Cornelia was found murdered, and Jo, Eunice and Rex found themselves in the midst of a great scandal. At first, Eunice and Rex were considered the prime suspects in the killing. Later, though, it was revealed that Cornelia's true murderer was her own housekeeper, Harriet Baxter.

After the Cornelia Simmons murder mystery was solved, most of the people in Henderson were content once again. Arthur and Jo rededicated themselves to a strong marriage; Eunice and Rex Twining married and moved to Puerto Rico; and even Jo's father, Frank, found happiness by marrying Stu Bergman's widowed mother. However, the younger members of the community were not as well settled as their parents at this time. Take, for example, Patti (Barron) Tate and Janet Bergman, who had grown into young women over the past several years. Along with their growth came the typical (or not so typical) problems of adulthood.

Janet Bergman met and fell in love with one of Jo's cousins, Bud Gardner. They later married and had a baby (Chuck). Things seemed very happy in the young Gardner household . . . until Bud left on a trip and presumably died in an accident.

Janet was overcome by grief and turned to a friend, Dr. Dan Walton, for comfort. She ended up marrying him. However, unbeknownst to her, Bud was still alive. In fact, Bud actually returned to Henderson while Janet and Dan were on their honeymoon. When they got back and discovered that Bud was alive, Janet was beset with the horrible dilemma of whom she should remain married to. Even though she really loved Dan, she felt Bud needed her more. Ultimately, Janet decided against her love for Dan, and moved in with Bud.

Stu Bergman, Janet's father, was aware of her brave choice; however, he knew that Bud could not make her truly happy. One night, he went to Bud's apartment to try to convince him to let her stay with Dan. Bud was not interested in Stu's concerns, though. Their "discussion" soon became a fight, and in the process, Stu was knocked out by Bud's quick fists.

When Stu regained consciousness, he discovered that Bud had died after falling from his apartment window; but Stu could not remember the circumstances under which the death had taken place. Thus, when the police came to investigate Bud's demise, he could not give any reasonable explanation. Stu was then arrested for Bud's "murder." Later, however, Jo came to Stu's rescue by finding a broken drainage pipe on the side of Bud's apartment building. After further investigation, police surmised that Bud Gardner, upon knocking Stu unconscious, mistakenly had thought *he* was dead and tried to flee his apartment quickly and quietly. In the process, Bud had grabbed the rusty drainpipe and it had apparently given way to his weight. Stu was now cleared of any criminal wrongdoing, and Janet was now free to live her life with Dan. Ultimately, Janet and Dan moved away from Henderson, and Stu and Jo continued their strong friendship.

As for Patti (Barron) Tate, she spent the early part of her young adulthood falling in love with the wrong men. First, she had an affair with a married man while visiting her grandparents in Arizona. Next, she romanced a rebellious, irresponsible youth named Ted Ashton. She later paid for that mistake by being involved in an accident which left her temporarily paralyzed. Jo realized after Patti's accident that while her own life had begun to settle down, she was now entering a new phase of motherhood — worrying mainly about the life of her adult daughter instead of herself.

By the early 1960s writers on *Search for Tomorrow* ceased to focus solely on the problems of Joanne Gardner Barron Tate. While she was still very important to the basic storyline, *Search* began to explore the lives of other characters as well as some of the more important social issues at that time. One of the most important social themes of the early sixties was alcoholism; and not-so-coincidentally, several stories of excessive drinking began to emerge in the tiny town of Henderson.

Arthur Tate was one of the show's most celebrated alcoholic victims. For years, he had regretted his business and financial losses as well as his extramarital escapades. Finally, when he could tolerate his guilt no longer, he turned to drinking. Together with a friend, newspaperman Fred Metcalf, Arthur spent many nights drowning his sorrows over his personal and professional shortcomings. One night, however, his excessive drinking precipitated a very serious heart attack. Arthur survived the initial cardiac arrest, but he was forced to change his alcoholic habits as well as to spend a long period of time recuperating from his attack. Arthur later died from another massive heart attack, but not until after he had truly changed his ways. Jo was devastated by her loss — not only had she loved Arthur, but she now found herself alone for the second time in her life.

While Jo was trying to deal with her own problems, daughter Patti was adding to her troubles as well. Patti continued to fall in love with the wrong men. This time, she complicated that habit by becoming pregnant by an older, married doctor named Everett Moore. Everett was the victim of an unhappy marriage, so he often sought comfort wherever he could find it. Patti seemed to be a very likely candidate for his affection, since by now she had developed a highly emotional need for older, married men. After discovering her pregnancy, Patti considered marrying Everett. (He was now free to wed since his wife had committed suicide.) However, by this time, she also recognized the fact that the marriage would not be for love; it would only be for the sake of the baby. Her consideration became groundless after awhile, however, because in the midst of her confusion, Patti was involved in an auto accident and subsequently miscarried her unborn child. Unfortunately, the accident had long-term ramifications as well as pain from the immediate tragedy: After sustaining several major injuries, Patti was told that she should never try to have another child.

Needless to say, both Jo and Patti were very vulnerable during this time, as they tried desperately to put the pieces of their lives back together again. Jo was especially committed to having her life in order before she entered into any new relationships. Thus, it came as quite a surprise when she found herself falling in love with her former enemy—a successful business entrepreneur named Sam Reynolds.

Sam was known as a carpetbagger who had come to Henderson for the sole purpose of acquiring many of its businesses. In the process of building his local empire, Sam had successfully taken Tate Enterprises away from Jo's husband, Arthur. Jo felt that Sam's ruthlessness in business had shortened Arthur's life, and she vowed never to forgive him for his actions. Despite Jo's strong resolve to hate Sam, however, she found herself becoming more attracted to him with each passing day. Sam was equally attracted to Jo—and because of the pain he had caused her through Arthur's business losses, he made a special attempt to make her happy.

For a while, Jo resisted Sam's charms, but before long, neither could deny the love they felt for each other. Unfortunately, though, Sam had a problem: His wife, Andrea Whiting Reynolds, was separated from him, but refused to give him a divorce. Andrea had enjoyed spending Sam's money so much that she was not anxious to lose any part of it. Previously, there had been no problems with her, for Sam had never cared enough for another woman to seek a divorce. His relationship to Jo, of course, was different. So Andrea set about to ruin Sam's relationship with her. And she stopped at nothing in her vicious schemes. She even convinced Sam's estranged son to come to Henderson and spy on his father, using the assumed name of "Len Whiting."

Sam was obviously unaware of Andrea's plot; he was busy enjoying his romance with Jo as well as Patti's relationship with a newcomer in town . . . named Len Whiting. After several months, Len and Patti truly fell in love, and planned to marry. Andrea was even more furious at the thought of her son's defection. In fact, on the day of their wedding, Andrea surprised everyone by coming to the ceremony and vowing to cause more trouble for Sam and Jo as well as for Patti and Len. Needless to say, both potential marriages were put aside once more.

But each couple continued to find happiness together despite Andrea's attempts to thwart it. As a result, she continually renewed her resolve to destroy all of them. One night, Andrea tried to kill Sam by spiking his drink with a dangerous drug. Unfortunately for her, though, their drinks were switched inadvertently and she was poisoned instead. She ultimately survived, but Sam was then arrested for attempted murder. His trial was long and gruesome; however, he was later acquitted, and Andrea finally agreed to seek psychiatric counseling and to give him the divorce for which he had waited so long.

All the same, Sam and Jo's troubles did not end with Andrea's change of heart. Shortly before they planned to be married, Sam was sent to Africa on a special mission for the United Nations. While he was away, Jo busied herself with their wedding plans as well as helping Patti and Len to work out a reconciliation. The young couple still loved each other very much, but their combined emotional problems made an easy relationship impossible. After awhile, however, Patti and Len resolved their differences and subsequently were married. By now, though, their love had become more complicated, because Len had had an affair with a lovely woman named Grace Bolton during the time of his separation from Patti.

Grace and Len had met because of Grace's incurable medical condition. But despite the depressing long-term odds, they had sought comfort from each other and, along the way, had conceived a child (unbeknownst to Len). After he renewed his relationship with Patti, Len did not think about Grace (who, by now, had moved to California). However, he later discovered that she had died in childbirth. Beset by grief as well as concern for his newborn baby, Len persuaded Patti to adopt the little boy, whom they named Chris. He neglected to tell her that he was Chris's real father. Jo was also unaware of Chris's true parentage, but one day, she succeeded in piecing together the obscure information surrounding his birth. She was so shocked by her realization that she had an accident with the car she was driving at the time.

Jo nearly died in the car crash; as a matter of fact, she survived her massive injuries only by the grace of God and the quick thinking of Dr. Tony Vincente, as physician at Henderson Hospital. Despite her miraculous survival, however, Jo became blinded temporarily. And Jo's temporary blindness, combined with her later discovery that Sam had "died" in Africa, caused her to fall into a severe depression.

By now, Tony and Jo had become close friends, so he did his best to ease her pain after she received the devastating news of Sam's death. Later, their friendship blossomed into love; Jo became healthy once again; and they agreed to marry after Tony received a divorce from his nasty wife, Marcy. But just as they began to look forward to their wedding, Sam Reynolds returned from the "dead."

It seemed that the authorities in Africa had mistakenly identified another body as his months before, and Sam had come back to Henderson as soon as he had discovered the administrative mix-up. Sam, of course, still wanted to marry Jo, but she had since developed deep feelings for Tony. Jo agonized over the question of whom to marry for awhile.

However, she later decided that she was obligated to wed Sam, even though she really loved Tony.

Despite Jo's strong resolve to be happy with Sam, her emotional health began to fail during this period. As her wedding day approached, Jo's emotions took over completely, causing her blindness to return (although this time the cause was psychosomatic). But Sam was determined to marry her at any cost, and didn't care about Jo's worsening emotional condition. He continued to carry out their marriage plans, even after she begged him to postpone the ceremony. He later kidnapped her when she refused to marry him, told her friends and family that they were eloping, and took her to an isolated cabin in the woods.

Initially, Jo's family was not very concerned about her strangely "secret" marriage and extended honeymoon, for Sam continued to keep in touch with them and falsely indicated that they were very happy. Jo, of course, became more nervous as each hour passed. Her nervousness later escalated into sheer terror, however, when she and Sam were attacked by a man and woman in their cabin. In the ensuing scuffle, Sam was fatally wounded by a stray bullet, and Jo was left unconscious. Later, after the family became suspicious over Jo and Sam's whereabouts, they traced her to Sam's hideaway cabin. They subsequently rescued her; Jo regained her sight as well as her consciousness; and she and Tony married soon after she had recuperated from her ordeal.

Thus, by the early seventies, Joanne Gardner Barron Tate Vincente had entered into marriage for the third time. Her family had changed enormously over these years, too (see Figure 37). Patti and Len Whiting had adopted Len's son, Chris, and Patti had ultimately overcome her emotional problems and the accompanying drug dependency. From time to time, Patti and Len still had marital difficulties (including the dramatic period when a mentally unbalanced woman named Emily Hunter tried to seduce Len away from Patti and take Chris away as well); but overall, they endured as a strong couple throughout the years.

Elsewhere during this time, Henderson was shocked by the news that Marge Bergman, Stu's devoted wife for many years, had died suddenly. Stu was beside himself with grief, but tried to display a brave front as he worked at being a good single parent to his young son, Tommy. After a while, he hired a woman named Ellie Harper to help with some of the household duties. Stu and Ellie eventually fell in love and were married, but not until they had lived through several difficult ordeals in their relationship.

It all started shortly after Marge's death, when Stu discovered that Dan Walton, his daughter Janet's husband, had also passed away. Janet was now left alone to raise their two children, Liza and Gary. Janet had truly loved Dan, but she was still a relatively young woman; so after a while, she found herself falling in love with a psychiatrist named Wade Collins. But

FIGURE 37

Prominent Families on SEARCH FOR TOMORROW (early 1970's)

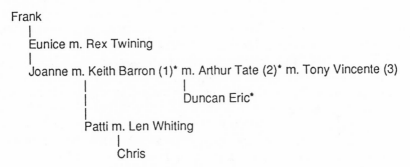

THE GARDNERS

Frank
|
Eunice m. Rex Twining
|
Joanne m. Keith Barron (1)* m. Arthur Tate (2)* m. Tony Vincente (3)
        | |
        | Duncan Eric*
        |
      Patti m. Len Whiting
         |
         Chris

* indicates deceased

---

her daughter, Liza, was not enthusiastic about her mother's remarriage. In fact, in the early stages of Janet and Wade's courtship, Liza spent a great deal of time trying to ruin their romance. Later, though, Liza realized that her mother's remarriage would not detract from her late father's memory, and she heartily endorsed Wade and Janet's union.

After that marriage, Stu and Tommy moved in with the Collins family, and Stu became an especially close confidante to his granddaughter, Liza. Liza needed all the advice she could get during this time, for she found herself in and out of love many times. One of her first young paramours was a ward of Jo's named Bruce Carson. Liza later broke up with Bruce, however, and fell in love with one of her friend's brothers, Steve Kaslo, instead. Liza wanted to marry Steve right away, but they later decided to live together for a while before marriage. Janet and Wade Collins were terribly upset by Liza and Steve's decision, but they tried to trust their judgment and hope for the best. Indeed, Liza and Steve were married eventually, and they were happy—for a short time. But as their relationship continued to mature, they found that Steve's music career conflicted with Liza's modeling aspirations. Ultimately, they worked out their professional difficulties, but shortly thereafter, Steve discovered he had leukemia. He tried to hide his condition from Liza; he even worked overtime to record a special song for her. But just before he completed his record, Steve collapsed and died. Liza was totally devastated by his death.

As Stu's family problems continued to mount, Ellie Harper began to feel that she was no longer an important part of his life. Finding herself being hurt by his "indifference," Ellie decided to leave Stu to his family, and she fled to Henderson. Later, however, she rushed back to his side during a family crisis. They subsequently were married and enjoyed several happy years together before Ellie ran away with a chef from a local country inn.

While Stu and his family were experiencing great difficulties, Jo's household was no more serene than that of her best friends. After many years, Jo's sister, Eunice, returned to Henderson, having divorced Rex Twining and remarried a man named Doug Martin. As soon as she arrived, Jo knew that her personal life would become more complicated than ever. Indeed, she was right.

Shortly after Eunice and Doug had resettled in Henderson, Eunice met a very wealthy, attractive lawyer named John Wyatt. John had come to town to acquire some local businesses, and one of his first acquisitions was a magazine where Eunice later became a freelance writer. John was then interested in becoming Eunice's lover. Even though she was tempted, Eunice decided against complicating her life in that fashion. Doug Martin, Eunice's husband, was not so convinced of Eunice's fidelity, however. They fought constantly, and Doug ultimately moved into a motel. Eunice then went to John Wyatt's cabin to reconsider her situation.

While she was at the cabin, Eunice was visited by John's secretary, Marian Malin, who confessed that she was in love with John—and warned Eunice that Doug was on his way to the cabin to win her back. By the time Doug got there, however, Karl Devlin, the previous owner of John Wyatt's magazine, was also with Eunice and Marian. Karl had become mentally unstable since he'd lost his business, and he decided that the only way to gain back his magazine company was to kill everyone whom he felt had taken it from him.

When Doug arrived, Karl was holding Eunice and Marian at gunpoint. He immediately attacked Karl and was critically injured in the process. Later, Doug discovered that his injuries were permanent: He had been paralyzed by a gunshot wound and would be an invalid for the rest of his life. After he found about about his future, he asked Eunice for a divorce and quickly left Henderson. Eunice was now free to accept John's proposal to marry, which she eventually did.

Back at the Vincente house, Jo's husband, Tony, had started to suffer from some severe health problems. In fact, his colleagues cautioned him that if he were not careful, he could fall victim to a fatal heart attack. But Tony, a very dedicated doctor, found it almost impossible to lighten his schedule. As a result, Tony ignored his friends' advice and later died from a massive coronary while trying to save a patient from an attack by a local mobster.

Jo, once again widowed, really didn't know what to do with her life now that she was alone. Naturally, she turned to her friend, Stu Bergman, for advice, and he suggested that they buy a country inn together. For a while, Jo was happy to bury herself in her work; but it didn't take long for her to become embroiled (once again) in another complicated romance.

John Wyatt, now Eunice's husband, had been disenchanted with his marriage for quite some time. Eunice had never been able to forgive herself for Doug Martin's paralysis, so she decided to punish herself (and John) by refusing any sexual intimacy. John loved Eunice, but he was still virile enough to want to make love. He subsequently sought extramarital affairs to relieve his sexual tensions.

John's first liaison was with Jennifer Phillips, a seductive temptress who was determined to make him her next husband. Together with a friend, a pretty nurse named Stephanie Wilkins, Jennifer searched for ways to have John move in with her so that she could completely destroy his marriage to Eunice and ultimately marry him. Unfortunately, Jennifer went beyond all bounds of credibility with her lies to win John's sympathy. He soon became aware of her schemes and later walked out on her. Jennifer, outraged at his rejection, quickly became obsessed with getting revenge on him for his actions. One night, she finally made him "pay" for rejecting her love by murdering Eunice and pinning the blame on him. Later, however, Stephanie intervened on John's behalf and made Jennifer confess her crime.

John was now freed from his conviction, but his personal life was more unsettled than ever. After his release from prison, Stephanie confessed that she had fallen in love with him. John, though, was more interested in Jo (because she reminded him of her sister, Eunice). Jo, meanwhile, was attracted to a new doctor in town named Greg Hartford. For months, the romantic excitement involving John, Greg, Stephanie and Jo was extremely high; however, ultimately things calmed down and John married Stephanie. They lived as a family with John's stepdaughter, Suzi Martin, and Stephanie's daughter, Wendy Wilkins. As for Jo, her desires for romance with Greg fizzled when he left Henderson with his daughter. Jo later met, married, and divorced a professional gambler named Martin Tourneur. By the end of her fourth marriage, Jo decided that she had lived with more than enough men in her life. She concentrated instead on her business and friendship with Stu Bergman.

Besides keeping up with the trials and tribulations of many favorite characters, fans of *Search for Tomorrow* were able to greet several new personalities in Henderson during the late seventies and early eighties. Among these were Travis (Rusty) Tourneur Sentell, who came to town as the handsome heir to Tourneur Instruments. Travis immediately fell in love with

FIGURE 38

Prominent Families on SEARCH FOR TOMORROW (mid 1980's)

THE GARDNERS

Frank
- Eunice* m. Rex Twining (1) m. Doug Martin (2) m. John Wyatt (3)
  - Suzi m. Brian Emerson (1) m. Warren Carter (2)* m. Cagney McCleary (3)
    - Jonah
- Joanne m. Keith Barron (1)* m. Arthur Tate (2)* m. Tony Vincente (3)* m. Martin Tourneur (4)
  - Duncan Eric*
  - Patti m. Len Whiting
    - Chris
    - Sarah

THE BERGMANS

Stu m. Marge (1)* m. Ellie Harper (2)

Janet m. Bud Gardner (1) (3)* m. Dan Walton (2)* m. Wade Collins (4)*

Liza m. Steve Kaslo (1)* m. Travis Tourneur Sentell (2)*

— Chuck

— Gary

Tourneur

— Jimmy
— Tommy

THE KENDALLS

Lloyd m. Estelle

— Chase
— Alec
— Steve
— Rebecca (T.R.)

THE MCCLEARYS

Kate

— Hogan
— Quinn
— Cagney m. Suzi Martin (see above)

Jonah

— Adair

* indicates deceased

Liza Walton Kaslo and courted her until their marriage many months later. Travis and Liza subsequently had a little boy named Tourneur; but Travis never saw little Tourneur grow up because he (Travis) died tragically one day as he was flying to another country for an international business deal.

Another colorful character at this time was an attractive but mysterious stranger named Warren Carter. Warren spent a great deal of time conning most of Henderson. He later became the focus of a heated romantic competition between Suzi Martin and Wendy Wilkins. Warren subsequently died after he'd made too many enemies and committed too many crimes. However, his memorable stay in Henderson was still impressive even several years after his demise.

With appearances of people like Travis Sentell and Warren Carter, *Search for Tomorrow* began a new era in its colorful history. It began to phase out some of the older, more traditional men and women of Henderson, and concentrated instead on newer, more action/adventure romances with characters like Sunny Adamson, the McCleary brothers, and the newest town carpetbagger, Lloyd Kendall. Each of these people also had family ties in town, thus expanding the list of prominent families on the soap to include the McClearys and the Kendalls as well as Jo and Stu's clans (see Figure 38).

By 1986, however, ratings for this long-running soap opera were among the lowest in its broadcast history. As a result, the serial's writers decided to give *Search* a major facelift. They subsequently created a flood to ravage the small fictional town; killed off all the characters whom they deemed unpopular or unnecessary; and introduced a new cadre of people that they hoped would increase the soap's popularity. At this writing, however, *Search for Tomorrow*'s ratings have not increased greatly after the Henderson flood. If the situation does not soon change drastically, it is likely that NBC will reconsider the show's placement on the network schedule.

The Young and the Restless
First Broadcast: March 26, 1973 (CBS)

In the early 1970s, the daytime programming executives at CBS decided to develop a new serial which would compete successfully with the current, more youth-oriented soaps like *General Hospital, One Life to Live,* and *All My Children.* These efforts ultimately resulted in a slick contemporary story by William J. Bell and Lee Phillip. Bell and Phillip named their soap *The Young and the Restless,* and for over a decade, it has earned consistently high ratings by living up to its promising title.

Taking place in Genoa City, Wisconsin, the story originally focused

FIGURE 39

Prominent Families on THE YOUNG AND THE RESTLESS (1973)

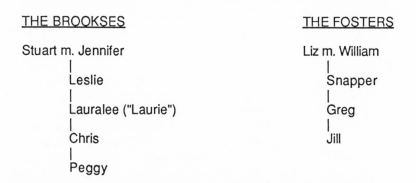

THE BROOKSES

Stuart m. Jennifer
|
Leslie
|
Lauralee ("Laurie")
|
Chris
|
Peggy

THE FOSTERS

Liz m. William
|
Snapper
|
Greg
|
Jill

on two families: the wealthy Brooks clan and the lower-class Fosters (see Figure 39). Stuart Brooks, the Brooks family patriarch, owned the only newspaper in town. Together with his socialite wife, Jennifer, he enjoyed the reputation of being one of Genoa City's richest citizens. He also enjoyed the power he could wield in that city while overseeing his four grown daughters: Leslie (a professional pianist), Lauralee or "Laurie" (a novelist), Chris (a journalist), and Peggy (a student).

The Fosters were a much less impressive family economically. However, they were no less respected than the Brookses in the community. After her husband, Bill, had deserted her and her family, Liz Foster worked hard at her job as a domestic to support her daughter and two sons. She fervently hoped that her work would cause them to be strong, ambitious and successful. For the most part, her dream was realized: son Snapper was now a medical student, and Greg was an attorney. Their sister, Jill, however, had never reached her goal of being a model. Instead, she worked in a beauty shop to help augment the family income.

When the story opened, a young former surgeon named Brad Eliot had just moved into town. Brad had changed his identity and come to Genoa City to start a new life as well as a new career. He made this move because he felt he had caused a young boy to die while he performed surgery on him. As a result, Brad wanted to abandon his work as a doctor and find a new way to make a living. Ultimately, he chose to come to Genoa City, and was now working as a reporter for Stuart Brooks' newspaper, *The Chronicle*.

Stuart Brooks was very impressed with Brad Eliot. He respected his work and liked the way he conducted his life in public. Thus, despite the fact that he knew very little about his background, Stuart encouraged Brad to court his daughter, Leslie.

Stuart was very worried about his eldest daughter at this time. He felt that she worked too hard at trying to be the "world's greatest" concert pianist, often to the detriment of her own personal life and social development. With Brad's self-confidence, Stuart hoped that Leslie might break out of her introverted shell. And indeed he was right; before long, Leslie became much more outwardly social, having been nurtured by Brad's love and affection. Unfortunately, however, Leslie's happiness with Brad proved short-lived when her sister, Laurie, set about to have Brad for herself.

Laurie worked very closely with Brad at *The Chronicle*. Because she was so attracted to him, she used their professional relationship to sabotage Brad's romance with her sister. Many times, for example, Laurie would "forget" to forward their messages to each other. Or, for some unclear reason, she might force Brad to spend a long night at the newspaper office with her. Needless to say, Leslie's fragile confidence began to crumble almost immediately when she felt that Brad was no longer interested in her; conversely, Brad could not understand Leslie's growing "indifference" to him. Finally, Laurie succeeded in seducing Brad away from her sister. She proposed to him and he accepted, feeling that his chances with Leslie were gone. Before they were to marry, however, Brad discovered Laurie's lies and cover-ups. He subsequently found Leslie in New York (wandering about aimlessly), declared his love for her and confessed his past. Soon after, they were married, and were happy for awhile. Unfortunately, though, they later divorced after Brad developed serious physical problems and was separated from Leslie for long periods of time.

While Leslie and Laurie Brooks were dealing with their love crises, their sister, Chris, was having romantic problems of her own. She had fallen deeply in love with Snapper Foster, much to her father's chagrin. Stuart objected to Snapper for two reasons: He felt that the young couple's economic class differences would interfere with any long-term relationship, and he wasn't at all sure that Snapper returned Chris's love.

Stuart was definitely correct in assessing Snapper's lack of devotion to his daughter, for Snapper was too busy working his way through medical school while supporting his mother and siblings to spend his time dreaming about love. With Snapper's money woes, he clearly wanted to avoid any further commitments, especially to marriage. However, he was interested in finding a physical relationship — with no strings attached. Obviously, Chris Brooks was not the ideal mate for this pursuit, since she was too interested in marriage; so he decided instead to seduce a pretty waitress named Sally McGuire.

Snapper was not terribly astute in his judgments of Sally's naivete in their affair, though. While claiming to be disinterested in marriage, Sally felt completely the opposite. She plotted and schemed to become pregnant, thus forcing Snapper into marriage. But after discovering her pregnancy,

Snapper realized how much he truly loved Chris. She had shown him her devotion by moving out of her father's large mansion to a small apartment (in which she, incidentally, was raped). In doing so, she had shown him she was not interested in the Brooks fortune. Upon learning of her love — and pain — Snapper proposed to Chris, and they began their fragile marriage.

Sally, now pregnant with Snapper's child, was devastated when she learned of Chris and Snapper's wedding. Her first thought was to commit suicide. However, she was ultimately saved from that horrible fate when Pierre Rolland, the owner of the nightclub where she worked, confessed that he had loved her all along and proposed marriage. Shortly after his proposal, Sally married Pierre (over his family's objections). Their happiness was destroyed abruptly, though, when Pierre died after being attacked by a mugger. After Pierre's death, Sally left town and had her baby, Chuckie. She later returned to Genoa City to harass Snapper about his illegitimate son, but then married an old boyfriend named Stan and left town permanently.

Snapper's brother, Greg, was very involved with Chris and Snapper's marital strain over Sally, since he had always been in love with Chris. However, after he discovered that Chris was pregnant and that his brother's marriage was out of jeopardy, he turned his emotions instead to one of his legal clients, Gwen Sherman. He later fell in love with her and they planned to marry. Unfortunately, though, Greg's dreams of happiness disappeared when he discovered that Gwen had been a prostitute before coming to Genoa City.

At first, Greg cancelled his wedding plans, vowing that he wanted nothing more to do with Gwen. But after a while, he mellowed in his anger and began to work toward a reconciliation with her. Their romance began to blossom again, and they even looked forward to marriage ... until Gwen's former pimp came to town and forced her to return to her old profession. Initially, Greg was terribly upset and confused at Gwen's odd behavior because he didn't know that she was being threatened. Later, however, he persuaded her to testify against her "old boss" in court. She did, and was finally freed from her checkered past.

Gwen and Greg never married, however, even after he saved her reputation. Eventually, Gwen became more spiritual and decided to live in a convent. Greg continued to find happiness in his work, serving as legal defense to many of his friends in town. He also spent time trying to bring his parents back together when Bill Foster returned to Genoa City after a nine-year absence.

Bill came back to his family after Snapper had finally convinced Liz to declare her husband legally dead. Since she hadn't heard from him in the more than seven years of their separation, Snapper felt Liz owed it to herself to begin a new life and remarry. She had recently fallen in love with a man named Sam Flowers. Sam was very good to her, and was anxious to make her his wife. Thus, after much soul-searching, Liz accepted Sam's proposal and started proceedings to declare herself legally widowed.

Just before his death declaration was finalized, however, Bill Foster returned. While his family resented his appearance at first, they soon changed their minds when they learned he was dying from lung cancer and wanted to make peace with his family again. Liz had never stopped loving Bill, so upon his return, she cancelled her engagement to Sam and offered to care for Bill until he died. They later "remarried" and lived together for a year, after which Bill died, and Liz was left a widow.

The other member of the Foster family, daughter Jill, was also involved in a romantic struggle during this time. Jill had never been truly happy as a beauty operator. She longed for the opportunity to break away from her mundane, everyday life, and fantasized about the future, when she would join the world of the rich and famous. One day, Jill actually got her wish. A wealthy customer of hers, Kay Chancellor, had been impressed with Jill's apparent ambition and drive. Mrs. Chancellor soon decided to offer Jill a job as her personal secretary; needless to say, Jill jumped at the chance.

After Jill accepted the job and moved into the Chancellor mansion, she did not take long to get used to her newfound lifestyle. She also realized quickly that Kay Chancellor was an alcoholic who was often irresponsible in the way she ran her household as well as in the way she treated her husband, Phillip. It came as no surprise, then, that within a few months, Phillip and Jill found that they were attracted to each other. However, Jill was uncomfortable with the notion of being a "homewrecker." She refused to become involved with Phillip until they were able to find some way to rehabilitate Kay.

Despite all their attempts, though, Kay seemed to continue on her self-destructive path ... until she realized that Jill and Phillip were falling in love with each other. She immediately began to recover, newly aware of the threat that she would lose Phillip. She also decided to look for ways to drive a wedge between her husband and Jill, for she was not about to lose Phillip to her former beautician.

One of Kay's schemes was to bribe her estranged son, Brock Reynolds, into charming Jill away from Phillip. Brock liked Jill, and he didn't want to hurt her. However, he soon realized that if he refused Kay's offer, someone else might accept it and ultimately destroy her. Thus, he agreed to draw Jill away from Phillip by proposing to her himself. They later had a "private wedding ceremony" (performed by Brock) and lived in a small cabin in the woods.

Brock's affection for Jill was only platonic, though; as a result, he and Jill agreed that they would not become intimate sexually until their love had grown deeper. Meanwhile, Phillip was furious at the thought that Jill had left him for his stepson. But in spite of his attempts to win her back, Jill refused to see him ... until she discovered she was pregnant. Of course, Jill knew that the child was Phillip's, since she hadn't had any physical relationship with Brock. She subsequently met with Phillip and told him about the baby.

Upon hearing that he would soon be a father, Phillip decided to divorce Kay immediately and marry Jill. His first act was to fly to the Dominican Republic for a quickie divorce. Unbeknownst to him, however, Kay was not as willing to terminate their relationship. In fact, she vowed to do anything to preserve their marriage — even if it meant killing him and committing suicide. Consequently, after Kay picked Phillip up at the airport, she drove her car over a cliff. Kay survived the "accident," but Phillip was not so lucky. He did live long enough to marry Jill, however, and establish her as heir to the Chancellor fortune. Unfortunately for Jill, though, Kay was not finished with her vendetta. She challenged the legality of Phillip's divorce and remarriage, claiming she had signed all of the documents under alcoholic duress. After several appeals, the courts finally invalidated Jill's claim to Phillip's estate. Jill then vowed revenge on Kay for killing her husband, leaving her young son (Phillip, Jr.) fatherless, and keeping her away from Phillip's estate.

Jill's revenge became ruthless, as she slowly drove Kay to drink again and led her to believe she was going insane by discussing Phillip as though he were still alive. After a while, Jill finally relented in her abuse, but by that time, Kay had already fallen back into alcoholism and had rededicated herself to making Jill's life as miserable as her own. Kay didn't stop at repossessing the Chancellor mansion, either; she also tried to get custody of Phillip, Jr., and successfully reduced Jill to pennilessness. Jill was outraged at her behavior, so she retaliated with her own venom. The vicious cycle went on and on.

Jill and Kay's mutual hatred never abated, even after the Phillip Chancellor affair. They continued to make each other miserable at every opportunity, even after they had each found new relationships.

Back at the Brooks household, life had developed major complications as well. Jennifer Brooks, Stuart's wife, had become increasingly disenchanted with her marriage after her family had grown. She felt that Stuart did not appreciate her as he should; she also fell in love again with an old flame of hers, Dr. Bruce Henderson. Unfortunately, however, Jen was unable to ask Stuart for the divorce she wanted because he suffered a severe heart attack just before she started to discuss it with him. Despite her silence, though, the Brooks daughters were well aware of her intentions, and they battled amongst themselves, trying to decide if they should support Jen in her intention to divorce. Laurie was most positive toward her mother, whereas Peggy despised Jen altogether. But their "split vote" made little difference to Jen; she went on with her plans anyway, after

Stuart was well enough to hear her news. Jen then left Genoa City to marry Bruce.

In spite of her marital intentions, however, Jen never became Mrs. Bruce Henderson. As soon as she moved to Chicago, she discovered a malignant lump on her breast, and underwent massive surgery. The resulting mastectomy left her emotionally drained, and she felt too unwomanly to be married to anyone. Stuart still loved her, though; and when he found out how bad she felt, he did everything within his power to convince her that she was still very beautiful. Jen ultimately reconciled with Stuart. They then resumed their marriage with renewed passion.

After Jen and Stuart were reunited, they began to face a series of problems with their children. Daughter Laurie's romances were among the most difficult. First, Laurie became involved with a married man named Jed Andrews. The elder Brookses were relieved when the unhappy affair finally ended. However, they were not prepared for the next shock: Laurie's romance and planned marriage to Mark Henderson (Bruce Henderson's son). Mark was a very nice young man—but unbeknownst to Laurie, he was her half-brother. After they were told the terrible family secret, Mark left town, and Laurie exiled herself from her parents. As far as she was concerned, they were no longer her family. She subsequently tried to hurt them as much as she could.

Unfortunately, Laurie's hurt over Mark Henderson later drove her to make some very irresponsible romantic choices. One such mistake was falling in love with Lance Prentiss, a wealthy playboy, who had once romanced her sister, Leslie (while Leslie was separated from Brad). Lance was handsome, dashing and seemingly perfect; however, he was very secretive about his background and family life. As it turned out, Lance was an extremely devoted son to his mother, Vanessa, a pathologically ill person who was jealous of anyone who interfered with her relationship with her son. It seemed that Vanessa and Lance had been trapped in a fire many years before. Vanessa was able to save her young son, but her face had become permanently disfigured in the process. Now, she saw any young and beautiful woman as a potential threat to her happiness with Lance. Laurie, of course, became her prime target, for Lance had fallen in love with her and they subsequently married.

Vanessa's hatred for Laurie grew with every day. And she tried anything and everything to drive her away from her son. First, Vanessa fired Lance from his chief executive post at Prentiss Industries; next, she told Laurie that Lance's unemployment would cause her great harm. Indeed, Lance started gambling and drinking heavily, and Laurie began to be victimized by his unhappiness. After a while, Laurie gave up and divorced Lance; but Vanessa was too obsessed at this point to stop threatening her. Finally, Vanessa went totally out of control and engineered her own death to make Laurie look like a murderer. Laurie was eventually acquitted, and she and Lance tried to reconcile. But by this time, their marriage had become too shattered to be rebuilt. Ultimately, Lance and Laurie went their separate ways, and both left Genoa City.

Laurie's sister, Leslie Brooks Eliot, also left town after much pain and trauma. Her brief affair with Lance Prentiss had resulted in a pregnancy. However, by the time Leslie discovered that she was carrying Lance's child, Laurie had already married Lance. Thus, Leslie decided to keep her baby's parentage a secret, raising him as a single parent. Leslie did not remain a "future" single parent for long, though. One day, Lance's long-lost brother, Lucas Prentiss, came to town and fell in love with Leslie immediately. After she told him about the baby, he offered to marry her before the child was born. She agreed, and when her tiny son, Brooks, came into the world, he was blessed with a legitimate name and two parents.

Leslie's newfound family situation should have made her happy; but she knew that she really loved Lance instead of Lucas. Fearing future problems, she decided to give Brooks to Lance and Laurie and leave Genoa City. Laurie was understandably appalled by Leslie's "gift" and fought with her viciously. In the end, Leslie ran away and was so distressed that she developed amnesia. Later, she returned to Genoa City (and Lucas), but she did not remain for long. Soon realizing that she no longer belonged there, she took Brooks and left town for good.

Thus, as *The Young and the Restless* entered into the early eighties, the Brooks family had almost evaporated, and new families came into prominence (see Figure 40). Among them were the Williamses and the Abbotts. These new characters, along with the Fosters, continued to bring high drama to Genoa City.

The Williams family was composed of Carl and Mary and their children, Paul, Steve and Patty. Carl was a policeman in town, and he was known for his kindness as well as his high standards of respectability. It came as no surprise, then, that he was terribly upset to discover that his son, Paul, had made a young teenage girl, April Stevens, pregnant. Moreover, Paul refused to assume his responsibility as the baby's father, and was perfectly happy to see the child grow up illegitimately.

Eventually, Carl and Mary forced their son to marry April and become a father to little Heather. The marriage, however, was shaky from the beginning. By this time, April had become accustomed to living without Paul. And even though she loved him, she was drawn to her family, who had promised to provide her and Heather with everything she'd need as long as she left Paul and Genoa City. Ultimately, April decided to follow her family. Paul was then left alone until he met and fell in love with a former prostitute named Cindy Lake. Cindy later died after being attacked by her former pimp. Paul then went on to marry the devious Lauren Fenmore.

Paul's sister, Patty, was also experiencing romantic problems during

FIGURE 40

Prominent Families on THE YOUNG AND THE RESTLESS (early 1980's)

THE FOSTERS

Liz m. William (1)*m. Stuart Brooks (2)
|
Snapper m. Chris Brooks
| |
| Chuckie
|
Greg m. Nikki Reed (1)
|
Jill m. Phillip Chancellor (1)* m. John Abbott (2) (see below)
|
Phillip, Jr.

THE WILLIAMSES   THE ABBOTTS

Carl m. Mary   John m. Dina (1) m. Jill Foster (2)
| |
Steve   Traci
| |
Patty --------------------m.--- Jack (1)
| |
Paul m. April Stevens (1) m. Lauren Fenmore (2)   Ashley
|
Heather

* indicates deceased

---

this period. She had fallen in love with a wealthy playboy named Jack Abbott — son of John and heir to the fortune of Jabot Cosmetics. Patty had never been in love before, but Jack's experience was different. He was older and much more worldly than she and had womanized his way through much of Genoa City before meeting her. In fact, at the time of his attraction to Patty, Jack was just recuperating from a messy affair with Jill Foster Chancellor.

Jack and Jill had become lovers after she had taken a job at Jabot Cosmetics. However, Jill soon realized that Jack was not really interested in marriage — unlike his father, John, who had fallen in love with her. Thus, Jill broke off her romance with Jack, and pursued John Abbott instead. Jack did not accept this loss graciously. He tried to fire Jill from Jabot, claiming that she was seducing his father for money and power. Jill filed a class discrimination suit against him, though, and he was forced to reinstate her into the company as well as accept the fact that she and his father would soon be married. It was in this heated atmosphere that Jack met and decided to marry young Patty Williams.

Needless to say, the Abbott household was extremely tense after Jill's marriage to John and Jack's marriage to Patty. And life continued to become more complicated when other members of the Abbott family came to live in Genoa City.

Two of the newer additions to the Abbotts were John's daughters (and Jack's sisters), Traci and Ashley, who had come home after college graduation. Ashley disliked Jill from the moment she met her, and was convinced she would be nothing but trouble for her father and brother. Indeed, Ashley was right: Jill and Jack continued to be sexually attracted to each other even after their respective marriages. Their interest in each other ultimately resulted in Jill's divorce from John, Jack's divorce from Patty, and Jack's dismissal from his father's business (before being reinstated as president of Jabot).

But Ashley had other, more personal problems to address upon her return. Several months after she became adjusted to her father's new marriage, Ashley's mother, Dina (a.k.a. Madame Mergeron), came to town. Dina's appearance after all these years was disturbing enough. However, it became totally devastating to Ashley when she discovered that Dina had had an affair during her marriage to John Abbott, and that a man named Brent Davis, not John, was Ashley's real father. For awhile, Dina and Brent's secret had been kept hidden; but one night, Brent (who was an alcoholic) confessed his guilt to Ashley. Ashley went out of her mind at the news and ran away. She was later found by a friend of hers, businessman Victor Newman. Victor had always been attracted to Ashley, and he worried about her condition after such an emotional shock. Victor spent a great deal of time trying to find Ashley. He ultimately rescued her from a would-be rapist, and convinced her to come home with him.

Since Victor was aware of the secret surrounding Ashley's parentage, he knew she would be uncomfortable at home. He offered to have her live with him and his second wife, Nikki, instead of going back to the Abbott mansion. Ashley accepted gratefully; Nikki, however, was not happy with the arrangement because she knew that her husband was very fond of her newest houseguest. Eventually Ashley returned to her home and accepted John as her true father, even though he was unaware that he was not her biological parent.

But Ashley's problems were not over. Her brother, Jack, had inadvertently discovered the secret of her true father, Brent Davis. He decided to blackmail her into resigning the presidency at Jabot Cosmetics, so that he could take over once again. Ashley eventually succumbed to Jack's threats because she didn't want to hurt John Abbott any more. After her resignation, she found solace with Victor Newman again. And since Victor was unhappy in his marriage to Nikki, this "comforting" friendship soon evolved into a full-blown love affair. Nikki vowed revenge.

While Ashley was working out the complications of her life, her sister, Traci, had some difficulties as well. Shortly after moving back to Genoa City, Traci developed a crush on a young singer named Danny Romalotti. Unfortunately, however, Traci felt inferior to Danny's other fans because she was overweight. And her feelings of inferiority soon turned to depression when slim, svelte Lauren Fenmore began to compete with Traci for Danny's affection. Lauren ultimately became engaged to Danny, leaving Traci totally bereft. At this point, Danny's sister, Gina Roma, took an interest in Traci and encouraged her to lose some weight.

After Traci went on a diet, she began to gather up the pieces of her life again. She became attracted to a professor of hers, Dr. Tim Sullivan, and he eventually became her first lover. Tim did not understand the depth of Traci's commitment, however, and he slept with other women as well as her. One day, Traci discovered she was pregnant with Tim's child. She rushed over to his apartment to tell him the good news. But when she got there, she found him in bed with another girl. Traci then ran off and tried to commit suicide. Danny Romalotti (no longer engaged to Lauren) followed her, however, and offered to marry her.

Meanwhile, Tim felt terrible about Traci's heartbreak; when he learned also that she was carrying his child, he tried desperately to reach her for a reconciliation. Despite his attempts, though, he never found her until she had married Danny and miscarried the baby. Tim was now out of her life completely.

As for Danny and Traci, they later agreed that they weren't well enough suited to stay married to each other, so they subsequently divorced. Danny continued his singing career, and Traci fell in love with a gardener in the Abbott mansion, Brad Carlton. They eventually married, and John Abbott gave his new son-in-law an important job at Jabot Cosmetics. Everything finally seemed to resolve itself for Traci . . . except for the fact that her brother, Jack, neither liked nor trusted Brad. And he was determined to see Brad fall out of grace with the Abbott family.

The Young and the Restless, like other long-running soap operas, has undergone several massive character changes in its history. At present, the major focus is on the Abbott family (see Figure 41) and its business, Jabot Cosmetics. Jack Abbott is a central figure from which most of the dramatic action occurs.

Since this formula has proven to be most successful (as witnessed by the soap's consistently high ratings and numerous Emmy awards), the basic story premise is likely to continue as it has for the past few years. However, viewers have begun to note some weak elements in this formula, and if the ratings begin to slide, several plotline changes may occur. They include:

    1. Storylines may be quickened. Many fans have complained recently

FIGURE 41

Prominent Families on THE YOUNG AND THE RESTLESS (1986)

THE ABBOTTS

John m. Dina (1) m. Jill Foster Chancellor (2)
```
       |   |
       |   Ashley
       |
Jack m. Patty Williams (1)
       |
Traci m. Danny Romalotti (1) m. Brad Carlton (2)
```

that some of the conflicts on *The Young and the Restless* take weeks (or sometimes months) longer to resolve themselves than they should. The reader will recall that in Chapter 1, *The Young and the Restless* was cited as one of the slowest-paced serials on daytime television today. To alleviate this problem, the writers will have to accelerate the dramatic action of their stories.

2. The storylines may become less simplistic in addressing important issues. Some viewers feel that "solving" a social problem like unwed motherhood by having characters singing songs about it might do more harm than good. *The Young and the Restless* has addressed many issues, such as dieting and terminal illness, with extreme sensitivity in the past. However, certain problems may not be as well suited to a simplistic storyline. As such, they should be avoided.

In summary, however, these criticisms are relatively minor. *The Young and the Restless* has proven to be successful for over a decade, and is likely to remain so in the near future.

Chapter Five

Summary and Conclusions

After reviewing the last several decades of soap opera history, it is clear that daytime drama's key elements of writing, characterizations and audience analysis have evolved according to the demands and preferences of the public. It is also evident that through the years, producers of this type of programming have maintained a certain standard of excellence. Otherwise, the genre of daytime serial drama would be found on the inside of a well-preserved time capsule instead of on the highly competitive programming schedules of all three networks.

At present, daytime television provides networks with 60 to 80 percent of their annual revenues. Since much of the programming during this time block is composed of soap operas, it's fair to say that daytime drama supports many of the networks' prime-time shows.[1] For example, the average cost of producing one episode of *Dynasty* is $1.2 million; an *entire week* of soap operas usually costs between $300,000 and $400,000.[2] Unfortunately, however, most of the networks' highest moneymakers often face severe limitations in program quality. In the case of daytime soaps, these limitations are usually reflected in budgetary and content restrictions.

Economically speaking, the allowance for most soap opera productions is based on a low investment/high yield principle. As a result, salaries for most writers and actors on daytime television are considerably lower than for their counterparts in prime-time. Also, the numbers of characters and "on location" scenes in each show are much more limited in afternoon soaps as compared to most nighttime series.

But budget constraints are only a part of the restrictions placed on daytime programmers. In addition to monetary limitations, TV serials on the afternoon schedule are not as likely to address "hot" topics such as homosexuality or interracial relationships (see Chapter 1).[3] Most network executives deny that any intentional censorship exists in these areas; they insist that these themes have been aired before and have not proven to be very popular with a daytime audience. However, some serial writers tend to disagree with the networks' denial of topic suppression. John Whitesell,

176

an executive producer for *Another World,* contends that network management and the corporations who own the shows fear that viewers in the South and in smaller, rural communities would be offended at controversial topics like a romance between a white man and a black woman.[4] Another writer, Steve Karpf (co-creator of *Capitol*), agrees with Whitesell, and adds that networks overreact when they oppose controversial storylines because of "small-town" viewers:

> I take great exception to the idea that people who live in these areas are racist. They are not. They will happily and easily accept black characters if the characters are well-written.[5]

Examples to support Karpf's claim include the popularity of David Banning's romance with Valerie Grant *(Days of Our Lives)* and Carla Gray's affair with Jim Craig *(One Life to live)* in the mid-seventies. In each case, the interracial relationship provoked huge amounts of viewer mail, prompting the plotline to continue for several months. As Sam Ratliff, a writer for *Capitol,* has learned: "Even if viewers are outraged, that could only add interest to the show. I think the more they complain, the more they watch."[6]

Regardless of the philosophical differences among network programmers and some daytime soap opera writers, the fact remains that networks are much more conservative about dramatic storylines in the afternoon hours than they are during prime-time. Even after several decades of broadcasting, the main ingredients for daytime drama are love and romance, as compared with nighttime television's abundance of sex, sin and high-level violence. Interestingly enough, however, while the networks' attitude may be seen as sometimes restrictive, it may also be the primary reason for the longevity of soap operas versus the relatively rapid rise and fall of prime-time serials.

In recent months, media critics have noted that the popularity of all nighttime soaps is slipping. For instance, in the 1984–1985 Nielsen ratings, *Dynasty* ranked as #1 among its competitors in prime-time; in 1985–1986, it slipped to #7. Similarly, *Dallas,* which was #2 in 1984–1985, dropped to #6 in 1985–1986. For other soaps, the news was even more discouraging: *Knots Landing* fell from #9 to #15 in the same time period; *Falcon Crest* went from #10 to #20; and *The Colbys* rarely got above a #47 for its first season. These shows, previously seen as unbeatable, were defeated by such fare as *The Cosby Show, Family Ties, The CBS Sunday Night Movie, Murder She Wrote, 60 Minutes* and *Cheers.*[7] Obviously, since soap opera drama has proven to be successful as a genre for many years, other areas must be explored to understand the recent ratings decline. One such factor has surely been the quick burnout of audience interest after the introduction of several of the highly controversial storylines mentioned earlier.

Usually themes of homosexuality and interracial relationships will earn astronomically high ratings initially (due to viewer curiosity). Their meteoric rise is usually followed by an equally dramatic fall, though, because these topics do not seem to generate a long-term fascination.

In addition to the controversial nature of nighttime storylines, other weaknesses must be considered to understand fully the true distinctions between daytime and nighttime soap operas. Because of several inherent differences, afternoon serials are better able to endure over many years. Prime-time soaps, on the other hand, are not destined for longevity.[8] Consider the following reasons:

1. Series Replication Overload. When *Dallas* enjoyed its huge success in 1978, networks raced to copy the formula of that success. By 1981, soap opera fans could choose an average of three hours of serial programming each night on Wednesdays, Thursdays and Fridays. However, as CBS President of Entertainment, B. Donald ("Bud") Grant noted: "Television always kills the goose that lays the golden egg. When a form works, it gets copied and viewers become saturated."[9] Thus, prime-time television's excessive duplication of the same basic plotlines, complete with cardboard heroes and villains (who differ only by business affiliation and location), may have hastened the demise of several well-intentioned serial dramas.

Like the nighttime soaps, all daytime dramas contain similar elements. But, as Chapters 3 and 4 have pointed out, there are some very specific individual differences, such as storyline pacing and characterization, that help viewers distinguish one program from another. Also, daytime soaps have moved away from the concept of defining their characters as totally "good" or totally "bad" (see Chapter 2) because they have learned that such an uncompromising attitude can restrict their long-term story plans. It is a lesson that prime-time needs to learn as well. Characters like Krystle Carrington and Alexis Carrington Colby Dexter of *Dynasty* have no real flexibility in their actions. The only question viewers usually have when they see them is *how* they will reflect their "goodness" or "badness" — not how they will *feel* in a specific situation. Despite the fine performances exhibited by both actresses in these roles (Linda Evans and Joan Collins, respectively), their inherent character limitations can cause them to become too predictable and uninteresting after awhile.

2. Viewer Boredom. Like all prime-time series, nighttime soap operas are now facing what is known as a "fatigue factor" on television. Network programming has always built its reputation on overnight successes, which are ultimately followed by overnight failures. After all, how much action and adventure can one show possibly create before it must repeat itself? And, since the overall pacing of prime-time television is so much faster than daytime drama, there is reason to believe that viewers also become tired of specific programs faster.

To their credit, nighttime soap operas have done fairly well, considering the odds against their success. Of the programs currently being broadcast, only *Love Boat* and *60 Minutes* have a longer history than *Dallas* — and *Love Boat* was cancelled after the 1986 season. Thus, it comes as no surprise that prime-time serial drama may be losing its grip in the ratings race.

3. *Actor Departures.* One of the greatest advantages to prime-time television is its ability to attract (and create) major celebrities. Unfortunately, however, this advantage can quickly become a liability when actors decide to leave the shows that brought them added fame, money and marketability. Probably the most dramatic example of the effect an actor's departure can have on a program was shown when *Dallas*'s ratings dropped significantly after actor Patrick Duffy, who played Bobby Ewing, left the show. Producers tried to create new characters like Matt, Bobby's best friend (Marc Singer), and Jack, Bobby's cousin (Dack Rambo), to replace him, but their attempts were largely unsuccessful. Eventually, Patrick Duffy was lured back to *Dallas* with increases in salary and artistic control, and the other characters were dropped from the program.

Afternoon soap opera producers often experience problems with actors who become strongly identified with specific characters. But in most cases, the daytime actors' departures are not as dramatic as those of their prime-time counterparts. As a matter of fact, sometimes daytime actors are confronted with a totally different problem — shedding their "soap opera" image after they've left the show. They often have a difficult time establishing their own name in place of their former character's identity. The reason behind this "identiy crisis" is that in daytime drama, actors are usually known for their portrayal of the characters; they are not hired for the celebrity status they will bring to the show, as in prime-time TV.

From time to time, however, daytime writers lose an actor whose character cannot be replaced, such as Don MacLaughlin as Chris Hughes on *As the World Turns* or Charita Bauer as Bert Bauer on *The Guiding Light*. In such cases, writers create scenarios where the characters die or leave town; a new character from the family usually arrives shortly afterwards to fill the family void.

4. *Competition from More Powerful Block Programming.* Unlike the afternoon programming block (which has previously been shown as a "low investment" time period), prime-time soap operas run the risk of bumping against very expensive, high-powered nighttime competition. There is no question that networks spend most of their money on prime-time television; and as the budget skyrockets, so does the potential quality and competitiveness of the programming. In addition, TV's viewing audience is more diverse at night, so shows can be more diverse and often more successful than the programming alternatives available during the daytime. As a result, shows like the slick police action/adventure series *Miami Vice* have successfully penetrated the ratings block formerly held by nighttime serials like *Falcon Crest*.

Since the monetary investment is so high in prime-time television, however, networks cannot afford to support a prime-time program while it goes through a dry spell of mediocrity. Consequently, shows such as *Falcon Crest* and *The Colbys* are more apt to face extinction than a soap opera like *Ryan's Hope* or *Search for Tomorrow,* even though each of the latter has had more significant declines in ratings over the years. In short, daytime serials may have smaller budgets with which to work, but they also have greater network patience over longer periods of time than nighttime soaps.

In summary, prime-time serial drama seems to be declining in viewer popularity, while daytime soap operas are stronger than ever.[10] And the influence of afternoon serials over other dimensions of American life is absolutely overwhelming. It is important to note the following:

• Most newspapers now run weekly summaries of all thirteen soaps.

• University English and Communication departments teach courses on soap opera analysis.

• Soap stars make numerous trips to state fairs, local TV talk shows and shopping malls, greeting thousands of fans wherever they go.

• A large telephone company offers a daily soap opera update called "Soap Scoop." It has proven to be profitable for several years already.

• Stores have noted an increase in sales of radios with a TV band so that fans can listen to their favorite soaps while at work.

• VCR sales are also rising rapidly, and one of their most popular features is their ability to tape serials while their owners are away.

• Dozens of soap opera and daytime TV fan magazines occupy space in crowded newsstands.

• A telephone soap opera called *Fair Oaks* is now available in selected areas of the country. For $.95, soap fans can listen to an original serial drama in 2½-minute segments each day.[11]

• Millions of dollars' worth of soap opera T-shirts, notepads, aprons, coffee mugs and shoelaces are sold annually.

• A popular board game based on *All My Children* now exists, with plans for future games if this one proves to be as profitable as is promised.

• Soap opera songs have risen on recording charts over the years. Among the most popular have been "General Hospital," "Nobody Loves Me Like You Do" (from *As the World Turns*), and "Friends and Lovers" (from *Days of Our Lives*).

• Plans exist for future network daytime dramas, serials on cable television, and even several syndicated shows.

Soap operas are unquestionably one of the most recognized genres on TV today. And, like their radio predecessors, they enjoy consistent audience devotion and popularity in a world where most success is as ephemeral as the last ratings period. Indeed, America's romance with daytime drama has endured for a very long time, and based on all the existing research available, the future of the afternoon soap is as secure as its past.

Appendix A
1983–1985 Content Analysis Survey

For purposes of studying thematic trends in daytime drama, weekly summaries of eleven soap opera plots were collected from two syndicated news sources (Jon-Michael Reed, in *The Detroit News,* and Noreen Rooney and Christine Schmuckal in the *Detroit Free Press*) between July 24, 1983, and July 22, 1985. The soap operas in this study included: *All My Children (AMC); Another World (AW); As the World Turns (ATWT); Capitol (C); Days of Our Lives (DOOL); General Hospital (GH); Guiding Light (GL); Loving (L); One Life to Live (OLTL); Ryan's Hope (RH);* and *The Young and the Restless (Y&R).* Research gathering was conducted in such a way as to let the categories emerge by extracting key words from sentences in the plot summaries. The resulting themes were then collected, enumerated and classified under major categories, if possible. In cases where there might be two or three categories for a theme, the context used most often was listed. For example, "rape" was used more in a personal, intimate sense than in a criminal environment; and "reconciliation" was a general term for friends, family and lovers. Thus, "rape" was listed under "romance/love/ sex" rather than "crime/punishment," and "reconciliation" was listed independently.

Table A.1 lists the themes and categories used in soap operas from 1983 to 1985. The numbers beside each theme indicate how many times they were used in the plotlines. Table A.2 gives theme/category breakdowns for each soap opera from 1983 to 1985. The numbers on the left represent occurrences from 1983 to 1984; the numbers on the right represent occurrences from 1984 to 1985.

TABLE A.1

THEMES AND CATEGORIES
USED IN SOAP OPERAS FROM 1983-1985

THEME/CATEGORY	1983/1984	1984/1985
PREGNANCY/CHILDREN		
Abortion	25	5
Adoption	31	14
Artificial Insemination	1	1
Baby	37	45
Birth Control	5	4
Custody	38	58
Miscarriage	11	22
Parenthood	298	230
ENGAGEMENT/MARRIAGE/ DIVORCE		
Annulment	9	2
Bridal Shower	1	-
Divorce	105	65
Elopement	10	6
Honeymoon	16	9
Househusband	3	-
Left at the altar	13	5
Marriage	133	94
Marriage Problems	50	114
Marriage Proposal	154	112
Prenuptial Agreement	4	4
TRAVEL		
International Travel	117	123
Investigation	159	246
Running Away	88	85
Surprise Visit	24	46
Vacation	33	18

Table A.1, continued

THEME/CATEGORY	1983/1984	1984/1985
CRIME/PUNISHMENT		
Arrest/Jail	125	128
Court Case	123	102
Crime	347	292
Crime Clue	206	168
False Identity	125	140
Fight	95	89
Fire/Bomb	47	44
Jailbreak	16	8
Kidnapping	42	70
Prostitution	17	28
Revenge	42	49
ROMANCE/LOVE/SEX		
Affair w/Relative	8	2
Gigolo	8	6
Homosexuality	7	1
Impotency	2	3
Jealous Lover	227	187
Making Love	72	74
Passion	37	36
Love	94	95
Rape	33	18
Rebounding	25	26
Romance	339	246
Romance Break-up	96	70
Romance Stumbling Block	143	112
Seduction	78	38
PERSONAL PROBLEMS		
Alcoholism/Drinking	59	81
Drugs	50	60
Drug Plant	10	8
Fantasies/Dreams	31	34
Diet	8	1
Gambling	16	19

Table A.1, continued

THEME/CATEGORY	1983/1984	1984/1985
"Ghosts"	19	20
Guilt	24	15
Psychological Problems	122	91

MYSTERY/INTRIGUE

Blackmail	106	104
Bribery	41	28
Deception	391	236
Hero-Villain	103	118
Secret	381	412
Mysterious /Threat/Obscene Call	15	20
Bugging/Eavesdropping	79	134

FINANCE/PROFESSIONAL

Business	106	142
Firing	50	32
Job	379	364
Media	98	101
Money	231	206
Suspension	22	14

ILLNESS/MEDICAL

Amnesia	12	31
Autopsy	1	5
Death	131	159
Grave	1	10
Illness/Injury	295	297
Surgery	72	37

MISCELLANEOUS

Airplane Trouble	5	8
Car Crash	18	13
Character Leaving	64	60

Table A.1, continued

THEME/CATEGORY	1983/1984	1984/1985
Character Returns	70	74
Disappointment	9	1
Fear	42	55
Friendship	102	86
Graduation	7	1
Gifts	25	36
Independence	4	-
Jealousy	33	24
New Character	68	78
Party	63	69
Political Election	43	12
Reconciliation	109	135
Rejection	146	91
Trust	39	20

TABLE A. 2
THEME AND CATEGORY BREAKDOWN
FOR EACH SOAP OPERA, 1983-1985

	AMC	AW	ATWT	C
PREGNANCY/CHILDREN				
Abortion	4/1	-/2	2/-	3/-
Adoption	8/-	6/-	5/3	1/5˙
Artificial Insemination	-/-	-/-	1/-	-/-
Baby	2/4	4/3	8/6	7/5
Birth Control	2/1	-/-	1/-	-/-
Custody	-/2	1/-	5/13	-/9
Miscarriage	-/7	-/-	-/1	1/-
Parenthood	21/24	14/9	39/18	31/15
ROMANCE/LOVE/SEX				
Affair with Relative	1/-	-/-	1/-	1/-
Gigolo	5/3	-/-	1/-	2/-
Homosexuality	7/-	-/-	-/-	-/-
Impotency	-/-	-/-	1/1	-/-
Jealous Lover	27/30	8/11	10/12	34/21
Making Love	14/7	1/2	7/4	4/6
Passion	8/6	-/1	1/3	4/3
Love	7/10	9/7	9/9	4/10
Rape	7/1	-/1	-/4	1/-
Rebounding	2/8	2/-	1/-	3/1
Romance	43/23	28/19	30/26	37/25
Romance Break-up	7/4	10/2	5/9	11/4
Romance Stumbling Block	7/10	3/6	20/16	28/16
Seduction	21/8	5/3	7/5	3/1
ENGAGEMENT/MARRIAGE/				
DIVORCE				
Annulment	1/-	-/-	2/2	-/-
Bridal Shower	1/-	-/-	-/-	-/-
Divorce	13/14	2/4	12/2	8/3
Elopement	2/-	-/-	-/-	-/2
Honeymoon	3/4	2/2	1/2	3/-
Househusband	1/-	-/-	2/-	-/-
Left at the Altar	3/11	2/-	2/1	-/-

DOOL	GH	GL	L	OLTL	RH	Y&R
-/-	-/-	3/2	9/-	-/-	1/-	3/-
2/1	3/-	-/3	1/-	1/2	3/-	1/-
-/-	-/-	-/-	-/-	-/-	-/1	-/-
2/6	-/-	4/6	1/6	3/6	2/1	4/2
1/-	-/-	1/-	-/-	-/2	-/-	1/-
2/3	13/5	-/3	-/5	2/10	7/5	8/3
-/-	1/4	2/4	3/2	-/-	1/2	3/2
7/12	27/15	33/46	31/23	25/20	32/9	38/39
1/-	-/-	-/-	1/-	1/1	-/-	2/1
-/-	-/-	-/1	-/-	-/-	-/1	-/1
-/-	-/-	-/1	-/-	-/-	-/-	-/-
-/-	-/2	-/-	-/-	-/-	-/-	1/-
21/17	13/29	21/8	20/13	26/9	27/15	20/22
4/8	4/10	10/8	8/9	6/4	10/13	4/3
3/2	3/1	4/6	5/3	5/3	-/5	4/3
8/10	4/3	17/10	9/11	10/9	9/8	8/8
3/2	3/-	11/2	6/-	-/4	2/1	-/3
3/2	2/5	2/3	3/2	2/3	2/1	3/1
35/27	19/21	23/16	35/28	42/25	37/7	30/29
11/7	2/4	12/10	11/10	11/9	7/5	9/6
12/13	15/6	10/11	14/14	5/7	13/10	16/3
9/4	5/2	3/4	9/3	6/1	6/3	4/4
-/-	1/-	1/-	-/-	3/-	1/-	-/-
-/-	-/-	-/-	-/-	-/-	-/-	-/-
2/3	5/6	18/5	21/14	9/6	1/4	14/4
1/2	-/-	-/-	1/-	2/2	1/-	3/-
1/-	1/-	2/-	-/-	-/-	1/1	2/-
-/-	-/-	-/-	-/-	-/-	-/-	-/-
1/1	-/-	1/-	-/2	3/-	-/-	1/-

Table A.2, continued

	AMC	AW	ATWT	C
Marriage	16/15	10/8	12/9	5/2
Marriage Problems	3/18	4/9	11/5	5/16
Marriage Proposal	17/22	9/5	13/15	13/6
Prenuptial Agreement	2/-	1/-	-/-	-/-
PERSONAL PROBLEMS				
Alcoholism/Drinking	15/5	3/1	4/3	2/5
Drugs	11/7	21/16	15/2	-/5
Drug Plant	1/2	4/1	1/-	-/-
Fantasies/Dreams	-/4	2/4	3/5	9/5
Diet	-/-	-/-	2/-	-/-
Gambling	7/-	-/2	-/9	4/3
"Ghosts"	1/5	-/3	-/-	1/-
Guilt	-/1	3/-	2/2	3/2
Psychological Problems	22/9	6/10	10/14	10/4
TRAVEL				
International Travel	12/10	12/8	14/9	14/11
Investigation	9/15	22/21	24/37	27/24
Running Away	10/12	6/4	16/9	5/7
Surprise Visit	1/4	1/3	2/7	-/5
Vacation	8/5	-/-	3/1	1/3
MYSTERY/INTRIGUE				
Blackmail	7/22	11/3	10/2	9/9
Bribery	1/3	4/-	7/3	4/4
Deception	34/36	31/8	65/18	36/19
Hero-Villain	15/12	4/20	14/12	2/10
Secret	34/41	18/35	43/35	43/41
Mys./Threat./Obscene Call	1/3	1/3	-/2	2/2
Bugging Eavesdropping	-/17	5/14	6/10	3/13
CRIME/PUNISHMENT				
Arrest/Jail	14/17	11/9	18/18	5/3
Court Case	3/15	20/5	13/10	3/9
Crime	42/25	32/24	31/20	29/12
Crime Clue	13/9	16/27	14/27	14/14
False Identity	1/4	8/15	16/6	11/16

DOOL	GH	GL	L	OLTL	RH	Y&R
13/8	4/13	14/11	7/8	16/8	12/5	18/7
3/11	8/13	3/9	3/15	3/3	3/7	4/8
24/9	6/8	22/12	6/7	18/14	10/8	16/6
-/1	-/1	1/-	-/-	-/-	-/2	-/-
3/3	4/1	9/11	6/7	-/1	8/4	5/9
2/8	5/6	7/12	2/-	6/1	1/1	11/2
1/3	-/1	3/-	-/-	-/-	-/1	-/-
7/2	-/1	3/2	-/2	-/2	5/6	2/1
-/-	-/-	1/-	-/-	-/-	-/1	5/-
-/-	5/-	-/4	-/-	-/1	-/-	-/-
8/-	1/-	2/6	2/2	3/1	1/1	-/2
4/1	5/4	2/3	3/-	1/-	1/1	-/1
7/6	10/9	13/12	34/3	1/17	2/5	7/2
7/13	14/14	7/13	4/1	10/13	15/10	8/11
18/25	4/29	13/23	1/10	16/22	11/15	14/25
13/8	9/6	10/8	5/9	8/10	7/4	8/4
6/4	1/4	1/3	1/1	5/6	5/8	1/1
6/1	3/2	2/2	2/-	2/1	1/-	5/2
11/3	6/15	13/13	9/10	6/3	10/2	14/22
6/1	4/1	1/3	-/3	9/5	1/-	4/5
44/21	33/22	17/30	25/16	43/20	35/22	28/24
14/15	12/7	9/16	2/3	9/12	10/7	14/4
37/28	23/47	40/50	37/19	4/47	29/26	33/43
5/-	-/2	1/-	2/5	1/2	-/1	2/1
6/7	8/13	9/16	7/4	8/15	18/16	9/9
23/13	10/13	12/13	5/8	15/17	7/11	5/6
13/9	23/13	13/8	10/2	11/7	4/21	10/3
44/50	41/43	27/25	11/20	43/34	22/24	25/15
39/20	20/19	17/19	14/7	27/15	16/9	16/2
18/19	21/7	9/4	3/20	18/17	11/12	9/20

Table A.2, continued

	AMC	AW	ATWT	C
Fight	5/10	7/5	6/8	2/7
Fire/Bomb	5/5	3/4	7/8	-/-
Jailbreak	1/-	2/1	1/-	1/-
Kidnapping	5/9	1/7	8/9	1/-
Prostitution	2/4	2/3	-/-	3/-
Revenge	1/5	5/3	2/8	2/1
FINANCE/PROFESSIONAL				
Business	15/9	15/10	14/12	6/4
Firing	3/6	3/2	1/2	2/4
Job	31/30	39/28	33/34	19/42
Media	2/15	5/3	10/6	17/23
Money	17/36	21/21	17/22	10/14
Suspension	3/2	-/1	5/3	-/-
ILLNESS/MEDICAL				
Amnesia	-/2	-/5	-/4	-/-
Autopsy	-/-	1/-	-/2	-/-
Death	6/14	18/10	8/22	5/12
Grave	-/2	-/-	-/3	1/2
Illness/Injury	17/38	22/29	37/31	39/22
Surgery	2/1	1/3	10/6	9/12
MISCELLANEOUS				
Airplane Trouble	-/1	1/1	1/-	1/-
Car Crash	3/2	2/4	1/2	1/1
Character Leaving	11/6	7/5	4/5	2/6
Character Returns	13/7	7/9	5/7	3/4
Disappointment	3/-	-/-	-/-	2/-
Fear	1/8	-/4	-/9	6/4
Friendship	21/5	10/7	11/9	11/9
Graduation	1/-	-/1	-/-	-/-
Gifts	4/3	1/3	3/2	4/3
Independence	2/-	-/-	1/-	1/-
Jealousy	2/3	1/1	3/3	5/3
New Character	5/6	3/9	8/9	3/8
Party	4/7	6/6	4/4	13/8
Political Election	1/2	-/-	-/-	15/6
Reconciliation	9/14	7/4	13/21	11/8
Rejection	4/16	13/6	19/13	8/4
Trust	1/1	2/-	4/-	2/-

DOOL	GH	GL	L	OLTL	RH	Y&R
11/21	13/12	19/7	11/4	7/6	6/5	8/4
7/6	9/1	7/8	-/-	4/8	5/3	-/1
10/1	-/-	-/2	-/2	1/2	-/-	-/-
7/6	7/4	1/14	2/5	3/10	2/4	5/2
2/12	2/-	2/4	1/-	1/-	2/-	-/5
6/7	5/4	3/3	5/5	7/3	1/7	5/3
7/12	14/11	8/22	7/28	13/17	4/12	3/5
4/2	9/1	4/7	11/3	7/-	3/4	3/1
11/33	39/26	37/33	31/34	68/28	38/43	33/33
3/5	15/12	6/4	9/5	14/16	10/7	7/5
14/9	25/26	21/19	25/13	36/24	16/10	29/12
-/1	4/1	3/4	4/-	2/2	1/-	-/-
3/-	3/2	2/6	-/1	4/3	-/1	-/7
-/-	-/2	-/1	-/-	-/-	-/-	-/-
20/23	15/13	14/15	6/13	15/15	9/12	15/10
-/-	-/-	-/3	-/-	-/-	-/-	-/-
12/28	20/29	52/42	17/27	27/18	31/11	21/22
3/1	12/2	14/7	1/-	2/2	8/2	10/1
-/1	-/-	-/1	1/-	-/1	1/3	-/-
1/2	3/1	1/-	-/1	2/-	1/-	3/-
2/5	10/6	6/9	5/-	5/10	8/9	4/9
11/5	5/6	-/9	4/6	7/9	4/4	1/8
1/-	-/-	-/1	-/-	3/-	-/-	-/-
5/5	6/6	4/-	5/7	4/6	4/2	7/4
3/9	6/8	10/12	10/6	7/7	6/5	7/9
2/-	2/-	-/-	-/-	1/-	-/-	-/-
1/4	-/3	1/3	2/1	2/4	2/1	5/4
-/-	-/-	-/-	-/-	-/-	-/-	-/-
2/2	5/1	2/2	-/4	5/-	3/1	5/4
8/10	12/8	8/11	12/4	4/8	1/3	4/2
7/6	2/11	6/12	8/2	2/3	9/8	2/2
2/2	13/-	5/2	4/-	-/-	3/-	-/-
5/7	15/23	8/10	8/12	12/14	5/8	16/14
10/4	13/9	19/16	24/4	16/7	10/5	10/7
3/1	2/2	3/2	3/8	2/2	2/2	5/2

Appendix B
1985 Viewer Attitude Survey

To better understand today's soap opera audience, a random survey of 600 subjects was taken during the last week of November, 1985. Interviewees were asked how much television they watched; which daytime programs they preferred; and, if they were soap opera viewers, why they chose to watch specific soap operas. The following questionnaire and tables represent the results gathered.

DAYTIME PROGRAMMING QUESTIONNAIRE

Interview Number: _____   Age: _____   Gender: Male   Female (circle one)

1. When you have a "free" afternoon during the week, how do you usually spend your time?

_____(A) watching television

_____(B) doing work inside your house/apartment

_____(C) going to a film

_____(D) doing some outside activity (specify) _____

_____(E) other (specify) _____

(NOTE: IF THE ABOVE ANSWER INCLUDED "WATCHING TELEVISION," PLEASE PROCEED TO THE NEXT QUESTION.)

2. What does most of your daytime viewing consist of? Please rank in order of preference.

_____(A) soap operas   _____(D) cartoons

_____(B) game shows   _____(E) other (specify)_____

_____(C) movies   _____

(NOTE: IF THE ABOVE ANSWER INCLUDED "SOAP OPERAS," PLEASE PROCEED TO THE NEXT QUESTION.)

3. Which soap operas do you watch consistently? (Check each one—there is no limit.)

____(A) All My Children ____(H) Loving
____(B) Another World ____(I) One Life to Live
____(C) As the World Turns ____(J) Ryan's Hope
____(D) Capitol ____(K) Santa Barbara
____(E) Days of Our Lives ____(L) Search for Tomorrow
____(F) General Hospital ____(M) Young/Restless
____(G) Guiding Light

4. Which would most aptly describe your economic class?

____(A) lower ____(D) upper-middle
____(B) lower-middle ____(E) upper
____(C) middle

5. Which would most aptly describe your educational level?

____(A) elementary school ____(D) college
____(B) high school ____(E) master's
____(C) community college ____(F) Ph.D.

6. In order of importance (1 = most important; 5 = least important), why do you watch your favorite soap opera? Please answer this question for every soap you watch regularly.

Name of Soap Opera _____
____(A) I like the characters
____(B) The plots are interesting
____(C) The program agrees with my schedule
____(D) My friends watch it
____(E) I "grew up" watching it

Name of Soap Opera _____
____(A) I like the characters
____(B) The plots are interesting
____(C) The program agrees with my schedule
____(D) My friends watch it
____(E) I "grew up" watching it

Name of Soap Opera _____
____(A) I like the characters
____(B) The plots are interesting
____(C) The program agrees with my schedule
____(D) My friends watch it
____(E) I "grew up" watching it

Appendix B

TABLE B.1

PREFERENCES FOR DAYTIME ACTIVITIES*

(A) watching television
(B) doing work inside house/apartment
(C) going to films
(D) doing an outside activity
(E) other

GENDER/AGE	(A)	(B)	(C)	(D)	(E)
Totals: 1-10 (24)	29.2	-	-	45.8	33.3
Males 1-10 (12)	41.7	-	-	50	25
Females 1-10 (12)	16.7	-	-	41.7	41.7
Totals: 11-20 (187)	77	12.3	2.1	25.7	19.8
Males 11-20 (59)	59.3	15.2	1.7	35.6	25.4
Females 11-20 (128)	85.2	10.9	2.3	21.1	17.2
Totals: 21-40 (249)	69.5	26.9	4	26.1	14.9
Males 21-40 (93)	59.1	18.3	5.4	35.5	12.9
Females 21-40 (156)	75.6	32.1	3.2	20.5	16
Totals: 41-60 (99)	47.5	46.5	-	31.3	10.1
Males 41-60 (36)	30.6	36.1	-	52.8	11.1
Females 41-60 (63)	57.1	52.4	-	19	9.5
Totals: 61+ (42)	54.8	35.8	2.4	19	28.6
Males 61+ (16)	50	31.2	6.3	25	25
Females 61+ (26)	57.7	38.5	-	15.4	30.8

*NOTE: The numbers in parentheses indicate the actual numbers of persons surveyed in each age/gender group. Column figures are expressed in percentages.

TABLE B.2

VIEWER'S CHOICE OF VIEWING*

(A) Soap Operas
(B) Game Shows
(C) Movies
(D) Cartoons
(E) Other**

GENDER/AGE	(A)	(B)	(C)	(D)	(E)
Totals 1-10 (7)	42.9	42.9	14.3	100	14.3
Males 1-10 (5)	40	40	20	100	20
Females 1-10 (2)	50	50	-	100	-
Totals 11-20 (144)	82.6	14.6	5.6	12.5	11.1
Males 11-20 (35)	51.4	20	14.3	34.3	17.1
Females 11-20 (109)	92.7	12.8	2.8	5.5	9.2
Totals 21-40 (173)	79.2	15.6	12.7	11	12.7
Males 21-40 (55)	47.3	18.2	21.8	27.3	30.9
Females 21-40 (118)	94.1	14.4	8.5	3.4	4.2
Totals 41-60 (47)	74.5	12.8	21.3	4.4	6.4
Males 41-60 (11)	27.3	27.3	54.5	18.2	18.2
Females 41-60 (36)	88.9	8.3	11.1	-	2.8
Totals 61+ (22)	54.5	40.9	27.3	-	13.6
Males 61+ (7)	42.9	57.1	28.6	-	-
Females 61+ (15)	60	33.3	26.7	-	20

*NOTE: The numbers in parentheses indicate the actual numbers of persons who selected "watching television" as one of their choices. Column figures are expressed as percentages. The total percentages will equal more than 100 percent because many listed two, three, or four choices.
**"Other" included news, PBS, Sports, MTV, old reruns, talk shows and first-run syndications.

TABLE B.3

WHY PEOPLE WATCH SOAP OPERAS*

(A) I like the characters
(B) The plots are interesting
(C) The program agrees with my schedule
(D) My friends watch it
(E) I "grew up" watching it

AGE GROUP SOAP OPERA	(A)	(B)	(C)	(D)	(E)
Total 1–10					
All My Children	-	-	-	-	-
Another World	4	1	3	5	2
As the World Turns	-	-	-	-	-
Capitol	-	-	-	-	-
Days of Our Lives	4	1	3	5	2
General Hospital	-	-	-	-	-
Guiding Light	-	-	-	-	-
Loving	-	-	-	-	-
One Life to Live	-	-	-	-	-
Ryan's Hope	-	-	-	-	-
Santa Barbara	3.5	1	3	4	3
Search for Tomorrow	-	-	-	-	-
Young and Restless	-	-	-	-	-
Total 11–20					
All My Children	2.2	2.2	3.2	3.6	4
Another World	2	2.7	4.7	3.3	2.7
As the World Turns	1.5	2	5	4	2.5
Capitol	2.7	3.5	2.7	3.5	5
Days of Our Lives	2.1	2.1	5	3.4	4
General Hospital	2.9	2.5	3.1	3.3	3.2
Guiding Light	2.1	2	2.9	4.4	4.2
Loving	1.9	1.9	2.6	3.4	4.6
One Life to Live	2.4	2.4	3	3.5	3.7
Ryan's Hope	1.6	2	3.6	3.6	4
Santa Barbara	2	1.8	3	4.2	4
Search for Tomorrow	2	1	3	5	4
Young and Restless	1.8	1.3	3.3	4.2	4.3
Total 21–40					
All My Children	2.5	1.6	3.4	3.9	3.8
Another World	2.2	1.4	2.6	4.6	4.2

*NOTE: Persons were asked to rank their preferences, "1" being most important, through "5" which was least important. In some cases, the averages add up to more than 15 (the totals of one through five). This was because some people may have marked three "1"s, "2"s, etc., or simply marked nothing after their first two choices.

Table B.3, continued

AGE GROUP SOAP OPERA	(A)	(B)	(C)	(D)	(E)
As the World Turns	2.3	1.9	2.8	4.6	3.5
Capitol	2.1	1.6	3.1	3.8	4
Days of Our Lives	2.4	2	3.1	3.7	3.4
General Hospital	3.2	2	2.9	3.7	3.5
Guiding Light	2	1.6	3.9	3.9	3.7
Loving	2.1	1.4	3	4.1	4.5
One Life to Live	2.2	1.9	2.9	4.3	3.8
Ryan's Hope	2	1.8	3.1	4.2	4
Santa Barbara	-	-	-	-	-
Search for Tomorrow	-	-	-	-	-
Young and Restless	2.5	1.4	2.9	3.9	4.5
Total 41–60					
All My Children	2.5	1.5	2.6	4.1	4.2
Another World	1.5	2	3.3	4.5	3.8
As the World Turns	1.7	2	3.3	5	3
Capitol	1	2	3	4	5
Days of Our Lives	2	1.4	2.6	4	5
General Hospital	2.4	1.8	2.4	4	4.7
Guiding Light	2	1.7	3.3	4	4.3
Loving	-	-	-	-	-
One Life to Live	2.8	2.2	2.1	3.3	3.7
Ryan's Hope	2	1	3	4	5
Santa Barbara	2	1	3	4	5
Search for Tomorrow	-	-	-	-	-
Young and Restless	2.5	1.5	2.5	3.5	5
Total 61+					
All My Children	2	3	4	3	3
Another World	2.5	1.5	2.8	4.5	3.8
As the World Turns	2.3	2	2.8	4.3	4
Capitol	2.5	2.5	2.5	5	2.5
Days of Our Lives	2	1	3.5	4	4.5
General Hospital	1	2.5	2.5	4	5
Guiding Light	2	1.8	3	4	4.2
Loving	1	2	3	5	4
One Life to Live	1	2	3	4	5
Ryan's Hope	-	-	-	-	-
Santa Barbara	1	2	3	4	5
Search for Tomorrow	2	1	3	4	5
Young and Restless	-	-	-	-	-

Chapter Notes

Introduction

[1] Robert C. Allen, *Speaking of Soap Operas* (Chapel Hill: University of North Carolina Press, 1985), p. 3.

[2] Ibid., pp. 20-21.

[3] Ibid., p. 21.

[4] Paul F. Lazarsfeld and Frank N. Stanton, eds., *Radio Research: 1942-1943* (New York: Essential, 1944).

[5] Research from Lazarsfeld's Bureau of Applied Social Research included: Herta Herzog, "What Do We Really Know About Daytime Serial Listeners?", in *Radio Research: 1942-1943*, pp. 3-33; Rudolf Arnheim, "The World of the Daytime Serial," in *Radio Research: 1942-1943*, pp. 34-85; and Helen J. Kaufman, "The Appeal of Specific Daytime Serials," in *Radio Research: 1942-1943*, pp. 86-107.

[6] Muriel G. Cantor and Suzanne Pingree, *The Soap Opera* (Beverly Hills, Ca.: Sage, 1983).

[7] Natan Katzman, "Television Soap Operas: What's Been Going On, Anyway?", *Public Opinion Quarterly* 36 (Summer 1972), 200-212.

[8] Rose Goldsen, "Throwaway Husbands, Wives and Lovers," *Human Behavior* 35 (December 1976), 64-69.

[9] Bradley S. Greenberg, R. Abelman, and Kimberly Neuendorf, "Sex on the Soap Opera: Afternoon Delight," *Journal of Communication* 31 (Summer 1981), 83-89.

[10] Mary Cassata and Thomas Skill, *Life on Daytime Television: Tuning-In American Serial Drama* (Norwood, N.J.: Ablex, 1983).

[11] From 1983-1985, eleven daytime dramas were studied via content analysis. The programs included in this research were *All My Children, Another World, As the World Turns, Capitol, Days of Our Lives, General Hospital, Guiding Light, Loving, One Life to Live, Ryan's Hope,* and *The Young and the Restless.* Results from this content analysis may be found in Appendix A. During the same period, several other daytime dramas aired, but were not included in the study for various reasons. *Edge of Night* was cancelled before the research was completed. *Rituals* and *Santa Barbara* debuted several weeks after the data collection had begun; *Rituals* was subsequently cancelled within a year. *Search for Tomorrow* was not consistently summarized, so the data were not considered reliable enough to determine thematic trends.

201

Chapter One. The Plots

[1]Robert Laguardia, *Soap World* (New York: Arbor House, 1983), p. 9.

[2]Muriel Cantor and Suzanne Pingree, *The Soap Opera* (Beverly Hills, Ca.: Sage, 1983), pp. 36–37.

[3]J. Fred MacDonald, *Don't Touch that Dial: Radio Programming in American Life from 1920 to 1960* (Chicago: Nelson-Hall, 1979), p. 233.

[4]LaGuardia, p. 12.

[5]Ibid., p. 20.

[6]MacDonald, p. 235.

[7]Ibid., pp. 241–243.

[8]Ibid., p. 243.

[9]Rudolf Arnheim, "The World of the Daytime Serial," in *Radio Research: 1942–1943,* eds. Paul F. Lazarsfeld and Frank N. Stanton (New York: Essential, 1944), pp. 38–85.

[10]Ibid., pp. 38–39.

[11]MacDonald, pp. 243–244.

[12]Arnheim, pp. 38–39.

[13]Ibid., p. 71.

[14]Ibid., pp. 81–85.

[15]To conduct this study, weekly summaries of eleven soap operas were collected from two sources (Jon-Michael Reed and Noreen Rooney and Christine Schmuckal) between July 24, 1983, and July 22, 1985. Research gathering was conducted in such a way as to let the categories emerge by extracting key words from sentences in the plot summaries. Because the writers from both sources remained constant, word choices also seemed constant. Two summaries for each plot each week also served as checks and balances for each other, and, as such, contributed to the reliability of the study.

Arnheim's data-gathering methods were quite different from those employed in this content analysis. Arnheim used 47 students; 39 female and 8 male. Each listened to one radio serial for three weeks from March 17 to April 17, 1941. For every daily installment reviewed, a report sheet was completed. Forty-three soap operas were covered in his survey.

Because today's soap operas are less numerous (though longer) than those studied forty years ago, the researcher felt that the content analysis should cover a longer period of time to compensate in numbers. Also, despite Arnheim's chosen method, he acknowledged the importance of content analysis at the outset of his study. His reason for choosing report sheets was simply a matter of expediency.

[16]LaGuardia, p. 39.

[17]See Tables 1 and 2, Appendix A.

[18]The lesbian plotline occurred from weeks November 21, 1983, to December 30, 1983. After that time, the character (played by Donna Peskow) left Pine Valley, never to return again. However, *All My Children* was not alone in trying controversial plots and subsequently dropping them. Other controversial issues in daytime drama which were tried and then abandoned from 1983 to 1985 incuded artificial insemination, birth control, abortion, impotence, life as a househusband and anorexia.

[19]MacDonald, p. 235.

Chapter Two. The Characters

[1]Robert J. Landry, "The Soaps Then and Now," *Variety,* 11 January 1984, p. 170.

[2]Today, a similar situation occurs in televised cartoons. Actors read from their scripts (rather than memorizing them), and may assume two, three, or more characters in the story. This is because the audience cannot differentiate the character from the voice.

[3]Landry, p. 170.

[4]"Sex and Suffering in the Afternoon," *Time* (January 12, 1976): 52.

[5]Christopher Schemering, *The Soap Opera Encyclopedia* (New York: Ballantine, 1985), pp. 315–317.

[6]Dan Wakefield, *All Her Children* (New York: Avon, 1976), pp. 41–43.

[7]Marc Gunther, "Peter Reckell's a Big Star. That's the Problem...," *The Detroit News,* 16 March 1986, p. F1.

[8]Rudolf Arnheim, "The World of the Daytime Serial," in *Radio Research: 1942–1943,* eds. Paul F. Lazarsfeld and Frank N. Stanton (New York: Essential, 1944), p. 50.

[9]Ibid., footnote 8, pp. 50–51.

[10]Ibid., p. 52.

[11]Ibid., p. 51.

[12]Edith Efron, "The Soaps—Anything but 99-44/100 Percent Pure," in *Television,* 4th ed., ed. Barry G. Cole (New York: Free Press, 1973), pp. 156–162.

[13]Ibid., p. 157.

[14]Ibid., p. 159.

[15]Mary Cassata and Thomas Skill, *Life on Daytime Television: Tuning-In American Serial Drama* (Norwood, N.J.: Ablex, 1983), p. 33.

[16]Leslie Rubinstein, "Confessions of a Soap Opera Addict," *McCall's* (March 1986): 84–90.

[17]Wakefield, pp. 62–63.

[18]Ibid., p. 65.

[19]The amount of personal versus professional activity varied from serial to serial, but most daytime dramas showed a preference for personal drama rather than professional problem-solving.

[20]This feature, the common person acting more expert than the expert, is a well-established phenomenon in crime books. See Arnheim, p. 64.

[21]Ibid., pp. 43–44.

[22]"The Code of Sudsville," *Time* (March 20, 1972): 94.

[23]Marya Mannes, "Everything's Up-to-Date in Soap Operas," in Cole, pp. 163–164.

[24]Terry Ann Knopf, "Daytime Money and Power on the Soaps," *Boston Globe TV Week,* 1 February 1981, p. 12.

[25]Ibid., "Politicians: New Soap Scoundrels," *Boston Globe TV Week,* 22 March 1981, p. 10.

[26]Since many of the characters fit into more than one category, these percentages reflect a total higher than 100 percent.

[27]Arnheim, p. 42.

[28]Robert LaGuardia, *Soap World* (New York: Arbor House, 1983), p. 238.

[29]Schemering, p. 3.

[30]Michelle Lynn Rondina, Mary Cassata and Thomas Skill, "Placing a 'Lid' on Television Serial Drama: An Analysis of the Lifestyles, Interpersonal Management Skills, and Demography of Daytime's Fictional Population," in Cassata and Skill, pp. 3–21. It is important to note that the researchers defined "primary" as the main characters in today's soaps; "secondary" types occurred less often, but were extremely important in storyline development. Also worthy of mention is that the authors developed this classification model by looking at results from other studies,

and modifying their study accordingly. The two previous works which most influenced Rondina, Cassata and Skill's lifestyle research were:

1) Ronald Frank and Marshal Greenberg, *The Public's Use of Television* (Beverly Hills, Ca.: Sage, 1980). Frank and Greenberg included nine elements in their profiles: being socially stimulating; status enhancement, unique creative achievement; escape from problems; family ties; understanding others; greater self-acceptance; escape from boredom; and intellectual stimulation and growth.

2) Philip Kotler, *Principles of Marketing* (Englewood Cliffs, N.J.: Prentice-Hall, 1980). In this book, Kotler cited a Chicago-based ad agency which developed eight lifestyle categories: successful professional; chic suburbanite; elegant socialite; traditional family man; militant mother; frustrated laborer; happy homemaker; and retiring homebody. While these classifications were initially designed to describe consumer groups (not fictional characters), Rondina *et al.* felt it served as a good basis from which to categorize soap opera characters.

[31]Rondina, Cassata and Skill, pp. 15–16.

[32]Ibid., p. 20.

[33]Knopf, 1 February 1981.

[34]Alice Burdick Schweiger, "*Loving:* Ann Arbor Actress Enjoys Juicy Role on Soap," *Detroit Free Press,* 9 January 1986, p. 1B.

Chapter Three. The Audience

[1]James Thurber, *The Beast and Me* (New York: Hearst Corporation, 1948).

[2]Muriel G. Cantor and Suzanne Pingree, *The Soap Opera* (Beverly Hills, Ca.: Sage, 1983), p. 116.

[3]Hooper ultimately went out of business, and A.C. Nielsen eventually concentrated all of its efforts in television. Today, A.C. Nielsen provides only TV ratings; Arbitron services both radio and television.

[4]Bettelou Peterson, "Services Compete to Tell Who Is Watching the TV Shows," *Detroit Free Press,* 9 February 1986, p. 46.

[5]A "rating" is the percentage of persons tuned in to a specific show as compared with all the households in the area that contain television sets (whether on or off); a "share" is the percentage of persons tuned in to a specific show as compared to all households with television in use at the time. Understandably, a "rating" is always lower than a share; and the ratings during daytime hours are always lower than at night. For this reason, evening hours are referred to as "prime-time."

[6]Todd Gitlin, *Inside Prime Time* (New York: Pantheon, 1985), p. 49.

[7]Herbert H. Howard and Michael S. Kievman, *Radio and TV Programming* (Columbus, Oh.: Grid, 1983), pp. 167–171.

[8]According to Howard and Kievman (pp. 210–211), weekly network schedules are divided into six program blocks: evening prime-time (8:00 pm–11:00 pm EST, Monday through Saturday, and 7:00 pm–11:00 pm Sundays); evening news (one half-hour each day); daytime (10:00 am–4:00 pm EST, Monday through Friday); early morning (7:00 am–9:00 am EST, Monday through Friday); late night (11:30 pm–1:00 am or 1:30 am EST, Monday through Friday); and weekend daytime (Saturday and Sunday mornings and afternoons).

[9]According to Howard and Kievman, this direct mail company also updates all of the phone directories in the country, some of which are selected by Arbitron.

[10]Cantor and Pingree, p. 117.

[11]Todd Gitlin, *Inside Prime Time* (New York: Pantheon, 1985), pp. 47–55.

[12]Ibid., pp. 49–50.

[13]Ibid., p. 54.

[14]Ibid., pp. 32–42.

[15]Sometimes these questionnaires ask open-ended questions, but they are usually yes/no or multiple choice.

[16]Gitlin, p. 33.

[17]Ibid., p. 37.

[18]Ibid., p. 40.

[19]Robert C. Allen, *Speaking of Soap Operas* (Chapel Hill: University of North Carolina Press, 1985), pp. 135–136.

[20]This study was conducted by fifty broadcast programming students in November, 1985. The students distributed 600 questionnaires to random subjects, attempting to answer the following questions:

1) Who watches daytime television?

2) Of those who watch daytime television, which program types are most popular?

3) Who watches which soap operas?

4) How many soap operas does the average viewer watch?

5) Why do people watch soap operas?

The sample questionnaire and several tables which illustrate the results are found in Appendix B.

[21]Allen, pp. 135–136.

[22]Ibid., p. 136.

[23]Herta Herzog, "What We Know About Daytime Serial Listeners," in *Radio Research: 1942–1943*, eds. Paul F. Lazarsfeld and Frank N. Stanton (New York: Essential, 1944), pp. 3–33.

[24]Herzog made an interesting observation while testing for phone use in her "sophistication index." When comparing women of the same economic level who owned phones to those who did not, she found more serial listening was done by non-phone households. Because the Hooper ratings service conducted all of its interviews by phone, Herzog felt that the daytime serial audience was vastly underrated. (See Herzog, p. 9, footnote 3.)

[25]Ibid., pp. 8–12.

[26]Actually persons 61 and over were more active in each category than the other age groups. Perhaps this was due to their large amount of discretionary time as compared with younger adults.

[27]In all studies dealing with randomly selected subjects, researchers run the risk of creating samples which are not totally representative. In this study, 600 people were randomly selected in several areas of the country. However, because college students served as the data-gatherers, it is possible that the resulting sample was somewhat skewed educationally and economically. This does not take away from the fact that today's viewers are educationally and economically better off than in the forties—other studies have confirmed this trend. However, it is important to note that the percentages may be higher in this analysis than in other research.

[28]Helen J. Kaufman, "The Appeal of Specific Daytime Serials," in Lazarsfeld and Stanton, pp. 86–107.

[29]Kaufman used two surveys for this study, and defined "young" as women up to 35; "old" meant women over 35 years of age.

[30]According to Kaufman, Helen Trent remained 35 for several years—the lack of visibility in radio made this easier to accomplish.

[31]Ibid., pp. 95–96. While found in Kaufman's study, these quotations are actually taken from a study done by Herta Herzog entitled, "On Borrowed Experience," in *Studies in Philosophy and Social Science,* 1941.

[32]Several soap operas were not summarized for various reasons. *Loving,* according to the survey, showed no real distinction in any category — in fact, most people interviewed said they watched it because they were on lunch break or because they were waiting for *All My Children. Ryan's Hope* showed most popularity with females 41–60, but was not a first choice among most. *Santa Barbara* still seemed to be searching for its identity in 1985, having just begun in the summer of 1983. And *Search for Tomorrow* seemed to be the least popular of all soaps in November, 1985. However, this may be partially due to the fact that *Search* does not air in as many broadcast markets as the other serial dramas.

[33]Herta Herzog, 1944.

[34]Ibid., p. 24.

[35]For specific age/gender statistics, see Appendix B, Table B.3.

Chapter Four. A Synopsis of Trends in Today's Soap Operas

[1]The information for each soap opera summary was gathered from and combined with several sources:

1) viewing experience;

2) viewer interviews (and most especially, the helpful insights of Carolyn Matelski, Teri Haymer and Joan Coffey);

3) syndicated plotline summaries from Jon-Michael Reed, found in many newspapers, including *The Detroit News;*

4) syndicated plotline summaries from Noreen Rooney and Christine Schmuckal found in many newspapers, including the *Detroit Free Press;*

5) Christopher Schemering's *The Soap Opera Encyclopedia* (New York: Ballantine Books, 1985);

6) Robert LaGuardia's *Soap World* (New York: Arbor House, 1983); and

7) Mary Ann Cooper's edited series of soap opera stories, entitled *Soaps and Serials.* Available from Procter and Gamble Productions, Inc. (Rocky Hill, Conn.: Pioneer Network, Inc., 1986), these paperbacks recount stories taken from actual soap opera script. Included in the collection are *Another World, As the World Turns, Capitol, Days of Our Lives, The Guiding Light,* and *The Young and the Restless.*

Chapter Five. Summary and Conclusions

[1]Diane Haithman, "Soap Writers Rule Daytime TV with a Godlike Hand," *Detroit Free Press,* 25 November 1984, p. 1G.

[2]These figures were gathered from a 1985–1986 list of production costs found in *Variety.*

[3]Haithman, p. 1G.

[4]"Soap Writers Say Some Taboos Remain," *TV Guide* (May 3–9, 1986): A-48.

[5]Ibid.

[6]Ibid.

[7]Marc Gunther, "Prime-Time Soaps Hit the Spin Cycle," *The Detroit News,* 19 January 1986, pp. 1H and 4H.

[8]Ibid.

[9]Ibid., p. 1H.

[10]Mike Duffy, "Interest in Soap Operas Bubbling," *Detroit Free Press,* 23 August 1981, pp. 1C and 8C.

[11]"Over-the-Phone Soap," *Variety,* 14 May 1986, p. 12.

Bibliography

Books

Allen, Robert C. *Speaking of Soap Operas*. Chapel Hill: University of North Carolina Press, 1985.

A scholarly analysis of television research methodology, this text provides a fine history of daytime drama as well as several pedagogical approaches for future research.

Buckman, Peter. *All for Love: A Study on Soap Opera*. Salem, N.H.: Merrimack, 1985.

Buckman takes a mythological perspective in his analysis of soap operas, and maintains that the combination of fantasy with age-old stories makes daytime drama a perennial success.

Cantor, Muriel, and Pingree, Suzanne. *The Soap Opera*. Beverly Hills, Ca.: Sage, 1983.

This is one of the most highly regarded texts in the area of daytime drama. Cantor and Pingree combine past research with their own research to provide the reader with backgrounds in soap opera history, production and audience analysis.

Cassata, Mary, and Skill, Thomas, eds. *Life on Daytime Television: Tuning-in American Serial Drama*. Norwood, N.J.: Ablex, 1983.

This text, in many ways, is considered the latter-day equivalent to Lazarsfeld and Stanton's *Radio Research: 1942–1943* because of its amount of statistical research. It addresses plotlines, characterizations and audience views as well as some of the more aesthetic dimensions (such as musical themes) in daytime drama.

Cole, Barry G., ed. *Television*, 4th ed. New York: Free Press, 1973.

Cole includes a series of authors to critique all areas of television. Most noteworthy in daytime drama are Edith Efron and Marya Mannes (who are mentioned in Chapter 2 of this text). Efron and Mannes provide a good perspective of early seventies' attitudes towards television soap operas.

Goldsen, Rose. *The Show and Tell Machine: How Television Works and Works You Over*. New York: Dial, 1977.

Goldsen adopts a "social effects" approach to all facets of television; her section on soap operas is only a small part of this very interesting work.

207

Greenberg, Bradley S. *Life on Television.* Norwood, N.J.: Ablex, 1982.
This is another text which deals with the general effects of television, but many of Greenberg's comments on daytime drama are insightful and worth reading.

Lackman, Ron. *TV Soap Opera Almanac.* New York: Berkeley, 1976.
Lackman answers many of the questions daytime viewers ask about soap operas, e.g., the first broadcast of shows, actor's bios, plotlines, etc.

LaGuardia, Robert. *Soap World.* New York: Arbor House, 1983.
This book is also filled with soap opera trivia, but LaGuardia provides an extra bonus by narrating the plotline/character histories in a very interesting, readable manner.

Lazarsfeld, Paul F., and Stanton, Frank N., eds. *Radio Research: 1942-1943.* New York: Essential.
This work, containing chapters from Rudolf Arnheim, Herta Herzog and Harriet Kaufman, contains the seminal study on which most later research (including this text) was founded. It is truly a classic in the field of daytime drama.

Lemay, Harding. *Eight Years in* Another World. New York: Atheneum, 1981.
One person's perspective on being involved with a soap opera. *Another World* fans will enjoy this account.

MacDonald, J. Fred. *Don't Touch That Dial: Radio Programming in American Life from 1920 to 1960.* Chicago: Nelson-Hall, 1979.
As evident from its title, this book does not deal specifically with soap operas, but MacDonald's insight into the genre within the radio framework is invaluable for anyone researching daytime drama in its early years. Also, MacDonald writes in an easily readable manner.

Newcomb, Horace. *TV: The Most Popular Art.* New York: Anchor, 1974.
As one of the industry's best-known media critics, Newcomb's chapter on soap operas is typical of his other work: well-written and interesting.

Schemering, Christopher. *The Soap Opera Encyclopedia.* New York: Ballantine, 1985.
Another soap opera lover's trivia book, but more updated than the others. Provides very interesting statistical information, especially in its appendices. All soap operas, radio and television, are presented here.

Wakefield, Dan. *All Her Children.* New York: Avon, 1976.
Wakefield writes a wonderful behind-the-scenes account of Agnes Nixon and her famous creation, *All My Children.* It is informative, colorful and very easy to read.

Articles

Alexander, Alison. "Soap Opera Viewing and Relational Perceptions." *Journal of Broadcasting and Electronic Media* **29** (Summer 1985): pp. 295-308.
"Are Soaps Only Suds?" *New York Times Magazine,* 28 March 1943, pp. 19, 36.
"Broadcast Serial Audiences Not Typed." *Broadcasting.* 26 April 1943, p. 19.
Buerkel-Rothfuss, Nancy L., and Mayes, Sandra. "Soap Opera Viewing: The

Cultivation Effect." *Journal of Communication* **31** (Summer 1981): pp. 108–115.

Carveth, Rodney, and Alexander, Alison. "Soap Opera Viewing Motivations and the Cultivation Process." *Journal of Broadcasting and Electronic Media* **29** (Summer 1985): pp. 259–273.

"The Code of Sudsville." *Time,* 20 March 1972, p. 94.

Compesi, Ronald J. "Gratifications of Daytime Serial Viewers." *Journalism Quarterly* **57** (1980): pp. 155–158.

Demeuth, Philip, and Barton, Elizabeth. "Soap Gets in Your Mind." *Psychology Today,* July 1982, pp. 74–78.

Dennison, Merrill. "Soap Opera." *Harper's,* April 1940, pp. 498–505.

Doob, Anthony N., and MacDonald, Glenn E. "Television Viewing and Fear of Victimization: Is the Relationship Causal?" *Journal of Personality and Social Psychology* **37** (1979): pp. 170–179.

Downing, Mildred. "Heroine of the Daytime Serials." *Journal of Communication* **24** (1974): pp. 130–137.

Estep, Rhoda, and MacDonald, Patrick T. "Crime in the Afternoon: Murder and Robbery on Soap Operas." *Journal of Broadcasting and Electronic Media* **29** (Summer 1985): pp. 323–331.

Fine, Marilyn G. "Soap Opera Conversations." *Journal of Communication* **31** (1981): pp. 97–107.

Goldsen, Rose. "Throwaway Husbands, Wives and Lovers." *Human Behavior* **35** (December 1976): pp. 64–69.

Greenberg, Bradley S.; Abelman, R.; and Neuendorf, K. "Sex on the Soap Opera: Afternoon Delight." *Journal of Communication* **31** (1981): pp. 83–89.

_____, and D'Alessio, Dave. "Quantity and Quality of Sex in the Soaps." *Journal of Broadcasting and Electronic Media* **29** (Summer 1985): pp. 309–321.

_____; Neuendorf, K.; Buerkel-Rothfuss, N.L.; and Henderson, L. "What's on the Soaps and Who Cares?" *Journal of Broadcasting* **26** (Fall 1982): pp. 519–536.

Gunther, Marc. "Peter Reckell's a Big Star. That's the Problem. . ." *The Detroit News,* 16 March 1986, p. F1.

Katzman, Natan. "Television Soap Operas: What's Been Going On Anyway?" *Public Opinion Quarterly* **36** (1972): pp. 200–212.

Keeler, John. "Soap: Counterpart to the 18th Century's Quasi-Moral Novel." *New York Times,* 16 March 1980, p. 34.

Kinzer, Nora Scott. "Soap Sin in the Afternoon." *Psychology Today,* August 1973, pp. 46–48.

Knopf, Terry Ann. "Daytime Money and Power on the Soaps." *Boston Globe TV Week,* 1 February 1981, p. 12.

_____. "Politicians: New Soap Scoundrels." *Boston Globe TV Week,* 22 March 1981, p. 10.

Landry, Robert J. "The Soaps: Then and Now." *Variety,* 11 January 1984, p. 170.

Lemish, Dafna. "Soap Opera Viewing in College: A Naturalistic Inquiry." *Journal of Broadcasting and Electronic Media* **29** (Summer 1985): pp. 275–293.

Lowry, D.T.; Love, G; and Kirby, M. "Sex on the Soap Operas: Patterns of Intimacy." *Journal of Communication* **31** (1981): pp. 90–96.

Media Probes. "Soap Operas." A production of Laybourne/Lambe, Inc. Broadcast by Public Broadcasting Service, 1981.

Nixon, Agnes E. "Coming of Age in Sudsville." *Television Quarterly* **9** (1970): pp. 61–70.

Rubenstein, Leslie. "Confessions of a Soap Opera Addict." *McCall's,* March 1986, pp. 84–90.

Rubin, Alan M. "Uses of Daytime Soap Operas by College Students." *Journal of Broadcasting and Electronic Media* **29** (Summer 1985): pp. 241–258.

Schweiger, Alice Burdick. "*Loving:* Ann Arbor Actress Enjoys Juicy Role on Soap." *Detroit Free Press,* 9 January 1986, p. 1B.

"Sex and Suffering in the Afternoon." *Time,* 12 January 1976, p. 46.

"Soap Opera." *Fortune,* March 1946, pp. 119–124, 146–148, and 151–152.

"Soap Operas: Men are Tuning In." *New York Times,* 21 February 1979, Section 3, p. 1.

Wiley, George. "End of an Era: The Daytime Radio Serial." *Journal of Broadcasting* 5 (Spring 1961); pp. 97–115.

Index